Learning and
Performance
Matter

Learning and Performance Matter

Editors

Prem Kumar
National Community Leadership Institute, Singapore

Phil Ramsey
Massey University, New Zealand

World Scientific

NEW JERSEY · LONDON · SINGAPORE · BEIJING · SHANGHAI · HONG KONG · TAIPEI · CHENNAI

Published by

World Scientific Publishing Co. Pte. Ltd.

5 Toh Tuck Link, Singapore 596224

USA office: 27 Warren Street, Suite 401-402, Hackensack, NJ 07601

UK office: 57 Shelton Street, Covent Garden, London WC2H 9HE

British Library Cataloguing-in-Publication Data
A catalogue record for this book is available from the British Library.

LEARNING AND PERFORMANCE MATTER

ISBN-13 978-981-277-192-6
ISBN-10 981-277-192-1

Typeset by Stallion Press
Email: enquiries@stallionpress.com

Printed in Singapore.

FOREWORD

DAVE ULRICH

LESSONS OF LEARNING

No one doubts that learning matters. Scholars have shown that leaders who are learning-agile are more responsive to changing conditions and likely to accomplish their goals. Organizations that have learning capability, or the ability to generate and generalize ideas with impact, also are more competitive. While these headlines are catching and appealing, it is important to go beneath them and figure out not only what is happening but why. Learning about learning requires more rigorous thought and analysis. When we know why something happens, we are more likely to be able to replicate it and it becomes a pattern rather than an isolated event.

This excellent anthology by leading thinkers in organizations offers thoughtful insights on lessons about learning. They probe deeper into learning processes so that these processes can be understood, mapped, and replicated. The lessons from these essays will help mangers manage change and leaders learn. A number of lessons jumped out at me as I read and re-read these essays:

- Learning matters and affects performance. Ramsey shows that the assumptions of learning are not separate from work but an intricate part of doing work and doing it better. Learning affects performance because all performance can be improved through learning. Singer and Edmondson show that learning, particularly in health care settings, has costs, but the benefits far outweigh the costs. When individuals, teams, and organizations embrace change and learn from failure, learning becomes an organizational capability that sustains high performance.

- Learning depends on social and technical software. Brown and Gray not only capture the history of learning but show that the future of learning will be embedded in a social network. Connectivity and choice flowing from new technologies will allow us to participate and learn with each other in new and remarkable ways.
- Learning is a social phenomenon that occurs among individuals.
- Learning requires knowledge management. Wheatley and Rogers show that in the information age, knowledge is pervasive. They articulate 7 principles that are foundational to knowledge management.
- Learning requires leadership commitment. Darling and Flanigan make the strong case that learning cannot be delegated or relegated to staff functions. They identify skills leaders must have to learn from action and to take action from learning. They also propose practices like After Action Review and Emergent Learning Maps that enable leaders to become learners.
- Learning must be woven into an organization's performance management system. Kleiner uses the cute phrase "doggie treats" to capture the analytics that ensure that learning becomes part of a performance map. He raises the challenges of measuring abstractions like learning and of making learning real to the organization.
- Learning affects strategy by making explicit controversial choices. Karnani does an outstanding job highlighting the importance of duality. Duality means that there are always choices, particularly around strategies an organization may take. With a learning mindset, executives are more willing to make these choices explicit. Doing so leads to debate, conversation, and more informed decisions. Without a learning mindset, strategy may end up as vacuous vision and value statements of the obvious.
- Learning means getting insights from outside the box. Blyde builds a strong case for the effective use of consultants who have the capacity to bring new ideas, or learning, into an organization. He lays out guidelines for finding and using consultants who can partner you in the learning journey. Consultants who foster learning engage in dialogue, participate in a learning journey, and bring in new ideas from outside.
- Learning pushes teams to do more than perform. Kayes shows that task teams focused on performance are not sufficient for overall team effectiveness. Teams

must also have the capacity to explore new alternatives. Team performance without learning will not be sufficient for long term success. He also shows what teams should do to foster learning.

- Learning requires new ways to measure outcomes. Ramsey, Tootell, and Mason show that learning may not fall neatly into pre-packaged outcome factors. To measure learning requires focusing on the means and examining behavioral gaps that learning can begin to close.

- Learning requires commitment to expertise. Jarvis shows that expertise is an important element in sustained learning. He also shows the process required to become an expert or someone who has unique knowledge and insight. These people are critical to the learning process.

- Learning can be undermined through bad management. Needham describes bullying in the workplace, where the manager as bully removes incentives and the desire to learn from employees as targets. Bullying may be explicit or implicit, but in either case they undermine and destroy a commitment to learning.

- Learning requires consistency more than perfectionism. Ramsey and Ramsey point out that those of us with perfectionist tendencies avoid learning in the quest to be perfect. We will need to be able to examine the World View that Shapes our efforts at work.

- Learning may apply at a societal level. Kumar shows how the principles of learning have helped shape the Singapore economy. Some of the remarkable successes of this country's economy may be explained by the learning processes that have been put in place.

So what do these lessons of learning mean?

First, learning affects performance at the individual, team, and organizational level. Individuals learn through curiosity and experimentation; teams learn by encouraging diversity of ideas and input; organizations learn by disciplines for continuous improvement and experimentation. When learning occurs, good things happen. Individuals have a more robust life and are more committed to work. Teams are more productive. And organizations more competitive.

Second, learning is a capability that can and should be embedded into an organization. An organization's capability refers to what it does well and what it is known for. As organizations capture, practice, and master learning disciplines, they become known for their capacity to learn. Organizations with a learning reputation will have intangible value for investors resulting in higher stock prices and becoming a preferred place to work for future employees.

Third, learning means to generate and generalize ideas with impact. As we struggle to make sense of learning, we realize that it requires some form of generalizing new ideas. These ideas may come from experiences, experimentation, continuous improvement, benchmarking, or other means, but learning begins with generating a new idea. But, learning cannot be maintained until that idea crosses a boundary. If a person has an idea, but it stays with that person, learning has not occurred. The boundary may be time as one person's (or organization's) experiences transfer to the next person or organization; it may be space as ideas move from one geographic region to another, or it may be business as ideas cross functional or business boundaries. In any case, the ability to generalize an idea is as important as the ability to generate the idea. Most large organizations are more enamored with the generation than generalization of ideas, which limits the capacity to learn.

Finally, learning is everyone's responsibility. It is not enough to say that someone else should learn. Each person is accountable to oneself and through that personal accountability should take responsibility for learning. This requires making choices, seeing consequences, and taking corrective action so that each cycle of behavior is better than the last.

As these and other lessons of learning move from principles to practices, the disciplines of learning become less of a fad and event and more of a pattern and an ongoing experience. They are assimilated into how people and organizations work to produce improved products and services.

This volume is a good push along the learning journey.

Dave Ulrich

Professor, University of Michigan

And

Partner, The RBL Group (www.rbl.net)

Contents

Introduction

Learning and Performance: Rethinking the Dance

PHIL RAMSEY

INTRODUCTION

This book is about a dance[1]; one that is currently going wrong in organisations around the world. It is about a dance that has been following the same pattern for so long that we are struggling to establish better ways of going about it. We could call it the 'Learning — Performing' Dance.

This chapter sets the scene for the contributions that follow. It aims to explain the nature of the dance and its importance to organisations today. It sets the issue within a cultural frame, suggesting that many organisations have established a way of acting that they no longer think about but which fundamentally shapes how they behave and the results they achieve.

This cultural frame emphasises the challenge people face when they try to implement concepts advocated in the book: while concepts and techniques may have a strong appeal, perhaps seeming to be just what your organisation needs, they will often run counter to the culture of your organisation, generating resistance that may surprise you. This is not meant to dissuade you from implementing ideas that appeal; rather, it is meant to prepare you for the challenge.

To establish the frame, we can start by considering the nature of 'Learning' and 'Performing', the values that keep appearing throughout this book. We take the view that these are more than *actions*. They are *values* which are fundamental

---

[1] In their book *Building Cross Cultural Competence*, Charles Hampden-Turner and Fons Trompenaars use the term 'corybantic' to describe the way peoples' values may dance between two ends of a continuum.

to the successful operation of organisations, key dimensions around which organisational cultures form.

Consider what this means.

DILEMMAS — THE FOUNDATION OF THE DANCE

Every year — sometimes several times during a year — an argument breaks out all over New Zealand. The cause? The naming of players selected to play for the All Blacks, New Zealand's national Rugby Football team. The nature of the argument is always the same: should the selectors choose the best player in each position, or should they select players with the potential to be the best at some point in the future?

While the argument is always heated, it becomes white-hot when an outstanding player — past his best but still clearly better than others who play in his position — nears the end of his career. The intensity of the argument reflects the love New Zealanders have of rugby and for the All Blacks. It matters to them that their team wins and keeps winning. And tradition is involved: playing for the All Blacks is one of the greatest achievements to which a New Zealander can aspire. For many, it rankles to see people selected when they have not yet proved they deserve the honour.

The job of the selectors is difficult. They know the traditions and honour associated with the All Blacks better than most. They have had to prove themselves in order to become selectors. What's more, their jobs hang on the success of the team. But they are also deeply aware of the need to develop players for the future. Retirement and injury are part of the game. And playing a test match — a game between international teams — is of far greater intensity than any other match; it is difficult for a new player to adjust quickly to the new demand. Each selection, therefore, presents the selector with a dilemma of whether to give greater weight to the need for performance, or to the need for learning.

'Performance' refers to meeting the demands that are placed upon you. It involves using whatever resources or capacity you have available to achieve required results. For a sports team, the demands are very clear: the desired result of each game is to win. For teams like the All Blacks and to their supporters, failure is devastating.

'Learning' is a very different way of acting. Rather than using existing capacity, learning involves building that capacity so that it can be used at some point in the future. Learning also involves a very different view of failure: the only way to avoid failure is to stick to what you know you can achieve, avoiding anything new. Therefore, failure is a sign that you are challenging yourself — that you are, in fact, learning — with the added bonus that it can be diagnostic, clarifying where improvements need to be made.

Why do we call the choice between performance and learning a dilemma? The word *dilemma* literally means "two propositions". If you are given the choice between (1) performing now, or (2) learning for the future, you are confronted with two attractive propositions. Rather than having to choose, many people would prefer to do both.

Experts on culture Charles Hampden-Turner and Fons Trompenaars have developed what they term 'Dilemma Theory'[2] to explain how culture forms and influences behaviour. As the name suggests, they believe dilemmas are the key to understanding culture and values; dilemmas give us a means of understanding what shapes differences between communities and how differences can be reconciled. Dilemma Theory is our basis for saying that Performing and Learning are more than actions; potentially they are values that can help define the character of a community.

To understand what this means, imagine you are facing a dilemma. You have the choice of two ways of acting, but feel you must select one. The situation requires that you make a choice, so you do. If the choice brings the result you want, what will you do the next time the dilemma arises? Likely, you will choose the same option. And if you repeatedly make the same choice, after a time you will become 'skilled', selecting your preferred option without conscious thought.

Anything done often enough becomes a skill: something you can perform without thinking. You probably cannot recall the conscious effort involved in learning to tie shoelaces or read even simple words. Yet over time these become actions that can be performed while you direct your attention elsewhere. In the

---

[2] See their book *Building Cross-Cultural Competence* (New Haven: Yale University Press, 2000).

same way, responding to a dilemma may initially take effort, but once a preference is established, it can seem like there is no choice involved. One of the propositions stands out as obviously more attractive than the other.

Both individuals and groups form unconscious preferences in this way. When presented with dilemmas, and repeatedly choosing one proposition ahead of the other, they establish their preference as a 'value': a choice that does not have to be justified because it has become "the way we do things around here."[3] The culture of a community can be understood as a pattern of values that distinguishes it from other communities. In other words, a culture is the collection of different ways a community deals with dilemmas.

Dilemmas, then, help us to understand the process by which culture forms. If you have travelled, you have no doubt experienced the result of this process. When arriving in a new community, you will notice the differences, the things local people do that distinguish them from your home community. The difference you notice — whatever that difference might be — is the result of a dilemma. Both communities faced the same dilemma regarding how things ought to be done. The local community formed a preference for one proposition and your home community formed a preference for the other. And because these preferences were formed in the distant past, people in both communities take their own actions for granted. The actions are 'values' in that they are chosen as an unconscious preference. For people in each community, choosing the other proposition would feel uncomfortable, even wrong.

DANCE STEPS OF CULTURES

While a dilemma may seem like a very limited, 'either/or' choice, people — both individuals and as communities — find dynamic ways of responding to the two propositions. Imagine a continuum running between the two propositions of a dilemma. A person's response to the dilemma is like a dance they establish in moving back and forth between the propositions. Some people will dance back and forth along the whole length of the continuum while others will limit themselves to one end while watching others dance at the opposite end.

---

[3] Marvin Bower used this phrase to define what is meant by the term 'culture'.

A number of principles and processes shape how people dance along dilemma continua.

Firstly, the two ends of the continuum are *complementary*. The reason we experience a choice as a dilemma is because both propositions are attractive. In choosing one proposition, we neglect the other and miss out on the benefits it may provide. The longer we neglect a value, the more we need it, even if it seems to be opposite to our established values.

Despite this complementarity, people struggle to move smoothly back and forth along the continuum. Difficulties can arise when we encounter people who, when faced with the same dilemma, have formed a preference for the proposition we unconsciously neglect. It might seem absurd to us that a person chooses to do the opposite of what to us is 'obviously' the best way. Further, we find it easy to see the problems they experience by neglecting what we value, but may not make the link between our own problems and the values we are neglecting. Seeing someone who prefers the alternative proposition of a dilemma can make us more determined that the proposition we value is best.

The anthropologist Gregory Bateson coined the term *schismogenesis* to refer to the way complementary values can become split apart when people with opposite ways of acting encounter one another. In reaction to what they see each other doing, each party confines itself to its preferred end of the continuum. When the process of schismogenesis is in operation, people become determined to stick to what they value rather than responding to what the situation really demands.

The nature of values also gives rise to what learning expert Chris Argyris refers to as 'skilled incompetence'. This is where people have formed an unconscious preference for a way of acting that gets them into trouble. The power of our unconsciously held preferences — our values — is so strong we can recognise a problem created by our preference for one proposition on a continuum, espouse a shift to the proposition at the opposite end, yet continue acting in line with the proposition we say we want to move away from. For this reason, there is often a significant gap between the values people espouse and those that they live by.

Finally, people find ways to *reconcile* dilemmas; ways of acting that honour both the propositions. Reconciliation allows people to view the continuum as something other than an 'either/or' choice. They have the option of dancing along its full length. When a dilemma is reconciled, people from communities with opposing values can even learn to dance together.

DANCING TOWARD PERFORMANCE

There is a growing concern that organisations are dysfunctional in the way they dance on the Learning — Performing continuum. The dance floor seems dramatically tilted toward Performing.

People are, of course, aware of the need for learning in their organisations. Many executives have espoused the need for their organisations to become 'learning organisations'. Plenty of managers speak of the need for people to become tolerant of failure. Yet, reconciling the dilemma involves much more than espousing a shift to a value that has been neglected. Despite what executives are saying, organisations continue to over-emphasise performance to the neglect of learning. No doubt you have seen evidence of this in organisations you come into contact with.

One way the value of performing is evident is the way people unconsciously react to efforts that emphasise learning. In organisations around the world, people report that learning consistently comes a distant second behind performing. Often, learning is viewed as a luxury the organisation cannot afford when times get tough. Yet when times are good, people may be too busy for learning activities. Further, people are required to justify learning efforts with proof that these will generate increased levels of performance.

Another source of evidence can be derived from people's emotional experience of organisational life. Researcher Mihalyi Csikszentmihalyi has established that our experience of life depends on the interplay of the challenges we face and our capacity to meet those challenges. When our capacity exceeds the level of challenge we may initially feel "in control", but this gives way to boredom if the demands on us become too low. When we are faced with challenges that exceed our capacity we might initially feel aroused, but as the level of challenge rises, we become stressed and anxious. Eventually our capacity can become 'burned out'.

In organisational systems everywhere, people report an epidemic of stress. People report feeling over-extended and exhausted, unable to meet the challenges that confront them. In many places, being stressed has become so commonplace people treat it as unavoidable, even healthy. In reality, it is symptomatic of a dysfunctional dance where performing to new levels of challenge is consistently given priority over building capacity through learning. Organisations are not growing capacity at the same rate as they are raising the level of challenge.

ASSUMPTIONS

The tilted dance floor is also evident in the assumptions people make regarding learning, performing and work. These are deeply held beliefs that shape people's actions, even though they might find it hard to articulate just what the beliefs are. You might find that some of the assumptions expressed below reflect the way you think about work and shape the decisions you make.

"Learning isn't work": When people talk about learning, the expressions they use often indicate they think of learning and work as separate. If you are taking time to reflect on an event or to discuss work issues with a colleague, you may find yourself thinking "I should stop this and get back to work." Participants on a training course may think that when the course finishes, they will go "back to work". In these instances, learning is thought of as something other than work; the term 'work' is set aside as one that only applies to performing. Ironically, people express this view even though they find learning exhausting. The mental effort involved in learning shows that it is not only work, it is *hard* work.

Of course, the consequence of thinking that learning is something separate from work is that learning becomes an activity that must always be justified. Like a guest in the house, it is not part of the family; there is no natural home for learning in the workplace. And, like a guest that members of the family appreciate yet find exhausting, people are happy when learning leaves and the workplace can return to normal.

"We learn in order to perform": Western nations in particular have a strong cultural preference for analytical processes. One way this expresses itself is in the desire to differentiate between means and ends. It seems natural to think of events as a series of means leading to various ends. Yet, while it is happening, life is not

so easily divided up. We are constantly doing 'means' and experiencing the 'ends' of our own and others' actions. On top of that, our understanding of systems thinking has highlighted the 'circularity of causality'. Means lead to ends which cause us to pursue other means to new ends and so on. In any complex system, it is meaningless to say that one part of a cycle comes before another.

Despite this, many people are determined that learning is a means to improved performance. Further, they feel that performance is the only 'end' that can justify an investment in learning.

Timothy Gallwey, author of *The Inner Game of Work*, has pointed out that the result of learning is increased capacity. This may lead to improved performance or it may not. It may also produce a rich variety of other beneficial results. Learning may simply result in people experiencing work as more enjoyable and less stressful as their capacity comes into line with the challenges they face.

Of course, learning and performing are cyclical: performing highlights the need for learning just as learning can create the capacity for new levels of performance. So, it is also possible to work off the assumption that the purpose of performance is to stimulate learning: that performing is the 'means' and learning is the 'end'.

Even though the assumption that learning must lead to performance is arbitrary, the impact of the assumption is powerful. Because increased capacity is intangible, measuring the direct result of learning can be difficult. Executives feel that they are being reasonable when they insist that there must be a tangible, measurable outcome to investments in learning, and this should be performance. Delays or complex links between learning and performing can give the impression that learning investments have achieved nothing. Consequently, in many organisations, the assumption acts to block investment in learning.

"We can't afford to fail": You may have heard people say that in their organisation, "failure isn't an option". Many people treat failure as unacceptable; as something that diminishes a person. No one wants to be known as a "failure".

Yet failing is a necessary part of learning. Chris Argyris goes so far as to define learning as the detection and correction of error. The implication of this definition is that people who cannot detect errors cannot learn. Happily, detecting effort, mistakes and failure should not be too hard for anyone because it is characteristic of all human endeavours, despite the levels of performance we might aim to achieve.

Why do people react so badly to failure, when it is so common? As mentioned above, some people think that their work is so important they must not fail. For others, they feel they cannot afford to be seen to fail by customers, competitors or other stakeholders. Some find failure damaging to their ego, undermining their sense of identity. Whatever the reason, people expressing the need to avoid failure are clearly placing a high value on performing, and limiting their dance along the Performing — Learning continuum.

How do organisations deal with the mismatch between (1) the assumption that failure is unacceptable and (2) the fact that failure is a normal part of human activity which happens constantly? Sadly, in many organisations, the mismatch gives rise to a culture of blame. People try to disguise their own mistakes by either hiding them or blaming others. Some people limit their activity to areas they feel they are certain to succeed. Others distort measures to hide failure and give the impression that success is being achieved. But these efforts make error harder to detect, and the process of learning is squeezed out of organisational life.

The challenge for organisations is to encourage a healthy view of failure, allowing learning to flourish. Doing so can provide a context in which people can build capacity and thus generate the levels of performance to which they aspire.

"Management is all about measurement and results": Managers are naturally interested in generating results through other people, and ensuring that the results they get are valuable to their organisation. How can this best be done?

For many, the answer lies in becoming skilled in the use of measures. Many assume that a professional manager does not require a deep understanding of the work of the organisation. Rather, they need to be able to use measures to specify for people what results are required, and then to reward people according to the level of their achievement. Measures are the levers through which performance is generated.

There is growing unease in many organisations about the use of measures as the basis of management. Many people are aware of how measures produce undesirable behaviour. For those assuming management is fundamentally about measurement, undesirable behaviour simply indicates that current measures need to be adjusted. "If only we can get the scorecard balanced, we will get the performance we need."

Thomas Johnson has written extensively on the flaws in thinking we can manage by results. He contends that this assumption encourages managers to form mistaken views of their level of control, and to believe they can arbitrarily alter the way their organisations work. Managers might believe they can, simply by declaring it as a target and measuring whether it is achieved, reduce costs by 5%.

Johnson shares the view of systems thinkers like Russell Ackoff, that any system is perfectly designed to produce the results it is producing. Changing those results requires an understanding of the process by which they are produced and the careful re-design of that process. In other words, to get the performance we want, we must do more than 'command and control' performance from people. We need to learn how to create an organisational system where the desired results are the natural consequence of how people work. Learning in this way is inextricably linked to achieving the performance we want.

The assumption that management is about achieving performance without this learning is an example of schismogenesis: the splitting apart of what should be deeply interconnected. What is the consequence of this split? Managers may become better and better at achieving results that are easily expressed through measures and which can be achieved by people willing to comply with the 'command and control' approach to management.

"Learning will take care of itself": Learning is a naturally occurring process because humans are natural learners. We find ways to adapt to the situations we encounter. And over time we get better at the jobs we do. It might seem that this would lead to it finding a natural home in organisations. Unfortunately, the 'naturalness' of learning often has the opposite effect. Given the challenges that learning presents, managers can find that, by doing nothing, the situation seems to take care of itself.

People are self-organising. They do not require everything to be done for them. People seek help with the challenges that confront them, naturally form developmental relationships in which they can discuss issues that puzzle them, experiment with alternative ways of meeting challenges and ponder the results of their actions. In other words, people learn for themselves.

Of course, what people choose to learn may not be what an organisation needs or desires. In particular, people are social learners, naturally learning lessons that help them become part of a community they find attractive. At times, this can mean learning what it takes to join a community within an organisation that is undermining the organisation's interests.

Further, people pay attention to what they value; people are ready to learn in those areas already supported by the organisation's culture. But, as we saw earlier, some values within an organisation may be over-emphasised and others neglected. Allowing learning to take care of itself will lead to more effort in the areas already receiving too much emphasis and further neglect of what is really needed.

This 'success to the successful' situation has contributed to the current interest in organisational learning. Without guidance, people naturally attend to *individual* learning: that which helps them get better at their particular jobs. While we might hope that people will also use their natural capacity for learning to find ways to collaborate with one another, it does not happen. Organisations have to make an effort to ensure that such learning happens.

"I'm paid to know the answers": A final assumption is that people in work are meant to know the answers. Often, people feel that the further they have progressed in an organisation or the more they are paid relative to others, the more responsibility they have to know what you are doing. The problem with this thinking is that the need to appear to be an expert prevents people from admitting what it is they do not know.

Politicised organisational environments particularly make it important for people to act as experts. It may not feel safe to be tentative about your views or open to the thinking of others. All of this creates an environment in which learning will not flourish.

The problem with 'knowing the answers' is that it assumes there is a right answer to know. In some fields, there are right answers. In particular, right answers are possible where people are dealing with simple, non-living systems. Many of the organisational challenges we face are not like this. They involve living systems: individuals and communities who care about what the answer is, having differing values they think should be represented in any answer, feel strongly about how they should be treated in the process of establishing an answer, and will play crucial roles in implementing whatever is decided upon.

A situation like this is complex in a variety of ways. In his book *Solving Tough Problems*, Adam Kahane talks of three types of complexity: dynamic, social and generative. Dynamic complexity is characteristic of highly interconnected systems, where a change to one variable will affect other parts of the system that may be distant from the change in both distance and time. Social complexity exists when a situation involves a diverse group of people who need to work together in order to produce desired results. And generative complexity exists when the issues faced are new, where past solutions do not help because innovative solutions need to be generated.

Situations involving these layers of complexity are increasingly common. Consequently, issues where there is a right answer to be known are increasingly rare. Organisations face situations which demand that people learn how to handle issues about which they are not experts. People pretending to be experts do not help.

COMMITTING TO A BETTER DANCE

The assumptions described above are challenging because they are so commonplace. You will encounter them in organisations throughout the world. And wherever you do they will be affecting the way people engage in the Performing — Learning dance. Typically the dance will be distorted and people will be suffering as a result.

Why is it good to be aware of these assumptions as you start a book like this? They are not presented to dissuade you from reading or to stop you from experimenting with the ideas you encounter. The purpose is to help you understand the challenge that you and your organisation face.

Promoting learning might appear to be simple. It might seem ludicrous that anyone should object if you were to advocate for greater learning. And yet they do. In fact, many people find that the more they advocate learning, the more resistance they encounter. While this is perplexing, it is understandable when you consider that learning is a *value*. When people act in ways that encourage learning they are, perhaps unwittingly, advocating a shift in values: a culture change. Advocating learning is like suggesting to a group of people that they change the character or identity of their community. It involves addressing values and assumptions that help people define who they are.

Nevertheless, we urge you not to be daunted. Learning *is* needed in organisations. Our hope is that this book will help you take up the challenge.

Learning's Place in Organisations

A Short History of Learning*

JOHN SEELY BROWN AND ESTEE SOLOMON GRAY

When contemplating performance and learning in today's organizations, it's a challenge to find a balanced, reasonable position. Depending on your inclination, you might be buoyant that our understanding of organizational learning has come so far, or disappointed at the level of ignorance that remains. To get some perspective on where we are, let's consider the history of organizational learning efforts and what they have achieved.

Of course, like all historians, we will have our own idiosyncratic views of how we got to where we are. Rather than treating this naturally occurring bias as undesirable, we aim to use it as a basis for learning. Capturing our reflections on the past prompts us to consider the challenges that lie ahead. What follows, then, is a short history of learning followed by a somewhat longer consideration of what the future requires of us.

IT TAKES 20 YEARS...

It was in 1990, with Peter Senge's *The Fifth Discipline: The Art and Practice of the Learning Organization*, that learning was first catapulted from the peripheral corporate domains of training and development departments to a place much closer to the center of business discourse. E-mail was still a creature of early adopters and large institutions, and *PowerPoint* (or its aptly named predecessor, *Persuasion*) was just coming onto desktops and into conference rooms across the world.

---

* We are indebted to Teddy Zmrhal for their help on this chapter and more generally to Paul Duguid for his continual contributions to our understanding of social practice.

Because each technology purported to change the way people communicate rather than what they think, neither was considered particularly relevant to learning. In contrast, the five disciplines — personal mastery, mental models, shared vision, team learning, and systems thinking — appeared as tools to change the organization precisely by changing its thinking (and its thinking about thinking) and were easily recognized as valuable management tools for a knowledge-based, competitive era.

For those paying attention, the management conversation about learning had begun almost two decades earlier, when Chris Argyris and Donald Schön published *Theory in Practice*. They challenged organizations to recognize the limitations of "single-loop learning," familiar to the quality movement, which fosters the ability to detect and correct errors within the frame of current assumptions and policies, and to aspire instead to "double-loop learning," the ability to detect, determine, and perhaps even modify the organization's underlying norms, policies, and objectives.[1] The first type of learning implies *assimilation*, the domain of experience curves, which is relatively straightforward — both for people and for organizations. The second, considerably harder, implies *accommodation* — altering one's frame of reference or basic assumptions about the world. Double-loop learning involves changing the kinds of stories we construct to make sense of the world and, using the terms of gestalt therapy, requires a fresh, unbiased hearing of the "other." It is the ultimate goal of any learning culture. In corporations, double-loop learning is also the domain of strategic shifts. When Senge's five disciplines showed up on management's radar screens, they provided instant utility to the many organizations then engaged in strategic efforts to reframe existing markets and envision new business models. Yet Agryris's Model II learning organizations remain rare to this day.

Meanwhile in the mid-1980s, from a more personal perspective, a community of researchers at and around Xerox PARC (Palo Alto Research Center) resolved to crack the learning problem by coming at it with multifocal conceptual lenses. One result was the founding in 1987 of the independent Institute for Research on Learning (IRL), a multidisciplinary community that undertook research to explore

---

[1] See C. Argyris and D. Schön, *Theory in Practice: Increasing Professional Effectiveness* (San Francisco: Jossey-Bass, 1974). For additional information on Argyris, see http://www.infed.org/thinkers/argyris.htm

"everyday learning." Merging the practices of diverse fields — cognitive science, computer science, social linguistics, educational technology, and ethnography — proved painful but instructive. By the early 1990s, IRL began to inject a new, more social constructivist voice into the business conversations cascading from the learning organization work.[2] Amplified on one flank by workplace practitioners who worked with companies to enact new products, markets, and business models and on its other flank by educational practitioners who were elaborating new means to teach secondary school physics and mathematics, IRL put forth two fundamental understandings. First, that *learning is fundamentally social* and second, that learning *about* is quite different from learning *to be*, which is a process of enculturation.

Building on observations in workplace, school, and craft settings, IRL researchers noted that successful learning happens with and through other people and that what we choose to learn depends on who we are, who we want to become, what we care about, and which communities we wish to join. In this frame, learning is also a matter of changing identity, not just acquiring knowledge. Learning of this nature occurs primarily through the process of gaining membership in a community of practice and is critically enabled by what Jean Lave and Etienne Wenger described as "legitimate peripheral participation" — the essence of classical apprenticeship. By this measure, a marketing manager has learned enough about wireless networking to drive his or her company's participation in that market when and only when she or he can understand the goings-on at an insider's wireless conference or have a mutually satisfying conversation with a committed member of the wireless community. Practice is not merely the measure of learning but the medium of it. In communities that arise less through organizational fiat (the authorized infrastructure of work) and more through pursuit of common work by the ecology of crafts, disciplines, and personalities needed to accomplish that work (the emergent infrastructure of work) practice is invented — and learning captured — each step of the way.[3] Members in such communities are co-constructing knowledge, which is literally embodied in their practice. Practice

---

[2] For a complete list of IRL's 7 Principles of Learning, see http://www.linezine.com/6.2/articles/phuwnes.htm and http://www.newhorizons.org/trans/abbott.htm.
[3] Our colleague at IRL, Susan Stucky, first put forth the idea of "authorized" and "emergent" as parallel types of organization.

is not the stuff in libraries but *knowing in action*. Words, books, simulations, tool kits, and the like are artifacts deliberately crafted to transfer knowledge by evoking practice in the participant; they are not the knowledge itself.

In 1995, 20 years after Argyris and Schön, five years after *The Fifth Discipline*, and a year after the extended IRL community's first corporate client retreat, a pair of former *Harvard Business Review* editors launched *Fast Company*, a "handbook of the business revolution" targeted at readers "old enough to make a difference and young enough to be different." Readers were enjoined to "leap into the loop" by using e-mail to interact with the editors — a novel thought at the time — and to watch for a Web site yet to be constructed. By this time, PowerPoint was fully established as the first-language tool of business. Conference rooms were filled with people engaged in shoulder-to-shoulder knowledge sharing, literally returning to the ancients' practice of reading and writing knowledge on the walls, although this time with beams of light instead of charcoal, chalk, or pigment.

Learning was so central to the new rules of business that an article by the two of us entitled "The People Are the Company" anchored the core Big Idea section of the magazine's first issue. "Work Is Personal ... Computing Is Social... Knowledge Is Power" blared the cover art. "Learning is about work, work is about learning, and both are social," we wrote. In one of the most-cited articles in the publication's history, we asserted that the Community of Practice is the "critical building block of a knowledge-based company," the place where peers in the execution of real work create and carry the competencies of the corporation. Veterans of numerous internal change initiatives, we quietly faced down the tanks of prevailing workplace ideology by proclaiming, "Processes don't do work, people do." We pointed out that "the real genius of organizations is the informal, impromptu, often inspired ways that real people solve real problems in ways that formal processes can't anticipate. When you're competing on knowledge, the name of the game is improvisation, not rote standardization." We also took on the sister shibboleths behind the traditional corporate approach to learning and knowledge; namely, that learning means individual mastery and that everything knowable can be made explicit. We did so in the way we knew would work: by telling stories. We told stories about Xerox field reps using radios and an "electronic knowledge refinery" called

Eureka, and about how National Semiconductor's PLL (for "phase locked loop," a specialized kind of circuit) designers coalesced almost instantly into a powerful, strategic, and ultimately much emulated presence in the company simply by being given the language, the license, and, eventually, the funding to organize. On one hand, these stories about the tacit and collective dimensions of learning and work eased quite naturally into readers' experiences. On the other hand, partly by design, the words *emerge* and *social* seemed to jump off the pages into people's faces — simple and familiar yet mysterious and somehow uncomfortable.

A DECADE DISTILLED

Internet-time was upon us. The knowledge economy roared in, reshaping mainstream and management culture. It inflated. Burst. Rolled on. It was exciting to be part of the community of practitioners concerned with organisantional learning. As a result of our experiences, we can say things now that couldn't have been said before. We can begin to comprehend the fruits of the first decade of the knowledge economy.

What have we learned? What changes have we seen in the way we (and those we have worked with) approach work and learning?

Whether as individuals, as corporate entities or as smaller productive groups (teams, communities, groups, business units, etc), we all have struggled to adapt to the economic, cognitive, and social implications of speed and globalization. We came to understand on a very practical level that learning is the strategic competence for an entity experiencing change. We quickly recognized that becoming a learning organization entails deliberate culture change. With that, we began to abandon our old instincts to reify and broadcast and to develop new skills in and around cultivating new business practices. We struggled to honor local differences. And we learned to celebrate the unique power of narrative in conveying knowledge across otherwise formidable epistemic boundaries.

Whether we consider ourselves skeptics or optimists, we are aware that a different model of the human at work is emerging. People need to be trusted; work and therefore decision-making must be distributed. Relationships among workers — as learners — are key. People need to be given tools, as well as the social and informational spaces to interact as voluntary members of communities and as self-governing citizens. The outcome of investments in learning must be measured in new ways — in actual performance in real work. Thus, to the optimist's eye, the globally teamed workplace is beginning to seem like the norm; authority is naturally reaching down the ladder and closer to the customer, where the real knowledge is anyway. Meanwhile, to the skeptical eye, all this collaboration is a hair's breadth from enforced coordination; members of communities are being manipulated or, worse, exploited in their pursuit of personal and professional goals. But the signs of change are unmistakable.

Whether our early professional identities are rooted in the sciences or the arts and humanities, we are busily incorporating new metaphors and intuitions drawn from the theory and practice of adaptive systems, ecologies, and other biological models. We are elaborating new approaches to organizational design and to civic activity. We are recrafting the standard tools of the learning trade — such as technology, classrooms, and coaching — and integrating the lessons of first-generation online communities. We are more articulate and deliberate about the social systems underlying learning. We are slowly but surely deploying systems that enable and honor learning — *in situ*.

Reflecting upon the learning trajectory of the last decade captured so well in this volume, the days when *learning* usually meant *training*, *knowledge* meant *information*, and "content was king" seem to be fading. Community of Practice is now a common term in business language and a sanctioned, funded approach to global knowledge sharing and postmerger competence integration in leading companies. Learning is clearly no longer synonymous with individual mastery. It is now tacitly expressed in practice that not everything knowable can or should be made explicit, that content must be delivered in context to be effective. High-performance workscapes are built less through training and more through creating opportunities for collaboration and continual renewal, usually through teams, communities, networks, or forums. The words "social" and "emergent" no longer crimp business conversations about learning cultures but spark them.

CREATING LEARNING CULTURES: WHAT'S NEXT?

So, what do practitioners and stakeholders in the art and practice of creating learning cultures need to learn next? Not surprisingly, our response begins with a critique of current practice — individual and collective. For all we have learned and for all that learning cultures have ostensibly changed, there is surely more learning and changing ahead of us.

We, as corporate practitioners, are still not taking advantage of authentic practice, and until we do so, we cannot master the dual art of knowledge-sharing and innovation. The key to spreading actionable knowledge is understanding how shared practice provides the rails on which knowledge travels. Shared practice (which usually reflects shared roots) carries with it a shared worldview, which, in turn, enables people to trust the meaning of one another's words and actions. Without shared practice, knowledge tends to resist transfer, or "stick". The documents, tools, or instructions intended to convey actionable knowledge across organizations are quietly ignored, judged inapplicable, misapplied or otherwise fail because, without shared practice, their recipients can neither decode their true meaning nor recode that meaning into appropriate local practice. Conversely, communities of practice are powerful learning venues and knowledge creation loci precisely because knowledge flows (or "leaks") so easily within their boundaries. Similarly, the looser (but sometimes equally durable) networks of practice to which many professionals now belong provide somewhat thinner rails for knowledge to travel quite well between practitioners in distant parts of an organization or in different companies. As a rule, knowledge *leaks* in the direction of shared practice and *sticks* where practice is not shared.[4]

Very often, sharing knowledge across an enterprise requires leaving the rails of a shared practice and jumping between two different practices (marketing/sales and research, or materials science and production engineering, for example) or organizational cultures. In these cases, we must literally find ways to bridge different

---

[4] J. S. Brown and P. Duguid, "Knowledge and Organization: A Social-Practice Perspective," *Organization Science* (July 2000), p. 14.

practices. Bridging practices is never easy, even (or especially!) when accompanied by process-imposing tools like Lotus Notes or enterprise systems like those from SAP, PeopleSoft or Oracle. Bridging requires nuanced knowledge brokers, people who can span practices and speak multiple languages at the same time. It requires intentional boundary objects — documents, prototypes, phase gates of a process, and the like, around which a negotiation-in-practice can be afforded. It is in reflection upon this negotiation that the second loop of learning occurs — the ability to accommodate, to change underlying models, methods, and our own view of others. Yet few strategies or technologies honor the role of practice — of action on the ground and meaning negotiated in the crucible of work, among people. And too many focus, instead, on the warm friendly notion of communities.

The common corporate goal of sharing *best practices* is related to but distinct from the challenge of having actionable knowledge jump across distinct communities of practice. In this case, it is crucial to realize that every best practice emerged in a highly situated way; it was grown and honed in a particular context. In order for it to travel, it must first be disassembled from that context and then re-embedded in a new context (that is, in a different part of an organization or in a different organization entirely). The process of re-embedding is highly problematic since the best practice must be viewed as a seed that is allowed to germinate in its new context and sprout in a form that honors the nuances of this new context. It takes time and a willingness to let the people influenced by this new best practice do their part to shape it and grow it, preserving its essence but also modifying it to fit its new circumstances.

Practice does not come in discrete pieces like Legos but in clumps and clusters of yarn like a knitter's remnant box after a three-year-old child has played in it. To move a strand from one community to another, from one type of product to another, from one country to another means to disentangle, snip, and re-entangle — without consuming the yarn.

We have not yet faced up to the imminent and gnarly challenge of "learning to unlearn." Reframing is clearly the order of the early twenty-first century. But we will continue to cultivate learning cultures that assimilate rather than accommodate unless we take the lead in inventing, adopting, and embedding a repertoire of new practices (techniques, technologies, processes, experiences) aimed at learning to see differently.

Let's start with a zero-digital-technology example of such a practice that builds directly on knowledge sharing and innovation. Say you want to transfer a new, hard-earned strategic shift from business unit A, where it was hammered out over 18 months, to business unit B, which faces a similar set of strategic issues and, furthermore, sits directly up- or downstream from A. Time is of the essence. There is very little shared practice between A and B, although there is significant hand-off and therefore some history of communication. Bridging A and B, we know, will take nuanced brokering, mediating boundary objects, and time–time to negotiate meaning in practice and time to dis-embed and re-embed key innovations.

The technique is called $2 \times 2 \times 2 \times 2 \times 2$: Take two people from group A and two from group B, and bring them together for two meetings, each two hours long, two days apart. Ideally, there is a preexisting positive professional relationship between one of the As and the one of Bs. Perhaps they are both current or formers members of a particular engineering network of practice; perhaps they both served on a corporate change-initiative task force related, even tangentially, to the strategic issues on the table; perhaps they have functioned as customer and supplier to one another within the organization's value chain. Equally important is the relationship between the two members of each unit. Within their dyad, they must be able to reflect on and articulate elements of the practice they share; they must be able to share stories, hash out details, follow each other's leads, and refine each other's thoughts. What happens around the table the first day (and it really should be a physical table if possible) is intense. It takes tacit teaming by each side to establish and maintain the conversation — one talking while the other watches body language or searches for the next example. During the two hours, A1 and A2 help B1 and B2 enter into the new way of thinking and doing by describing, showing illustrative artifacts, answering questions, identifying, and if possible addressing objections, and working with B1 and B2 to map the new way into at least two specific situations or practices under way in B. Each of these situations is explored in depth, often primarily in dialogue between the two Bs with by now only intermittent interjection by an A. These situations then become the subject of continued exploration and experimentation in practice by the two Bs over the next two days. Success rests on the fact that with two representatives (the smallest possible representative of a community that is still a community), each side can bring its practice into the room. The second meeting brings all four people back to reflect and continue verbally negotiating meaning. Reframing occurs continuously. Repeat the last two steps as necessary. Unlearning alternates with learning throughout as the three sets of dyads (A1A2, B1B2; A1B1, A2B2; A1B2, A2B1) argue, test, witness, internalize, challenge, and change.

Almost every important new point of view or piece of technology, we argue, imposes a burden of unlearning on would-be adopters, often swamping or preventing the better known learning demands it makes. No more dramatic examples exist today than "naturalized" Internet citizens literally looking at internet-native genres like MMPOG (massive multiplayer online games). A fundamental act of reframing — learning to swap the periphery for the center — is necessary, we've learned, before one can begin to see the game. This is not an easy shift, unless you have a good guide plus an inclination to see.

In John's case, he realized early on how difficult it was to understand the culture being created by kids who grew up digital. Fortuitously, he met young author J.C. Herz,[5] who offered to be John's "reverse mentor." Over a year's time, J.C. structured a set of experiences that would give John a way in to the practice of this emerging digital culture, help him unlearn certain biases, and slowly construct a new set of conceptual lenses through which he could see, hear, and make sense of the massively multiplayer game world. For John, being reverse mentored also presented an opportunity to hone his ability to listen with humility and through engagement. What unfolded over the year was a slow realization that until then, John, like most adult game novices, had focused on the actual playing of the game — at the center of the game screen, if you will — while remaining moderately oblivious to the rich social activities transpiring around the edge of the game. There, at the edge, a rich constructivist ecology was evolving — the sharing of tricks and heuristics, the bartering of magical swords, avatars, and other objects of play , the general swapping of stories, and more. Suddenly, he realized that what he thought of as the center was in fact the periphery and that what he initially considered to be periphery (or context) was in fact the center (or content) of the game. The real game, he saw, is deeply social. The real action, he understood, lies in the new kind of nonlinear, multiauthored narrative being constructed collectively by the players.

---

[5] *Joystick Nation* (1997) and *Surfing on the Internet* (1995).

In Estee's case, the guides are her 15- and 11-year-old Internet native sons. For them, summer vacation begins when — and only when — they are allowed to devote *entire* days in succession to their favorite MMPOG, which this year happens to be the *Korean Ragnarok Online*. Being Mom, Estee worries about eyestrain, their relative lack of fresh air, sunshine, and exercise, and their willingness to forgo physically apprenticing with their father as he constructs an addition to our house. But, armed with a deeply internalized appreciation for the social and situated aspects of learning and prodded periodically by John to follow their experience closely, she does not worry about wasted time, social isolation, or (lack of) future memories of joyful togetherness. The boys prefer to play on adjacent computers in what they call the "downstairs computer room," where they are in constant verbal connection with each other. Occasionally, they or a friend are forced to use a third machine upstairs, which means they tie up two phone lines in order to keep up the conversation. Add to this the roughly 200 people with whom each interacts on a good Ragnarok day, in passing, as a close fellow traveler in their current party, as member of their latest guild, as famous personality players, and as buyer or seller of various items. Their ability to multitask is, well, awesome. To them, systems thinking seems natural. Later in the summer, letters from the younger to the older at overnight camp principally feature updates on what John has called a "new kind of nonlinear, multiauthored narrative." As John learned to see, the narrative is not about kills or game places visited or instances of deploying weapons, spells, or other skills — none of the foreground flora and fauna that capture the adult's eye when faced with the game. Rather, it's about how the game is evolving, what particular players are up to, the latest tidbit from one of the three or four user sites they graze, how the strategies they've been exploring are working out, what stupid or cool thing *Gravity* (the company that makes the game and runs the main servers) has done lately. "You know what I learned today, Mom?" starts the daily report. And as the 11-year-old talks, all the cyber-age shifts we talk about are manifest. He freely discovers, links, lurks, tries, asks, borrows, and navigates a complex n-dimensional space while his mom internally fights her need to know-before-acting and wishes for a place to start deducing what to do next. (She's wondering, is there a document, a set of base rules, something?) His digital world is social and constructivist from the get-go. Moreover, he is constantly shifting center and periphery — at will.

We have yet to deploy software that honors and energizes the emergent. The age of desktop computing has not given way to the era of social computing. "Almost without exception, companies applied these technologies to explicit work in the authorized organization; they flattened the formal. New digital technologies will enable companies to engage their employees and energize the emergent," we prophesied eight years ago. "Companies that embrace the emergent can tap the logic of knowledge work and the spirit of community. Those that don't will be left behind."

Enormous stocks of ink, budget, attention, engineering, and marketing elbow grease have certainly been devoted since then to technologies supporting communities, collaboration, and knowledge management. Few of these have engaged or energized their intended users beyond an early (often enforced) usage spike. For a time, unabashedly transaction-oriented marketplaces and exchanges hijacked both the noun *community* and the adjective *collaborative*. Knowledge management is often a synonym for taxonomy-driven content management. So-called collaboration systems are still primarily means for posting, retrieving, and, to a more limited degree, co-producing semistructured content. Even the live-events segment of the collaboration market was sold and purchased largely as a means to broadcast human-delivered presentations or lessons, until demand to replace face-to-face meetings with zero-travel e-meetings skyrocketed after September 11, 2001. New software that honors and activates the emergent has been barely visible.

In the last few months, the term "social software" has arced from the province of bloggers and tech early-adopter conferences to the pages of the *Wall Street Journal* and the *New York Times*. In most of those venues, the focus is on weblog creation tools including *blogs* — an instant personal publishing technology and practice that has enabled hundreds of thousands of people to find their individual voices over the last two years — and *wikis*, a group voice technology and practice, following on the heels of blogs, but entailing somewhat more structure and shared page ownership. *Social software* also encompasses instant messaging and other emerging forms of presence awareness technology, and hints of tools (still largely academic or researchy in flavor) for tracing, analyzing, and navigating social networks. Some observers include a gaggle of social networking services that interconnect registered individuals (and thereby, theoretically, their social networks) for numerous professional and personal purposes, depending on the service. Whether you believe recent groupware products such as peer-to-peer Groove or contextual collaboration offerings from IBM Lotus also fit the term is left for you, the reader, to decide. Undeniably, most of the Internet-native entries are better classified creatures of the emergent than the authorized. Moreover, the broader software or Web-services market of which they are a fresh part is showing signs of avoiding the tunnel vision that has traditionally excluded social sensibilities from the activities of information technology developers and purchasers. Social software developers and early adopters aspire to a new approach to building adaptive social applications that are easily deployed and can be humanized — not just customized — to support different types of online interaction and different modes of communication. They anticipate a new set of online genres reflecting a tremendous shift in human relationships: from episodic to always-on.[6] Many proudly point out the relative simplicity of blog and wiki technology. But the practice around their use is anything but.

Defined most clinically, social software is designed to be used by three or more people. It is much rarer than it sounds. Most interaction supported by technology is narrowcast (one-to-one), such as telephones and simple e-mail, midcast (one-to-small groups), such as e-mail using distribution lists and small ezines, or broadcast (one-to-many), as in standard publishing and large-scale ezines. Clay Shirky of New York University points out, "Prior to the Internet, the last technology that had any real effect on the way people sat down and talked together was the table. Beyond that, there was no technological mediation for group conversations. The closest we got was the conference call, which never really worked right..." We interject that a later midcasting technology, the copier, radically affected how people interacted around that table by giving each a copy of shared and sharable documents but agree with Shirky when he continues: "We've had social software for 40 years at most, dated from the Plato Bulletin Board System, and we've only had 10 years or so of widespread availability, so we're just finding out what works."[7]

---

[6] Lee Bryant and Livio Hughes, London http://www.headshift.com/moments/archive/sss2.html#_Toc38514168.

[7] Clay Shirky in a speech at ETech April, 2003 entitled "A Group Is Its Own Worst Enemy," published July 1, 2003 on the *Networks, Economics, and Culture* mailing list.

Designing social software that works is important for creating a culture of learning — inside and outside the corporation. It can, and already does in a few places, complement traditional IT systems designed to support the formal business processes and content stores of an organization but ignore the social fabric where learning and knowledge sharing happen. But social computing is hard, since we must now understand the emergent properties of groups of people, down to their social- and psychodynamics — both inside the corporation and in society at large. We must learn to distinguish the natural size and activity classes of various groups, communities, networks, and collections, and handle each appropriately. We learn from repeated online experience that by its very self-organizing nature, a community can quickly degenerate into the tyranny of the masses or be hijacked by weirdos, spammers, and the like. Designing social software is much more like designing a constitution than designing an operating system. The constitution needs to exhibit the right balance between supporting dissenting opinions and guaranteeing that the community's real work can get done. It must vary with each community; indeed, it must emerge and evolve along with the community. Borrowing Shirky's language again: "Groups are a run-time effect. You cannot specify in advance what the group will do, and so you can't substantiate in software everything you expect to have happen."

Designing and using social software is therefore like designing and living in ecology; moderators must honor diversity and husband the cross-pollination of opinions and ideas to keep the emergent ever present. There are also business challenges inherent in life on the emergent side of the enterprise in a cost-sensitive era. It can be difficult to garner revenue up front for things that don't yet exist or provide measurable outcome guarantees. If these design goals and business challenges can be met, social software can act as a true enhancer of our ability to learn from and with each other. We may yet tap the logic of knowledge work and the spirit of community.

CONCLUSION: A TWENTY-FIRST CENTURY INTUITION

It appears in big blue letters encased in a cloud-like form floating toward the top of the Darden Colloquium mural: *The 21st century mind is a collective mind*. We understand why. Learning is the strategic competence for meeting the economic, cultural, and cognitive implications of increased speed and globalization. A new, more social model of the human at work is emerging as biological metaphors, ecological models, and adaptive system approaches predominate. On a daily basis, twenty-first century first-world citizens engage in coproduction — as consumers, as coworkers, at play and in political life. E-mail is the lifeblood of business. Files that end in .PDF and .PPT are the universal currency of knowledge exchange. While corporate-learning practitioners are still not taking advantage of the rails of practice, non-Internet natives are still fundamentally confusing the center and the periphery when looking at genres like MMPOG, and industry has yet to deploy software that honors and energizes the emergent, alongside the authorized, as knowledge workers approach their keyboards with expectations beyond the twentieth-century information highway.

The Cartesian worldview of "I think, therefore I am" seems to be finally giving way. A next step, "We participate, therefore we are," better captures today's ethos, we think.

That next step is strongly in line with the African proverb, "It takes a village to raise a child." It takes a community to change a practice. If double-loop learning were a matter of intrapersonal, interpersonal, or even simple intracommunal learning, we would have seen more of it in the last 20 years. But our experience, our theory, and our intuition suggest this goal of all learning cultures, and most certainly twenty-first-century ones, is best achieved as an intercommunal dynamic. That is, it may take one working community pushing another in order to reconsider and recast working knowledge. Each center is the other's periphery. What ensues is a creative collision of craft, which — if it can take place in a fabric of trust, with appropriate brokering and cultivation practices — can recreate worlds.

The word "intuition" is purposefully chosen here. However, the twenty-first century plays out, none of us today knows how to create a twenty-first-century learning culture. In fact, most of us in charge today of the budget and resources for building tomorrow's learning cultures know we don't know how to build them for those coming up behind us. It takes courage to breach the barriers of current practice and head knowingly into the unknown. And it takes intuition to navigate there.

Let's distinguish for the moment between two kinds of intuition. One is the kind of personal intuition that arises from one's own experiences. The other arises from being embedded in a collective. It incorporates learning in the moment, listening with humility, and being able to tap tacitly held beliefs and sensibilities. It is about being able to discern a kind of group resonance. Mystical overtones notwithstanding, some leaders and strategists in the quotidian world already exhibit this ability to make sense at the collective level, but even here it is rarely articulated. As we move forward with the insights in this volume, both types of intuition are necessary.[8]

"I think, therefore I am" has paled. "We participate, therefore we are" is where we're heading. Here's to the next 20 years.

---

[8] John Seely Brown, in personal communication with Claudia Welss.

WHEN LEARNING AND PERFORMANCE ARE AT ODDS: CONFRONTING THE TENSION

SARA J. SINGER AND AMY C. EDMONDSON

INTRODUCTION

This chapter explores complexities of the relationship between learning and performance. We start with the general proposition that learning promotes performance, and then describe several challenges for researchers and managers who wish to study or promote learning in support of performance improvement. We also review psychological and interpersonal risks of learning behavior, suggest conditions under which exploratory learning and experimentation is most critical, and describe conditions and leader behaviors conducive to supporting this kind of learning in organizations. We illustrate our ideas with examples from field studies across numerous industry contexts, and conclude with a discussion of implications for theory and practice of this complex relationship for performance management.

We expect few readers to disagree with the suggestion that those who develop and exercise a greater capacity to learn are likely to outperform those less engaged in learning. Indeed, we might make the same unsurprising prediction about individuals, teams, or organizations. The positive relationship between learning and performance is both intuitive and relatively well documented. Research at individual, group, and organizational levels has provided both suggestive and reasonably conclusive evidence that learning promotes performance, as described below. Nonetheless, the aim of this chapter is to explore some of the problematic aspects of the relationship between learning and performance, a relationship that we suggest is not as straightforward as it first appears.

Why is this relationship problematic? First, although learning is clearly essential for sustained individual and organizational performance in a changing environment, the costs of learning may at times be more visible in organizations than its performance benefits. Learning can be messy, uncertain, interpersonally risky, and without guaranteed results. Moreover, not all learning leads to improved performance; it will depend on what is being learned and how important it is for particular dimensions of performance. Although some learning is straightforward (the knowledge is codified and readily used by newcomers), other forms of learning in organizations rely on experimentation and exploration for which outcomes are unknown in advance (Tucker, Nembhard, & Edmondson, 2005). Lastly, time delays between learning and performance may obscure or even undermine evidence of a clear causal relationship (Senge, 1990; Sterman, 1989).

In the sections that follow, we start by clarifying terms to build a foundation for our arguments. Next, we examine evidence for a positive relationship between learning and performance in organizations. We then explore challenges managers and scholars face when seeking to enhance or study this relationship. Finally, we propose conditions under which learning — especially in the form of exploration and experimentation — is most beneficial for organizations, and we describe circumstances conducive to learning behavior.

LEARNING AND PERFORMANCE IN TEAMS AND ORGANIZATIONS

We start with some definitions. *Performance* is conceptualized in this chapter as the achievement of goals. Performance usually includes multiple dimensions, some more important to stakeholders than others. For example, performance in hospitals typically includes achievement of clinical as well as financial goals. In addition, academic medical centers typically seek to achieve research and teaching aims. Group goals are often aligned, such that their mutual achievement is possible. However, some performance goals are not necessarily aligned, such as when an organization seeks to excel in innovation while also achieving superb quality and efficiency in an existing business (March, 1991). Where goals conflict, organizations inevitably need to make tradeoffs among competing objectives. In these situations, one aspect of learning is learning which performance variables to maximize. This requires learning how to manage the tensions that may exist between efficiency and cost versus clinical and customer experience.

Learning, whether for individuals or groups, is an active process of gaining information, understanding, or capabilities (Cannon & Edmondson, 2005; Edmondson, 2002; Garvin, 2000; Senge, 1990). *Collective learning* refers specifically to learning by groups or organizations, in which people must work together to organize the learning process — including such activities as collecting, sharing, or analyzing information, obtaining and reflecting on feedback from customers or others, and active experimentation. Most work in organizations and teams requires coordinated action among multiple individuals. The knowledge required to conduct work successfully takes many forms and resides in many locations. To be successful, groups must access this knowledge, develop a shared understanding of how best to apply it, and act in a coordinated manner that is reflective of new knowledge and insights. In short, work in groups frequently requires collective learning.

Learning behaviors enable groups to obtain and process data that allow it to adapt and to improve. Individual learning behaviors include asking questions, sharing information, seeking help, experimenting with unproven actions, and seeking feedback. Through these activities, groups can detect changes in the environment, learn about customers' requirements, improve members' collective understanding of a situation, or discover unexpected consequences of their previous actions. Team learning behaviors include collaborating, making changes, expecting to encounter problems that will require changes, and reflection-in-action (Edmondson, 1999). At the same time, these learning behaviors require willingness to take interpersonal risks such as discussing mistakes, which in teams and organizations requires that leaders work to create an environment conducive to learning (Edmondson, 2003b; Edmondson, 1999; Edmondson, Bohmer, & Pisano, 2001).

The ability to learn is increasingly recognized as a necessity of organizations operating in fast-changing environments (Banker, Field, Schroeder, & Sinha, 1996; Osterman, 1994; Safizadeh, 1991). Learning in teams is also recognized as having the potential to enhance continuous improvement of quality, innovation, customer satisfaction (Boyett & Conn, 1991; Cutcher-Gershenfeld, Nitta, Barrett,

Belhedi, *et al.*, 1994; Gupta & D, 1994; Hitchcock, 1993; Katzenbach & Smith, 2005; Tjosvold, 1991), improve employee satisfaction (Cohen & Ledford, 1994; Cordery, Mueller, & Smith, 1991), and reduce operating costs and improve response to technological change (Wellins, Byham, & Wilson, 1991).

LEARNING LEADS TO PERFORMANCE IMPROVEMENT

We start with the general premise that learning positively promotes performance. Supportive evidence of this relationship derives from various settings. Research has demonstrated performance benefits of individual learning behaviors, including for feedback seeking by individual managers (Ashford & Tsui, 1991), for teams seeking information and feedback from outside the team (Ancona & Caldwell, 1992), for research and development teams that experiment frequently (Henderson & Clark, 1990), and for discussing errors productively (Michael, 1976; Schein, 1993; Sitkin, 1992). These learning behaviors collectively were associated with perceived team performance in a study of 51 work teams in a furniture manufacturing company (Edmondson, 1999). In addition, among senior leaders in selected U.S. hospitals, a systems orientation, focused on improving system performance rather than blaming individuals, was associated with stronger perceived organizational safety culture (Singer & Tucker, 2005).

A study of surgical teams at 16 medical centers found a positive relationship between a team's ability to adapt to new ways of working and success in implementing a new technology, one type of performance (Edmondson, 2003b; Edmondson *et al.*, 2001). The study demonstrated that effective learning processes can overcome structural barriers to implementation of technologies that disrupt organizational routines, requiring both technical learning and new ways of communication and coordinating. Similar learning behaviors within teams and across teams were associated with team member assessment of team performance in an Australian hospital (Chan, Pearson, & Entrekin, 2003). The positive effect of team learning on team performance has also been reported by a number of prominent researchers (Cavaluzzo, 1996; Flood, MacCurtain, & West, 2001; Katzenbach *et al.*, 2005; Meyer, 1994; Roberts, 1997; Senge, 1992; Wheelan & Burchill, 1999). Team learning behaviors were also significantly related to organizational learning (Chan, Lim, & Keasbury, 2003).

Product design firm IDEO exemplifies a learning organization (Edmondson & Feldman, 2004a). The company's success in routinely coming up with great ideas is due in large part to IDEO's capacity to learn about, empathize with, and design products and services to meet the needs of end-users. Senior management's enabling attitude combined with personalized and flexible workspaces filled with idea-generating materials and technologies prompts highly technically skilled employees to think outside the box. IDEO's inclusive, collaborative culture fosters intensive, hands-on, collaborative work among non-conventional designers. Employees act on their ideas with little concern about what others might say. Company slogans include "Fail often in order to succeed sooner," and "Enlightened trial-and-error succeeds over the planning of the lone genius" (Kelley & Littman, 2001). Significant time is devoted to sharing stories, gadgets, and ideas. Regularly scheduled sessions provided opportunities for cross-fertilization and informal knowledge transfer across disciplines and promoted energy within the studio. IDEO's product development methodology involves brainstorming at every stage, which encourages new ideas and rapid prototypes. Good humor meets the inevitable failures associated with frequent small experiments. These organizational learning characteristics have enabled IDEO not only to win product design awards repeatedly but also to add new services to its repertoire successfully.

PERFORMANCE CAN APPEAR TO SUFFER FOLLOWING A COLLECTIVE LEARNING INITIATIVE

The positive association between learning and performance found in the studies described above does not represent the complete learning-performance story. Here, we focus on a more subtle aspect of this relationship. In some settings, learning activities result in either perceived or actual reductions in performance. That is, performance appears to suffer when collective learning goes up (See Fig. 1). At least two mechanisms can cause this phenomenon: the first we call the "visibility problem" and the second is the "worse-before-better problem."

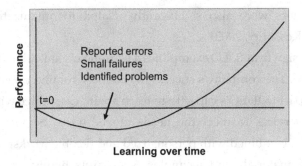

Figure 1. Hypothesized relationship between performance and learning over time.

The visibility problem

Making errors visible by reporting and tracking them is common in many settings, particularly in high risk settings where mistakes and exceptions frequently occur. However, humans tend to underreport errors, particularly where tracking them is difficult or labor intensive. For example, one hospital in Salt Lake City increased the number of identified adverse drug events (injuries caused by drug-related medical treatment) forty-fold after instituting an information technology system to predict and track errors (Evans *et al.*, 1992). The magnitude of this increase suggests that relatively few errors made in hospitals are reported.

The visibility problem refers to the phenomenon that occurs when some organizational groups report more errors than others and learn more as collectives, but appear to be performing worse than groups that report fewer errors because performance is assessed in terms of error frequency. That is, the errors are more visible than the benefits of learning from them.

As field research in the hospital setting has noted, documented error rates are a function of at least two influences: actual errors made and group members' willingness to report errors (Edmondson, 1996). Where errors are consequential, willingness to report may be the more important factor. Indeed, a study of hospital nursing units found — to the author's initial surprise — that higher documented error rates were correlated with *higher* perceived unit performance, quality of unit relationships, and nurse manager leadership (Edmondson, 1996). Recognizing that *documented* error rates may not reflect *actual* error rates, the research found the primary influence on detected error rates was unit members' perception of the risk of discussing mistakes openly. Interceptions of errors were also more prevalent in units in which members were less concerned about being caught making a mistake. The paper concluded that leadership behavior influenced the way errors are handled, which in turn led to shared perceptions of how consequential it is to make a mistake. These perceptions influenced willingness to report mistakes and contributed to a climate of fear or of openness that further influenced the ability of nursing units to identify and discuss problems. Thus, detection of error varied such that teams that needed improvement most were least likely to surface errors, and teams that learned most appeared to perform relatively poorly in terms of error rates.

In one survey of personnel from 15 California hospitals, an average of 38% of respondents felt embarrassed by their mistakes; 30% reported that it was not hard for doctors and nurses to hide mistakes; 10% felt that individuals in their department were not willing to report behavior that was unsafe for patient care; and 11% felt that reporting a patient safety problem would result in negative repercussions for the person reporting it (Singer *et al.*, 2003). There was substantial variation among hospitals in answer to these questions. These findings further suggest that an organization members' willingness and ability to catch and report errors may help to explain correlations between documented error rates and other measures of performance.

The worse-before-better problem

Learning new things inevitably results in making a few mistakes along the way. To be worth the effort, individuals must believe that the potential for gain is worth the cost. For example, if someone who hunts and pecks with two fingers on a keyboard makes an effort to learn to type, the speed and quality of his output is likely to get worse before it gets better. Nevertheless, in the long run, learning to touch type can improve performance substantially. Similarly, when trying to generate novel solutions to problems and new ideas for products, services, and innovations, groups must experiment to find out what works and what does not, so as to learn how to do things better. Experimentation, by its nature, will inevitably result in failures (Lee, Edmondson, Thomke, & Worline, 2004). According to traditional measures, an increase in these small failures would be interpreted as a decline in performance. Yet, without these failures, learning cannot occur.

Despite the increased rate of failure that accompanies deliberate experimentation, organizations that experiment effectively are likely to be more innovative, productive, and successful than those that do not take such risks (Thomke, 2003). Similarly, research and development teams that experimented frequently performed better than other teams (Maidique & Zirger, 1984). In addition, successful implementation of a new cardiovascular surgery technology required acknowledging the challenge and addressing the worse-before-better problem through preparatory practice sessions and early trials upon which team members shared their reflections and discussed opportunities for improvement (Edmondson *et al.*, 2001).

Small failures arise not only in the course of purposeful experimentation, but also when daily work is complex and interdependent. When problems inevitably arise during the course of business in these situations, workers can either compensate for problems, or they can seek to resolve the underlying cause by notifying those who can help to correct the problem. The former would likely go unnoticed, while the latter would expose poor performance. Nevertheless, compensating for problems can be counterproductive if doing so isolates information about problems such that no learning occurs. For example, in seeking to resolve problems themselves, hospital nurses wasted an average of 8% of their time coping with small process failures at significant financial cost associated with lost nursing time (Tucker & Edmondson, 2003).

In hazardous situations, small failures not identified as problems worth examination often precede catastrophic failures. Small failures are often the key early warning sign that could provide a wake up call needed to avert disaster down the road. Yet, in recognizing small failures in order to learn from them, individuals and groups must acknowledge the performance gaps.

LEARNING FROM FAILURE IS DIFFICULT

Where catastrophic failure is possible, mistakes are inevitable, or innovation is necessary, learning from failure is highly desirable. Yet such learning is hard to do.

Research suggests, for example, that hospitals typically fail to analyze or make changes even when people are well aware of failures (Tucker *et al.*, 2003). Few hospitals dig deeply enough to understand and capture the potential learning from failures.

Psychological and organizational barriers

A multitude of barriers can preclude learning in teams and organizations (Cannon *et al.*, 2005). These include limitations in human skills or cognition that lead people to draw false conclusions, and complex and cross-disciplinary work design that can make failures difficult to identify. Additional barriers include lack of policies and procedures to encourage and fund experimentation or forums for employees to analyze and discuss the results.

Learning about complex, interconnected problems also suffers from ineffective discussion among parties with conflicting perspectives. Status differences, lack of psychological safety, and lack of inquiry into others' information and experiences related to substantive issues can combine to ensure that a group as a whole learns little. Powerful individuals or respected experts can stifle dissent simply by expressing their opinions (Edmondson, 1996). Social pressures for conformity exacerbate the impact of leaders' actions, particularly when large status and power differences exist among leaders and subordinates (Edmondson, 2003c; Janis, 1982; Roberto, 2002). In addition, people in disagreement rarely ask each other the kind of sincere questions that are necessary for them to learn from each other (Argyris, 1985). People tend to try to force their views on the other party rather than educating the other party by providing the underlying reasoning behind their perspectives.

The human desire to "get it right" rather than to treat success and failure as equivalently useful data greatly impedes learning. This is true in routine work contexts, but it is particularly problematic when facing novel and unknown situations in which no one can know in advance all that is needed to perform well. Individuals prevent learning when they ignore their own mistakes in order to protect themselves from the unpleasantness and loss of self-confidence and self-esteem associated with acknowledging failure (Taylor & Brown, 1988). People may also deny, distort, or cover up their mistakes in order to avoid the public embarrassment or private derision that frequently accompanies such confessions, despite the potential of learning from them (Cannon, 1993). In addition, people derive greater comfort from evidence that enables them to believe what they want to believe, to deny responsibility for failures, to attribute a problem to others or the system, and to move on to something more pleasant. Similarly, groups and organizations have the tendency to suppress awareness of failures (Weick & Sutcliffe, 2001). Finally, organizational incentives typically reward success and frequently punish failure, creating an incentive to avoid and hide mistakes.

Teams and organizations are also predisposed to under-react to the threat of failure when stakes are high, different views and interests are present, and the situation is ambiguous. Such decision-making groups can fail to learn and hence make poor decisions (Edmondson, Roberto, Bohmer, Ferlins, & Feldman, 2004b). Multiple mechanisms can combine to inhibit responsiveness and preclude learning in these cases. First, people tend to filter out subtle threats (Goleman, 1985), blocking potentially valuable data from careful consideration. They also remain stubbornly attached to initial views and seek information and experts to confirm initial conclusions (Wohlstetter, 1962). Groups silence dissenting views (Janis, 1982), especially when power differences are present (Edmondson, 2002, 2003c). They spend more time confirming shared views than envisioning alternative possibilities (Stasser, 1999). Organizational structures often serve to block new information from reaching the top of the organization (Lee, 1993). Rather, they tend to reinforce existing wisdom (O'Toole, 1995).

Learning from small and large failures

Most organizations' inability to learn from failure stems from a lack of attention to small, everyday problems and mistakes. We hypothesize that organizations that embrace small failures as part of a learning process are more likely to innovate successfully. Likewise, organizations that pay more attention to small problems are more likely to avert big ones, especially where tasks are interconnected.

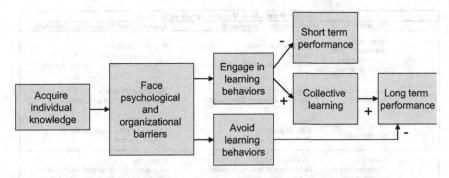

Figure 2. Impact of psychological and organizational barriers to learning.

Collective learning requires valuing failure and being willing to incur small failures in front of colleagues. It requires being willing to enhance rather than reduce variance. Learning groups must proactively identify, discuss, and analyze what may appear to be insignificant mistakes or problems in addition to large failures (Cannon *et al.*, 2005). When organizations ignore small problems, preventing larger failures becomes more difficult (Tucker *et al.*, 2003). (See Fig. 2.)

THE LEARNING MINDSET ACROSS DIFFERENT LEVELS OF ANALYSIS

Given the above challenges, this section describes some of the theoretical alternatives for promoting organizational learning that enhances future performance. We tie together different but related ideas from research on organizational learning at several levels of analysis (See Fig. 3). Specifically, advocacy and inquiry describe contrasting communication behaviors that originate in human cognition (Argyris & Schon, 1978), and advocacy and inquiry orientations have been used to describe distinct approaches to group decision making (Garvin & Roberto, 2001). Exploratory and confirmatory responses have recently been used to describe distinct ways that leaders can orient individuals and groups to respond to potential failures or problems (Edmondson *et al.*, 2004b). Similarly, learning and coping have been used to compare the ways in which leaders can orient team members to a new challenge or innovation (Edmondson, 2003d). Like inquiry and advocacy, exploration and exploitation describe distinct behavioral characteristics of firms

Learning Mindsets at Multiple Levels of Analysis			
Dimension		Performance Orientation	Learning and Innovation Orientation
Individual & group	Behavioral characteristics of individuals and group members	Advocacy orientation - Lack of listening - Reliance of quantitative data	Inquiry orientation - Openness, tolerance for ambiguity - Reliance on intuition and interpretaion
	Leader response to problems	Confirmatory response - Reinforce accepted assumptions	Exploratory response - Experiment to test assumptions
	Leader approach to environment	Coping - View as threat - Technically oriented	Learning - View as exciting opportunity - Team oriented
Organization	Behavioral characteristics of organizations	Exploitation - Appropriate in mature markets - Focus on execution	Exploration - Appropriate in uncertain environments - Focus on learning & experimentation
	Leader mindset and organizational design	Organize to execute - Ask, "Did we do it right?" Promote first order learning	Organize to learn — Ask, "Did we learn?" - Promote second order learning

Figure 3.

(March, 1991), and leaders can organize to learn or organize to execute respectively to promote these organizational orientations. We compare each set of terms below.

Advocacy and inquiry orientations

As discussed above, group structures and processes can severely inhibit the ability of a group to incorporate effectively the unique knowledge and concerns of different members. Key features of group process failures include antagonism; a lack of listening, learning and inquiring; and limited psychological safety for challenging authority. These kinds of individual and interpersonal behaviors have been collectively referred to as an *advocacy orientation* (Argyris et al., 1978). For example, simple but genuine inquiry into the thinking of other team members could have generated critical new insights about the threat posed by the foam strike to the Columbia space shuttle (CAIB, 2003). Instead, NASA managers spent 17 days downplaying the possibility that foam strikes on the shuttle represented a serious problem and so did not view the events as a trigger for conducting detailed analyses of the situation (Edmondson et al., 2004b).

A recent analysis concluded that NASA's response to the foam strike threat was characterized by active discounting of risk, fragmented, discipline-based analyses, and a wait-and-see orientation to action. When engineers became concerned about the foam strike, the impact of their questions and analyses was dampened by poor team design, coordination and support. In contrast to the flat and flexible organizational structures that enable research and development (Hayes, Wheelwright, & Clark, 1988), NASA exhibited a rigid hierarchy with strict rules and guidelines for behavior, structures conducive to aims of routine production and efficiency (Sitkin, Sutcliffe, & Schroeder, 1994). The cultural reliance on data-driven problem-solving and quantitative analysis discouraged novel lines of inquiry based on intuitive judgments and interpretations of incomplete, yet troubling information. In short, the shuttle team faced a significant learning opportunity but was not able to take advantage of it due to counterproductive organizational and group dynamics.

In contrast, effectively conducting an analysis of a failure requires a spirit of inquiry and openness, patience, and a tolerance for ambiguity. Such an *inquiry orientation* is characterized by the perception among group members that multiple alternatives exist, frequent dissent, deepening understanding of issues and development of new possibilities, filling gaps in knowledge through combining information sources, and awareness of each others' reasoning and its implications (Argyris *et al.*, 1978). Such an orientation can counteract common group process failures. Learning about the perspectives, ideas, experiences, and concerns of others when facing uncertainty and high stakes decisions, is critical to making appropriate choices.

Confirmatory and exploratory responses

Leaders play an important role in determining group orientation to an observed or suspected failure. When small problems occur, leaders can respond in one of two basic ways (Edmondson *et al.*, 2004b). A *confirmatory response* by leaders to small problems — appropriate in routine production settings, but harmful in more volatile or uncertain environments — reinforces accepted assumptions, naturally promoting an advocacy orientation on the part of themselves and others. When individuals seek information, they naturally look for data that confirms existing beliefs. Confirmatory leaders act in ways consistent with established frames and beliefs, passive and reactionary rather than active and forward-looking.

In uncertain or risky situations or where innovation is required, an *exploratory response* may be more appropriate than seeking to confirm existing views. An exploratory response involves challenging and testing existing assumptions and experimenting with new behaviors and possibilities, the goal of which is to learn and to learn quickly. By deliberately exaggerating ambiguous threats, actively directing and coordinating team analysis and problem solving, and encouraging an overall orientation toward action, exploratory leaders encourage inquiry and experimentation. Leaders seeking to encourage exploration also actively foster constructive conflict and dissent and generate psychological safety by creating an environment in which people have an incentive, or at least do not have a disincentive, to identify and reveal failures, questions, and concerns. This form of leader response helps to accelerate learning through deliberate information gathering, creative mental simulations, and simple, rapid experimentation.

Rather than supporting existing assumptions, an exploratory response requires a deliberate shift in the mindset of a leader — and of others — altering the way they interpret, make sense of, and diagnose situations. When leaders follow an exploratory approach, they embrace ambiguity and acknowledge openly gaps in knowledge. They recognize that their current understanding may require revision, and they actively seek evidence in support of alternative hypotheses. Rather than seeking to prove what they already believe, exploratory leaders seek discovery through creative and iterative experimentation (Garvin, 2000).

Several years ago, at Children's Hospital and Clinics in Minnesota, the new chief operating officer, Julie Morath, exhibited an exploratory response that promoted an inquiry orientation among group members (Edmondson, Roberto, & Tucker, 2005). Upon taking up her new position, she first strengthened her personal technical knowledge of how to probe deeply into the causes of failure in hospitals through a variety of educational opportunities and experiences. She learned from prominent experts that rather than being the fault of a single individual, medical errors tend to be embedded in complex interdependent systems and have multiple roots. In addition, she overcame organizational barriers by making structural changes within the organization to create a context in which failure could be identified, analyzed, and learned from. Notably, Morath instituted a "blameless reporting" system to encourage employees to reveal medical errors right away and to share additional information that could be used in analyzing causes of the error. This was in part an attempt to shift the culture to one that supported learning. More concretely, she created several specific forums for learning from failure, including focused event studies in response to all identified failures, small and large, and a leadership team called the Patient Safety Steering Committee (PSSC). The PSSC proactively sought to identify failures and opportunities for improvement throughout the organization, and ensured that all failures were analyzed for learning. In addition, cross-functional teams, known as safety action teams, spontaneously formed in certain clinical areas to better understand how failures occurred, to proactively improve medical safety. One clinical group developed something they called a "Good Catch Log" to record information that might be useful in better understanding and reducing medical errors. Other teams in the hospital quickly followed their example, finding the idea compelling and practical.

Learning-oriented and coping-oriented approaches

When implementing an innovation, such as a new technology or practice, leaders can orient those who will be responsible for implementation by responding in one of two ways. They may view the innovation challenge as something with which they need to cope or as an exciting learning and improvement opportunity (Edmondson, 2003d). A coping approach is characterized by protective or defensive aims and technically oriented leadership. In contrast, learning-oriented leaders share with team members a sense of purpose related to accomplishing compelling goals and view project success as dependent on all team members.

In the study of 16 cardiac surgery departments, mentioned above, implementing a minimally invasive cardiovascular surgery technique, successful surgical team leaders demonstrated a learning-oriented approach rather than a coping approach (Edmondson, 2003d). Learning-oriented leaders explicitly communicated their interdependence with others, emphasizing their own fallibility and need for others' input for the new technology to work. Without conveying any loss of expertise or status, these leaders simply recognized and communicated that in doing the new procedure they were dependent on others. In learning-oriented teams, members felt a profound sense of ownership of the project's goals and processes, and they believed their roles to be crucial. Elsewhere, the surgeon's position as expert precluded others from seeing a way to make genuine contributions beyond enacting their own narrow tasks, and it put them in a position of not seeing themselves as affecting whether the project succeeded or not. Learning-oriented teams had a palpable sense of teamwork and collegiality, aided by early practice sessions.

In addition, team members felt completely comfortable speaking about their observations and concerns in the operating room, and they also were included in meaningful reflection sessions to discuss how the technology implementation was going. In teams that framed the innovation as a learning opportunity, leaders enrolled carefully selected team members, conducted pre-trial team preparation, and multiple iterations of trial and reflection. Dramatic differences in the success of learning-oriented versus coping-oriented leaders suggest that project leaders have substantial power to influence how team members see a project, especially its purpose and their own role in achieving that purpose.

Organizational exploitation and exploration

Inquiry and advocacy orientations describe individuals and groups; exploration and exploitation are terms that have been used to describe parallel characteristics of organizations (March, 1991). In mature markets, where solutions for getting a job done exist and are well understood, organizations tend to be designed and oriented toward a focus on execution of tasks and *exploitation* of current products or services. In more uncertain environments, knowledge about how to achieve performance is limited, requiring collective learning — or *exploration* in which open-ended experimentation is an integral part. In sum, exploration in search of new or better processes or products, is conceptually and managerially distinct from execution, which is characterized by planning and structured implementation and amenable to formal tools such as statistical control (Sitkin *et al.*, 1994).

Organizing to learn and organizing to execute

In the same way that leader's response drives group member orientation, the mindset of organizational leaders as well as the structures and systems they initiate play a large role in determining firm behavior and capabilities. *Organizing to learn* and *organizing to execute* are two distinct management practices, one suited to exploration and the other to exploitation respectively (Argyris *et al.*, 1978).

Where problems and processes are well understood and where solutions are known, leaders are advised to *organize to execute*. Organizing to execute relies on traditional management tools that motivate people and resources to carry out well-defined tasks. When reflecting on the work, leaders who organize to execute are well advised to ask, "Did we do it right?" In general, this approach is systematic, involves first-order learning in which feedback is used to modify or redirect activities, and eschews diversion from prescribed processes without good cause.

In contrast, facing a situation in which process solutions are not yet well developed, leaders must *organize to learn*: generating variance, learning from failure, sharing results, and experimenting continuously until workable processes are discovered, developed, and refined. Motivating organizational exploration requires a different mindset than motivating accurate and efficient execution. Leaders must ask — not "Did we succeed?" but rather — "Did we learn?" In this way, organizing to learn considers the lessons of failure to be at least as valuable as the lessons of success. Such a managerial approach organizes people and resources for second-order learning that challenges, reframes, and expands possible alternatives (Edmondson, 2003a). Practices involved in organizing to learn include promoting rather than reducing variance, conducting experiments rather than executing prescribed tasks, and rewarding learning rather than accuracy (Edmondson, 2003a; Sitkin *et al.*, 1994).

Creating systems to expose failures can help organizations create and sustain competitive advantage (Cannon *et al.*, 2005). For example, General Electric, UPS, and Intuit proactively seek data to help them identify failures. GE places an 800 number directly on each of its products (Tax & Brown, 1998). UPS allocates protected time for each of its drivers to express concerns or make suggestions (Sonnenfeld & Lazo, 1992). Intuit staffs its customer service line with technical designers, who directly translate feedback from customers into

49

product improvements (Heskett, Sasser, & Schlesinger, 1993). At IDEO, brainstorming about problems on a particular project often enables engineers to discover ideas that benefit other design initiatives (Hargadon & Sutton, 1997). At Toyota, the Andon cord, which permits any employee to halt production, enables continuous improvement through frequent investigation of potential concerns (Mishina, 1992; Spear, 1999).

LEARNING COMES AT A COST TO CURRENT PERFORMANCE

Learning often comes at a cost to current performance. First, learning involves acquiring new skills, behaviors, or routines, that, by definition, one has not yet mastered. Therefore, learning can lead to performance decrements in the short term. Second, learning from small problems or process failures, requires eschewing quick fixes and workarounds, and instead stopping to take the time to analyze and seek to address root causes of the problem. Therefore, resolving problems to prevent recurrence is likely to take longer than working around the problem, harming efficiency in the short-term.

These short-term costs of learning are particularly problematic when workers face fragmented tasks or heavy workloads that preclude the necessary slack for learning. For these reasons, problem solving techniques recommended in the quality literature were used infrequently by front line caregivers in hospitals (Tucker & Edmondson, 2002). In this in-depth observational study, nurses were often overwhelmed by their workloads and primarily concerned about their ability to continue providing patient care, virtually eliminating the possibility of contributing to system improvement. Lack of processes and resources needed to tackle improvement efforts, including time to engage in second order problem solving, effective mechanisms for communicating across boundaries, and access to a support person who could facilitate investigation and implementation of solution efforts, discouraged learning behavior.

Despite short term costs, learning can enhance future performance. Interruptions caused by small problems increased the likelihood of performing a task incorrectly (Leape *et al.*, 1995; Osborne, Blais, & Hayes, 1999; Reason, 1990).

Solving recurring problems, prevents their recurrence and saves time in the long run. In contrast, working around problems has no effect on the frequency of future problems because nothing is done to ensure that similar events do not recur.

LEADING ORGANIZATIONAL LEARNING

Although group and organizational leaders may agree about the benefits of learning, they face a variety of challenges in their efforts to manage organizations effectively. These include recognizing and responding to the need for learning versus execution, embracing the small failures from which organizations can learn, and maintaining the ability to shift nimbly between learning and execution as needed.

Diagnose the situation and respond accordingly

Rather than vary their style as appropriate for the situation, in practice leaders tend to employ a consistent approach. Frequently they gravitate toward organizing to execute, particularly when associated practices are consistent with the organization's culture. However, being good at organizing to execute can hamper efforts that require learning. When leaders facing a novel challenge organize to execute rather than employing a learning approach, their organizations miss opportunities to innovate successfully.

For example, a major telecommunications firm studied in late 1999 was organized to manage precise execution of established work processes (Frei, Edmondson, & Hajim, 2001). In trying to expand into DSL, the organization was undertaking a technological challenge that required fast collective learning. Management practices honed for ensuring superb execution were not well suited for the uncertainty and rapid experimentation needed to discover the new routines that would ensure successful delivery of DSL services. In short, the firm's excellence in execution did not translate easily into a successful launch in the new technologically novel service.

In contrast, Julie Morath at Children's Hospital exemplified a mindset of organizing to learn. Emphasizing that she did not have the answers, she invited people throughout the organization to join in a learning journey, aimed at discovering how to ensure 100% patient safety.

Embrace failure

Organizing a team to experiment and learn about an unknown process requires a management approach that embraces failure rather than seeking perfect execution. Discovery and expeditious trial and error are the keys to successful learning. In the Electric Maze,[1] an interactive learning exercise adopted at Harvard Business School, participants recognize how unnatural collective learning is for most managers (Edmondson & Rodriguez-Farrar, 2004c). Teams of students must get each member from one end of the maze to the other without speaking. Individuals step on the maze until a square beeps, at which point the individual must retrace the steps back to the start.

To optimize the learning process, the team should "embrace failure" (symbolized in the Electric Maze® exercise as "beeps going forward") and systematically collect as many "failures" as quickly as possible. More typically, however, the need to learn with and in front of others is hampered by the perceived interpersonal risk of "failing" in front of colleagues by stepping on a beeping square. In reality, only by stepping on beeping squares can the team learn quickly and discover the true path forward. The exercise offers a palpable experience to show managers that the desire to look as if one never makes mistakes hinders team and organizational learning.

Maintain flexibility and shift as needed

Some business situations require innovation and execution simultaneously, or in rapid sequence. However, shifting from organizing to learn to organizing to execute can be difficult. Participants in the Electric Maze Exercise face and come to

---

[1] Electric Maze® is the registered trademarked name by Interel, a company that produces interactive learning tools and devices.

appreciate this challenge as well. To find the correct path through the maze requires organizing to learn. Once the path is discovered, teams are required to have participants walk through the path as quickly as possible with minimal error. In practical terms, this means the teams must shift their behavior from learning to execution. Most teams have a difficult time switching from the discovery task to the execution task.

The Maze exercise illustrates that managing a team for superb execution of a known process calls for a different approach than managing a team to experiment and discover a new process. Discovery through expeditious trial and error is the key to the first part of the exercise. In contrast, careful adherence to specification helps teams achieve error free execution in the second part. Discovering the path requires teams to organize to learn. Getting all team members successfully through the path requires teams to organize to execute. Organizational effectiveness is maximized when learning and executing situations are clearly framed as such, yet shifting between organizing to learn and organizing to execute is difficult, as noted earlier. The ability to recognize situations that require learning and the flexibility to shift from execution to learning requires awareness as well as skillful management, posing significant challenge to many leaders and competitive advantage to leaders with such ability.

IMPLICATIONS FOR PERFORMANCE MEASUREMENT

Implications of the complex relationship between learning and performance for performance measurement are worth a brief discussion. In execution contexts, performance is easier to measure. In exploratory learning contexts, performance is more difficult to measure in the short term, even if it contributes to clear performance criteria in the long term. Consider the Electric Maze exercise again. In the second phase, excellent performance is error free, rapid completion of the task — every member traversing the discovered path. In the first phase, success requires encountering and learning from failures, but how many is the right number? How fast should experiments be run? As in this example, the success of experimentation is far more difficult to assess than the success of execution.

Clearly, there are situations in which it is appropriate to measure performance against quality and efficiency standards. This is true when tasks are routine. However, employee rewards based primarily on indices measuring routine performance, such as accuracy and speed, can thwart efforts to innovate. Stated goals of increasing innovation are more effective when rewards promote experimentation rather than penalize failure (Lee *et al.*, 2004). At Bank of America, for example, innovation was an espoused value (Thomke & Nimgade, 2002). Leaders targeted a projected failure rate of 30% as suggestive of sufficient experimentation. However, few employees experimented with new ideas until management changed its reward system from traditional performance measures to those that rewarded innovation. Truly supporting innovation requires recognition that trying out innovative ideas will produce failures on the path to improvement.

Leaders need to align incentives and to offer resources to promote and facilitate effective learning. Supporting improvement requires understanding that mistakes are inevitable in uncertain and risky situations. Organizations must reward improvement rather than success, reward experimentation even when it results in failure, and publicize and reward speaking up about concerns and mistakes, so others can learn.

Policies that reward compliance with specific targets or procedures encourage effort toward those measures but may thwart efforts toward innovation and experimentation. For example in healthcare, pay-for-performance incentives have gained popularity in recent years among policymakers and practitioners (Rosenthal, Fernandopulle, Song, & Landon, 2004). Most performance pay systems reward organizations that meet standards of evidence-based practice (Rosenthal *et al.*, 2004). The potential problem with such schemes is that while incentives to promote evidence-based care are appropriate in areas where evidence is clear, without comparable incentives for experimentation where evidence is more ambiguous, performance pay may unintentionally undermine learning behaviors where they are needed. Given that so much of the health care services delivered today is hazardous and uncertain, powerful pay-for-performance incentives may deter desirable learning.

Given the problematic nature of the relationship between learning and performance, to provide incentives for learning, performance measurement must examine learning, not just performance (Garvin, 1993). Useful tools include surveys, questionnaires, and interviews to examine attitudes toward and depth of understanding regarding new ideas, knowledge, and ways of thinking. Process measures are also helpful (Garvin, 1993; Lee *et al.*, 2004). Direct observation is useful for assessing behavioral change due to new insights. Finally, performance measurement must consider improvement by measuring results over time. Groups that improve more over a fixed time frame or that take less time to improve must be learning faster than their peers. Short learning cycles will translate into superior future performance.

In contrast, an evaluation of current pay-for-performance arrangements among healthcare organizations found no emphasis on quality improvement relative to baseline measures (Rosenthal *et al.*, 2004). Rather, a majority of programs sought to intensify competitive pressures between organizations, exacerbating incentives for organizations to emphasize exploitation in targeted areas. This trend highlights the need for better understanding of learning requirements in organizations and what it takes to meet them.

CONCLUSIONS

In this chapter, we have called attention to some of the challenges and tensions that exist when trying to improve team or organizational performance through proactive learning. We note several ways in which learning and performance in organizations can be at odds. Notably, when organizations engage in a new learning challenge, performance often suffers, or appears to suffer, in the short term. Struggling to acquire new skills or capabilities often takes a real, not just apparent, toll on short-term performance. Moreover, by revealing and analyzing their failures and mistakes — a critical aspect of learning — work groups may appear to be performing less well than they would otherwise. We reviewed work that has elucidated the challenges of learning from failure in organizations, including the challenges of admitting errors and failures and production pressure that make it difficult to invest time in learning. We argued that these challenges are at least partially addressed by managerial efforts to create a climate of psychological safety and to promote inquiry. Leadership is thus essential to foster the mindset, group behaviors, and organizational investments needed to promote today's learning and invest in tomorrow's performance.

REFERENCES

Ancona, D. G. & Caldwell, D. F. (1992). Bridging the boundary: External activity and performance in. *Administrative Science Quarterly, 37*, 4, 634.

Argyris, C. & Schon, D. (1978). *Organizational Learning: A Theory of Action Perspectives.* Reading, MA: Addison-Wesley.

Argyris, C. (1985). *Strategy, Change, and Defensive Routines.* New York: Harper Business.

Ashford, S. J. & Tsui, A. S. (1991). Self-Regulation for Managerial Effectiveness: The Role of Active Feedback Seeking. *Academy of Management Journal, 34*, 2, 251.

Banker, R. D., Field, J. M., Schroeder, R. G., & Sinha, K. K. (1996). Impact of work teams on manufacturing performance: A longitudinal field study. *Academy of Management Journal, 39*, 4, 867.

Boyett, J. & Conn, H. (1991). *Workplace 2000: The Revolution Reshaping American Business.* New York: Penguin.

CAIB. (2003). Final Report on the Columbia Space Shuttle Accident, Volume 1. Washington, D.C.: U.S. Government Printing Office.

Cannon, M. & Edmondson, A. (2005). Failing to Learn and Learning to Fail (Intelligently): How Great Organizations Put Failure to Work to Improve and Innovate. *Long Range Planning Journal, 38*, 3, 299–320.

Cannon, M. D. (1993). *Motivation and learning: A paradox for performance.* Paper presented at the 53rd annual Academy of Management Meeting, Atlanta, GA.

Cavaluzzo, L. (1996). Enhancing team performance. *The Healthcare Forum Journal, 39*, 5, 57.

Chan, C., Lim, L., & Keasbury, S. K. (2003). Examining the linkages between team learning behaviors and team performance. *The Learning Organization, 10*, 4, 228–236.

Chan, C., Pearson, C., & Entrekin, L. 2003. Examining the effects of internal and external team learning on team performance. *Team Performance Management, 9*, 7/8, 174–181.

Cohen, S. G. & Ledford, G. E. J. (1994). The effectiveness of self-managing teams: A quasi-experiment. *Human Relations, 47*, 1, 13.

Cordery, J. L., Mueller, W. S., & Smith, L. M. (1991). Attitudinal and behavioral effects of autonomous group working: A longitudinal field study. *Academy of Management Journal, 34*, 2, 464.

Cutcher-Gershenfeld, J., Nitta, M., Barrett, B., Belhedi, N., & *et al.* (1994). Japanese team-based work systems in North America: Explaining the diversity. *California Management Review, 37*, 1, 42.

Edmondson, A. (2003a). Organizing to Learn: HBS Publishing (Note-5-604-031).

Edmondson, A. (2003b). Managing the Risk of Learning: Psychological Safety in Work Teams. In M. West & D. Tjosvold & K. Smith (Eds.), *International Handbook of Organizational Teamwork and Cooperative Working*. London: John Wiley & Sons, Ltd.

Edmondson, A. & Feldman, L. (2004a). Phase Zero: Introducing New Services at IDEO, HBS Case #9-604-005. Boston: Harvard Business School Publishing.

Edmondson, A., Roberto, M. A., Bohmer, R. M., Ferlins, E. M., & Feldman, L. (2004b). The Recovery Window: Organizational Learning Following Ambiguous Threats in High-Risk Organizations. In M. Farjoun & W. H. Starbuck (Eds.), *Organization at the Limit: NASA and the Columbia Disaster*. London: Blackwell.

Edmondson, A., Roberto, M. A., & Tucker, A. L. (2005). Children's Hospital and Clinics, HBS Case #9-302-050. Boston: Harvard Business School Publishing.

Edmondson, A. C. (1996). Learning from mistakes is easier said than done: Group and organizational influences on the detection and correction of human error. *The Journal of Applied Behavioral Science*, 32, 1, 5.

Edmondson, A. C. (1999). Psychological Safety and Learning Behavior in Work Teams. *Administrative Science Quarterly*, 44, 2, 350–383.

Edmondson, A. C., Bohmer, R. M., & Pisano, G. P. (2001). Disrupted routines: Team learning and new technology implementation in hospitals. *Administrative Science Quarterly*, 46, 4, 685.

Edmondson, A. C. (2002). The local and variegated nature of learning in organizations: A group-level perspective. *Organization Science*, 13, 2, 128.

Edmondson, A. C. (2003c). Speaking up in the operating room: How team leaders promote learning in interdisciplinary action teams. *The Journal of Management Studies*, 40, 6, 1419.

Edmondson, A. C. (2003d). Framing for learning: Lessons in successful technology implementation. *California Management Review*, 45, 2, 34.

Edmondson, A. C. & Rodriguez-Farrar, H. (2004c). The Electric Maze Exercise, HBS Case No. 9-604-046. Boston: Harvard Business School Press.

Evans, R., Pestotnik, S., Classen, D., Bass, S., Menlove, R., Gardner, R., & Burke, J. (1992). Development of a computerized adverse drug event monitor. *Proceedings of the Annual Symposium on Computerized Applications for Medical Care*: 23–27.

Flood, P., MacCurtain, S., & West, M. (2001). *Effective Top Management Teams: An International Perspective*. Dublin: Blackhall Publishing.

Frei, F. X., Edmondson, A., & Hajim, C. (2001). Verizon: The Introduction of DSL, *HBS Case Number 602-070*. Boston: Harvard Business School Publishing.

Garvin, D. A. (1993). Building a learning organization. *Harvard Business Review*, 71, 4, 78.

Garvin, D. A. (2000). *Learning in Action: A Guide to Putting the Learning Organization to Work.* Boston, MA: Harvard Business School Press.

Garvin, D. A. & Roberto, M. A. (2001). What you don't know about making decisions. *Harvard Business Review, 79,* 8, 108.

Goleman, D. (1985). *Vital Lies Simple Truths: The Psychology of Self-deception.* New York: Simon and Shuster.

Gupta, Y. & D, A. (1994). Excellence at Rohm and Haas Kentucky: a case study of work teams introduction in manufacturing. *Production and Operations Management, 3,* 3, 186–200.

Hargadon, A. & Sutton, R. I. (1997). Technology brokering and innovation in a product development firm. *Administrative Science Quarterly, 42,* 4, 716.

Hayes, R., Wheelwright, S., & Clark, K. B. (1988). *Dynamic Manufacturing: Creating the Learning Organization.* New York: Free Press.

Henderson, R. M. & Clark, K. B. (1990). Architectural Innovation: The Reconfiguration Of Existing. *Administrative Science Quarterly, 35,* 1, 9.

Heskett, J. L., Sasser, W. E. J., & Schlesinger, L. A. (1993). People, Service, Success: The Service-Profit Link (video): VHS/NTSC (N. America).

Hitchcock, N. A. (1993). Employee participation paves way to product perfection. *Modern Materials Handling, 48,* 6, 44.

Janis, I. L. (1982). Groupthink, second edition. Boston: Houghton-Mifflin.

Katzenbach, J. R. & Smith, D. K. (2005). The Discipline of Teams. *Harvard Business Review, 83,* 7, 162.

Kelley, T. & Littman, J. (2001). *The Art of Innovation: Lessons in Creativity from IDEO, America's Leading Design Firm.* New York: Currency Books.

Leape, L., Bates, D., Cullen, D., Cooper, J., Demonaco, H., Gallivan, T., Hallisey, R., Ives, J., Laird, N., Laffel, G., & et al. (1995). Systems analysis of adverse drug events. ADE Prevention Study Group. *JAMA, 274,* 1, 35–43.

Lee, F. (1993). Being polite and keeping MUM: How bad news is communicated in organizational hierarchies. *Journal of Applied Social Psychology, 23,* 14, 1124–1149.

Lee, F., Edmondson, A. C., Thomke, S., & Worline, M. (2004). The mixed effects of inconsistency on experimentation in organizations. *Organization Science, 15,* 3, 310–326.

Maidique, M. & Zirger, B. (1984). A study of success and failure in product innovation: The case of the U.S. electronics industry. *IEEE Transactions on Engineering Management, 31,* 4, 192–204.

March, J. G. (1991). Exploration and Exploitation in Organizational Learning. *Organization Science,* 2(1, Special Issue: Organizational Learning: Papers in Honor of (and by) James G. March): 71–87.

Meyer, M. A. (1994). The Dynamics of Learning with Team Production: Implications for Task Assignment. *The Quarterly Journal of Economics, 109,* 4, 1157.

Michael, D. N. (1976). *On Learning to Plan and Planning to Learn.* San Francisco: Jossey-Bass.

Mishina, K. (1992). Toyota Motor Manufacturing, U.S.A., Inc., *HBS Case #693-019.* Boston: Harvard Business School Publishing.

Osborne, J., Blais, K., & Hayes, J. (1999). Nurses' perceptions: When is it a medication error? *J Nurs Adm, 29,* 4, 33–38.

Osterman, P. (1994). How common is workplace transformation and who adopts it? *Industrial & Labor Relations Review, 47,* 2, 173.

O'Toole, J. (1995). *Leading Change: Overcoming Ideology of Comfort and the Tyranny of Custom.* San Francisco: Jossey-Bass.

Reason, J. (1990). *Human Error.* Cambridge: Cambridge University Press.

Roberto, M. A. (2002). Lessons from Everest: The interaction of cognitive bias, psychological safety, and system complexity. *California Management Review, 45,* 1, 136.

Roberts, E. (1997). Team training: When is enough...enough? *The Journal for Quality and Participation, 20,* 3, 16.

Rosenthal, M., Fernandopulle, R., Song, H., & Landon, B. (2004). Paying for quality: providers' incentives for quality improvement. *Health Affairs, 23,* 2, 127–141.

Safizadeh, M. H. (1991). The Case of Workgroups in Manufacturing Operations. *California Management Review, 33,* 4, 61.

Schein, E. H. (1993). How Can Organizations Learn Faster? The Challenge of Entering the Green Room. *Sloan Management Review, 34,* 2, 85.

Senge, P. M. (1990). *The Fifth Discipline: The Art and Practice of the Learning Organization.* New York: Doubleday.

Senge, P. M. (1992). *The Fifth Discipline: Teh Art & Practice of the Learning Organization.* Milson Point, New South Wales: Random House Australia.

Singer, S. J., Gaba, D. M., Geppert, J. J., Sinaiko, A. D., Howard, S. K., & Park, K. C. (2003). The culture of safety in California hospitals. *Quality and Safety in Health Care, 12,* 2, 112–118.

Singer, S. J. & Tucker, A. L. (2005). *Creating a Culture of Safety.* Paper presented at the Academy of Management Annual Conference, Honolulu, Hawaii.

Sitkin, S. B. (1992). Learning through failure: The strategy of small losses. In L. L. Cummings & B. M. Staw (Eds.), *Research in Organizational Behavior, 14,* 231–266. Greenwich, CT: JAI Press.

Sitkin, S. B., Sutcliffe, K. M., & Schroeder, R. G. (1994). Distinguishing control from learning in total quality management: A contingency perspective. *Academy of Management. The Academy of Management Review, 19,* 3, 537.

Sonnenfeld, J. A. & Lazo, M. (1992). United Parcel Service (A), HBS Case #9-488-016. Boston: Harvard Business School Publishing.

Spear, S. J. (1999). *The Toyota Production System: An Example of Managing Complex Social/ Teaching Systems: 5 Rules for Designing, Operating, and Improving Activities, Activity-connections, and Flow-paths (dissertation).* Boston, MA: Harvard Business School.

Stasser, G. (1999). The uncertain role of unshared information in collective choice. In L. Thompson & J. Levine & D. Messick (Eds.), *Shared Knowledge in Organizations.* Hillsdale, NJ: Erlbaum.

Sterman, J. D. (1989). Modeling managerial behavior: Misperceptions of feedback in dynamic decision-making. *Management Science, 35,* 3, 321–339.

Tax, S. S. & Brown, S. W. (1998). Recovering and Learning from Service Failure. *Sloan Management Review, 40,* 1, 75.

Taylor, S. E. & Brown, J. D. (1988). Illusion and Well-Being: A Social Psychological Perspective on Mental Health. *Psychological Bulletin, 103,* 2, 193.

Thomke, S. & Nimgade, A. (2002). Bank of America (A), HBS Case No. 9-603-022. Boston: Harvard Business School Publishing.

Thomke, S. (2003). *Experimentation Matters.* Boston, MA: Harvard Business School Press.

Tjosvold, D. (1991). *Team Organization: An Enduring Competitive Advantage.* New York: Wiley.

Tucker, A., Nembhard, I., & Edmondson, A. (2005). The Effects of Learn-What and Learn-How on the Implementation Success of Improvement Projects. Unpublished manuscript.

Tucker, A. L. & Edmondson, A. (2002). Managing Routine Exceptions: A Model of Nurse Problem Solving Behavior. *Advances in Health Care Management, 3,* 87–113.

Tucker, A. L. & Edmondson, A. C. (2003). Why hospitals don't learn from failures: Organizational and psychological dynamics that inhibit system change. *California Management Review, 45,* 2, 55.

Weick, K. E. & Sutcliffe, K. M. (2001). *Managing the Unexpected: Assuring High Performance in an Age of Complexity.* San Francisco, CA: Jossey-Bass.

Wellins, R., Byham, W., & Wilson, J. (1991). *Empowered Teams: Creating Self-directed Work Groups that Improve Quality, Productivity, and Participation.* San Francisco: Jossey-Bass Publishers.

Wheelan, S. A. & Burchill, C. (1999). Take teamwork to new heights. *Nursing Management, 30,* 4, 28.

Wohlstetter, R. (1962). *Pearl Harbor: Warning and Decision.* Stanford, CA: Stanford University Press.

THE WORK OF KNOWLEDGE MANAGEMENT MADE REAL

MARGARET WHEATLEY AND MYRON ROGERS

Managing knowledge is crucial to achieving improved performance based on learning. But most of us don't adequately understand either learning or knowledge. This confusion can be a tremendous hindrance to an organization's efforts at achieving increased performance. Unfortunately, in many organizations, confusion is the norm. We are struggling because we still work from management concepts that haven't kept pace with the changes we continue to experience.

We really do live in the Information Age, a revolutionary era when the availability of information is changing everything. Nothing is the same since the world was networked together and information became instantly accessible. Information has destroyed boundaries, borders, boxes, distance, values, roles, and rules. The availability of information has dissolved the walls of repressive governments, dishonest executives, and it has the potential to create the greatest mass empowerment of all time.

Because of access to information, we are in new relationships with everyone: with medical doctors (we go to the web and learn more than they do,) with car salesmen (we know the real sticker price,) and with leaders of all kinds (we know when they walk their talk). The World Wide Web has created a world that is transparent, volatile, sensitive to the least disturbance, and choked with rumors, misinformation, truths, and passions.

This webbed world has changed the way we work and live. 24/7/365 is one consequence of instant access and the dissolution of boundaries. We no longer have clear lines between work and private life — if the cell phone is on and there's an Internet connection available, bosses and colleagues expect us to be available. Increasingly, it's impossible to "turn off," to find time to think, to take time to develop relationships, to even ask colleagues how they're doing.

Information has changed capitalism and the fundamental character of corporate life. Corporations now play in the global casino — focused on numbers moment to moment, suffering instant losses or gains in trading, merging to look powerful, downsizing to look lean, bluffing and spin doctoring to stay in the game. In this casino environment, long-term has disappeared, thinking for the future is impossible, and developing an organization that will still be around in twenty years can seem like a sentimental and wasteful activity.

These are only a few of the profound changes created by the Information Age. A September 2000 study by a futures group from the U.S. Military summed it up this way: "The accelerated pace and grand breadth of information exchange is *arguably beyond comprehension and certainly out of control.* With so much information to choose from, each day it becomes harder to determine what is real, right, and relevant to people's lives."

If information exchange is out of control, then much of our thinking about management needs to be reconsidered. In particular, our love affair with numbers gives us the impression that we are in control of whatever it is we are measuring. In the West, we live in a culture that is crazy about numbers. Starting in the sixth century BCE, numbers became the means we used to see reality. But over time, numbers became the only reality. Today, we make something real by assigning a number to it. Once it's a number, it's ours to manage and control. The poet W. H Auden years ago wrote about this Western obsession: "And still they come, new from those nations to which the study of that which can be weighed and measured is a consuming love."

We need to look again at the fundamental ideas on which we are basing our efforts to manage knowledge. First, though, consider why Knowledge Management is crucial and some of the prevailing ideas that need to be reconsidered.

KNOWLEDGE MANAGEMENT IS A SURVIVAL SKILL

In this time of profound chaos and newness, we still have to do our work. But what is our work? For those in human resources information management, there is relentless pressure to find ways for technology and people to support organizations through this tumultuous time. Organizations need to be incredibly smart, fast, agile, responsive. They need to respond and make smart decisions at ever-increasing speed, even as the unintended consequences of speedy decisions flare up in a nanosecond and keep leaders focused only on fire-fighting. The old days of "continuous improvement" seem as leisurely as a picnic from the past. In this chaotic and complex twenty-first century, the pace of evolution has entered warp speed, and those who can't learn, adapt, and change moment to moment simply won't survive.

Many of these organizational needs are bundled together today under the banner of *Knowledge Management*. The organization that knows how to convert information into knowledge, that knows what it knows, that can act with greater intelligence and discernment — these are the organizations that will make it into the future. We all know that our organizations need to be smarter. Knowledge Management (KM) therefore should be something eagerly accepted by leaders, it should be an incredibly easy sell. Yet KM appears at a time when all organizations are battered and bruised by so much change, entering the Information Age after decades of fads, and by investments in too many organizational change efforts that failed to deliver what was promised. These experiences have exhausted us all, made many cynical, and left others of us worried that we'll never learn how to create organizations that can thrive in this century.

Unlike past organizational change efforts, Knowledge Management is truly a survival issue. Done right, it can give us what we so desperately need — organizations that act with intelligence. Done wrong, we will, like lemmings, keep rushing into the future without using our intelligence to develop longer-term individual and organizational capacity. To continue blindly down our current path, where speed and profits are the primary values, where there is no time to think or relate, is suicidal.

BELIEFS THAT PREVENT KNOWLEDGE MANAGEMENT

How can we ensure that KM doesn't fail or get swept aside as just the most recent fad? How can we treasure it for the life-saving process it truly could be? For

Knowledge Management to succeed, we will need to lay aside these dangerously out-of-date beliefs:

- *Organizations are machines.* This belief becomes visible every time we create separate parts — tasks, roles, functions — and engineer (and reengineer) them to achieve pre-determined performance levels. It is the manager's role to manage the parts to achieve those outcomes. Strangely, we also act as though people are machines. We attempt to "reprogram" people with new training and technology, hoping that, like good robots, they will go off and do exactly what they're told. When people resist being treated as dumb machines, we criticize them as "resistant to change."
- *Only material things are real.* A great deal of our efforts focus on trying to make invisible "things" (like knowledge, commitment, trust, relationships) assume material form. We believe we have accomplished this when we assign numbers to them. This belief combines with the next one;
- *Only numbers are real.* Our centuries-old love affair with numbers makes us uncomfortable when they are missing. Once we assign a number to something (a grade in school; a performance measure; a statistic) we relax and feel we have adequately described what's going on. These two beliefs reinforce that;
- *You can only manage what you can measure.* We use numbers to manage everything: ROI; P/E ratios; inventory returns; employee morale; staff turn-over. If we can't assign a number to it, we don't pay it any attention. To keep track of increasingly complex measurements, we turn to our favorite new deity, which is the belief that;
- *Technology is always the best solution.* We have increasing numbers of problems, which we try to solve using technology. But this reliance on technology actually only increases our problems. We don't notice that the numeric information we enter in a computer cannot possibly describe the complexity of the experience or person we are trying to manage. By choosing computers (and numbers) as our primary management tool, we set ourselves up for guaranteed and repeated failures.

All of these beliefs show up strongly in Knowledge Management. We're trying to manage something — knowledge — that is inherently invisible, incapable of being quantified, and born in relationships, not statistics. And we are relying on technology to solve our problems with KM — we focus on constructing the right data base, its storage and retrieval system, and assume we have KM solved.

The Japanese approach KM differently than we do in the West. The difference in approach exposes these Western beliefs with great clarity. In the West, we have focused on explicit knowledge — knowledge one can see and document — instead of dealing with the much more important but intangible realm of "tacit" knowledge, knowledge that is very present, but only observable in the doing, not as a number. American and European efforts have been focused on developing measures for and assigning values to knowledge. Once we had the numbers, we assumed we could manage it, even though more and more people now acknowledge that "Knowledge Management" is an oxymoron.

Current approaches to KM in the West demonstrate that we believe that knowledge is a thing, a material substance that can be produced, measured, catalogued, warehoused, traded, and shipped. The language of KM is littered with this "thing" thinking. We want to "capture" knowledge; to inventory it; to push it into or pull it out from people. One British expert on KM, David Skyrme, tells that in both Britain and the U.S., a common image of KM is of "decanting the human capital into the structural capital of an organization." I don't know how this imagery affects you, but I personally don't want to have my head opened, my cork popped, my entire body tilted sideways so that what I know pours out of me into an organizational vat. This prospect is not what motivates me to notice what I know, or to share it.

These language choices have serious implications. They reveal that we think knowledge is an entity, something that exists independent of person or context, capable of being moved about and manipulated for organizational advantage. We need to abandon this language and, more importantly, the beliefs that engender it. We need to look at knowledge — its creation, transfer, its very nature — with new eyes. As we rethink what we know about knowledge and how we handle the challenges of knowledge in organizations, our most important work is to pay serious attention to what we always want to ignore: *the human dimension.*

Think, for a moment, about what you know about knowledge, not from a theoretical or organizational perspective, but from your own experience. In myself, I notice that knowledge is something I create because I am *in relationship*–relating to another person, an event, or an idea. Something pulls me outside of myself and forces me to react. As I figure out what's going on, or what something means, I develop interpretations that make sense to me. Knowledge is something I create inside myself through my engagement with the world. Knowledge never exists independent of this process of my being in relationship with an event, an idea, or another person. This process is true for all of us. Knowledge is created in relationship, inside thinking, reflecting human beings.

From biology, it is evident that we are not the only life form that engages in knowledge creation. Everything alive learns and creates knowledge for its survival. All living beings pay exquisite attention to what's going on in their environment, with their neighbors, offspring, predators, and even the weather. They notice something, and then decide whether they need to adapt and change. Living beings never engage in this process of noticing — reacting-changing because some boss tells them to do it. Every form of life is free to decide what to pay attention to and how to respond. Individuals decide how they will respond to their neighbors and to current conditions, and then they live or die as a result of their decisions.

This same autonomy describes us humans, but we tend to find it problematic if we're the boss. We give staff detailed directions and policies on how to do something, and then they, like all life, use their autonomy to change it in some way. They fine tune it, they adapt it to their unique context, they add their own improvements to how the task gets done. If we're the one in charge, however, we don't see this behavior as creativity. We label it as resistance or disobedience. But what we are seeing is *new knowledge*. People have looked at the directive, figured out what would work better in the present context, and created a new way of doing it, one that, in most cases, stands more chance of success.

I experienced this knowledge creation process months ago as I sat on an airport commuter bus and listened to the driver train a newly hired employee. For thirty minutes, I eavesdropped as she energetically revealed the secrets and efficiencies she had discovered for how to get to the airport in spite of severe traffic or bad weather. She wasn't describing company policy. She was giving a non-stop, virtuoso performance of what she had invented and changed in order to get her customers to their destination. I'm sure her supervisor had no idea of any of this new knowledge she'd been creating on each bus ride.

But this bus driver is typical. People develop better ways of doing their work all the time, and also like to brag about it. In survey after survey, workers report that most of what they learn about their job, they learn from informal conversations. They also report that they *frequently* have ideas for improving work but don't tell their bosses because they don't believe their bosses care.

SOME PRINCIPLES THAT FACILITATE KNOWLEDGE MANAGEMENT

Knowledge creation is natural to life, and wanting to share what we know is humanly satisfying. So what's the problem? In organizations, what sends these behaviors underground? Why do workers go dumb? Why do we fail to manage knowledge? Here are a few principles that I believe lead to answers to these questions.

1. *Knowledge is created by human beings.* If we want to succeed with KM, then we must stop thinking of people as machines. Instead, we must attend to human needs and dynamics. Perhaps if we renamed it "Human Knowledge" we would remind ourselves of what it is and where it comes from. We would refocus our attention on the organizational conditions that support people, that foster relationships, that give people time to think and reflect. We would stop fussing with the hardware; we would cease trying to find more efficient means to "decant" us. We would notice that when we speak of such things as "assets" or "intellectual capital" that it is not knowledge that is the asset or capital. People are.

2. *It is natural for people to create and share knowledge.* We have forgotten many important truths about human motivation. Study after study confirms that people are motivated by work that provides growth, recognition, meaning, and good relationships. We want our lives to mean something, we want to contribute to others, we want to learn, we want to be together. And we need to be involved in decisions that affect us. If we believed these studies, and created organizations that embodied them, work would be far more productive and enjoyable. We would discover that people can be filled with positive energy. Organizations would be overwhelmed by new knowledge, innovative solutions, and great teamwork. It is essential that we begin to realize that human nature is the blessing, not the problem. As a species, we are actually very good to work with.

3. *Everybody is a knowledge worker.* This statement was an operating principle of one of my clients. If everybody is assumed to be creating knowledge, then the organization takes responsibility for supporting all its workers, not just a special few. It makes certain that everyone has easy access to anyone, anywhere in the organization, because you never know who has already invented the solution you need. The Japanese learned this and demonstrated it in their approach to KM. I learned it on that bus ride.

4. *People choose to share their knowledge.* This is an extremely important statement, and the important word is "choose." Most KM programs get stuck because individuals will not share their knowledge. But it's important to remember that people are making a choice to not share what they know. They *willingly share* if they feel committed to the organization, believe their leaders are worth supporting, feel encouraged to participate and learn, and if they value their colleagues. Knowledge sharing is going on all the time in most organizations. Every organization is filled with self-organized Communities of Practice, relationships that people spontaneously create among colleagues to help them work more effectively or to help them survive the current turbulence. These communities of practice are evidence of people's willingness to learn and to share what they know. But the organization must provide the right conditions to support people's willingness. Some of these necessary, non-negotiable conditions are:

- people must understand and value the objective or strategy
- people must understand how their work adds value to the common objective
- people must feel respected and trusted
- people must know and care about their colleagues
- people must value and trust their leaders

If we contrast this list to the current reality in most organizations, it becomes obvious how much work is needed to create the conditions for effective KM. This is a proven list, with more than enough case studies and research to validate it. If we don't vigorously undertake creating these conditions as the real work of KM, then we might as well stop wasting everyone's time and money and just abandon KM right now.

5. *Measures are useful when used as feedback.* In creating conditions for effective KM, measurement is critical. Measures have no inherent value in themselves: they become useful when they provide us with feedback. All life thrives on feedback and dies without it. When we create systems for KM we need to be clear about the difference between measurement and the feedback that will allow systems to flourish. Unlike measurement, feeback:

- is self-generated, developed by the system to deal with whatever is important to it;
- depends on context and changes to fit circumstances; and
- allows new and surprising information to get in.

6. *Knowledge management is not about technology.* This would seem obvious from the preceding statements, but it feels important to stress because we modern managers are dazzled by technical solutions. If people aren't communicating, we just create another website or on-line conference; if we want to harvest what people know, we just create an inventoried data base; if we're geographically dispersed, we just put video cams on people's desks. But these technical solutions don't solve a thing if other aspects of the culture — the human dimension — are ignored. A few years ago British Petroleum successfully used desktop video cams to facilitate knowledge sharing among their offshore oil drilling rigs. But this wasn't *all* they did. They also worked simultaneously to create a culture that recognized individual contribution, and moved aggressively to create a new vision that employees could rally behind (BP became "Beyond Petroleum.)

And many organizations have learned from experience that if they want productive teams, they must bring people together in the same space several times a year. They're learning that in the absence of face-to-face meetings, people have a hard time sharing knowledge. It's important to remember that technology does not connect us. Our *relationships* connect us, and once we know the person or team, then we use the technology to stay connected. We share knowledge because we are in relationship, not because we have broader bandwidth available.

7. *Knowledge is born in chaotic processes that take time.* The irony of this principle is that it demands two things we don't have — a tolerance for messy, non-linear processes, and time. But creativity is only available when we become confused and overwhelmed, when we get so frustrated that we admit we don't know. And then, miraculously, a perfect insight appears, suddenly. This is how great scientists achieve breakthrough discoveries, how teams and individuals discover transforming solutions. Great insights never appear at the end of a series of incremental steps. Nor can they be commanded to appear on schedule, no matter how desperately we need them. They present themselves only after a lot of work that culminates in so much frustration that we surrender. Only then are we humble enough and tired enough to open ourselves to entirely new solutions. They leap into view suddenly (the "aha" experience,) always born in messy processes that take time.

Self-awareness and reflection are increasingly listed as critical leadership skills. Some companies created architectural spaces to encourage informal conversations, mental spaces to encourage reflection, and learning spaces to encourage journal writing and other reflective thought processes. These innovations, however, run contrary to the prevailing tendencies for instant answers and breathless decision-making. Too many of these sensible innovations fail because warp speed asserts its demands. People simply don't have time to use their journals or to sit in conversation-friendly spaces.

We have to face the difficult fact that until we claim time for reflection, until we make space for thinking, we won't be able to generate knowledge, or to know what knowledge we already possess. We can't argue with the clear demands of knowledge creation — it requires time to develop. It matures inside human relationships.

Although we live in a world completely revolutionized by information, it is important to remember that it is *knowledge* we are seeking, not information. Unlike information, knowledge involves us and our deeper motivations and dynamics as human beings. We interact with something or someone in our environment and then use who we are — our history, our identity, our values, habits, beliefs — to decide what the information means. In this way, through our construction, information becomes knowledge. Knowledge is always a reflection of who we are, in all our uniqueness. It is impossible to disassociate *who* is creating the knowledge from the knowledge itself.

It would be good to remember this as we proceed with Knowledge Management. We can put down the decanting tools, we can stop focusing all our energy on database designs, and we can get on with the real work. We must recognize that knowledge is everywhere in the organization, but we won't have access to it until, and only when, we create work that is meaningful, leaders that are trustworthy, and organizations that foster everyone's contribution and support by giving staff time to think and reflect together. In so doing we collapse the divide between learning and performing.

This is the real work of Knowledge Management. It requires clarity and courage — and in stepping into it, we will be contributing to the creation of a far more intelligent and hopeful future than the one presently looming on the horizon.

The Organisational Challenge

WHAT CAN LEADERS DO?

MARILYN J. DARLING AND DAVID C. FLANIGAN

Most of us know who in our organization owns the responsibility for training, but who owns the responsibility for learning?

This question is at the heart of understanding how to find an effective balance between learning and performance. It will also be important to operational leaders, because the ultimate goal of investments in learning in operational settings is to improve an organization's capacity to achieve excellent results.

In his ground-breaking book, *The Fifth Discipline*, Peter Senge described a cluster of "archetypes" or patterns that systems exhibit, including the organizations we live within. One of a handful of core archetypes is called "Shifting the Burden." It works like this:

> Symptoms of a problem start to surface. Someone sees a quick way to eliminate the problem (i.e., eliminate the symptoms) and makes the problem "go away." But of course the underlying problem remains and will surface again. The more fundamental solution to the problem requires more time and thought, takes time to implement, and often has delays between implementation and relief of the symptoms. So there is great pressure to rely on the quick intervention and, often, on the person or function that intervenes. Over time, the quick intervention can become institutionalized as the system resigns itself to depending on its permanent existence. (Senge, 1990)

In fact, this cycle of effects is almost synonymous with the structure of an organization. Not all organizations are "dys"-functional, but as soon as we create functional specialties, we create the conditions in which this archetype can begin its pernicious work. Functions wanting to justify their continued existence look for challenges to address. Operational leaders come to assume that these functional experts are producing the "best" solutions to the challenges they identified. The solutions may become more and more complex; creating a sort of barrier to entry that further protects functional experts. In the process, however, operational leaders lose touch with the original challenges, create delays between identified challenges and their resolution, and shift the burden to their experts. So what can these leaders[1] do? It is one thing to delegate the job of training to training and development experts. It is another to delegate the *responsibility* for learning. When leaders delegate not only the responsibility for execution of training programs, but also the responsibility for defining goals and measures of learning for their teams, they shift the burden to a functional specialty.

This chapter will reframe how we think about balancing learning and performance in a way that keeps our eye on the prize of achieving excellent results; it will make the case that the more fundamental solution to the challenge of building capacity is to ask operational leaders to maintain their responsibility for learning; and it will offer ideas about how to make this less onerous than it sounds.

THE STRUCTURE OF LEARNING IN A DYNAMIC ENVIRONMENT

The first step is to tease apart what it means to "learn" if the goal is to increase the capacity of teams in organizations to produce excellent results.

In a complex organization working in a complex environment, knowledge has a short shelf life. A lot of factors — from customers to competitors to other internal organizations to the economy and the weather — all have a vote in whether or not our own organization succeeds in its mission. They all interact with each other as well as with us. Some factors act randomly and some act purposefully; some may even work at counter-purposes. Together, they conspire to create a "perpetually

---

[1] By "leader," we are referring to anyone at any level in the organization who is responsible for creating a vision and defining outcomes for a team. Leaders can be found on the shop floor as well as in the Board Room.

novel" environment where the exact situation never repeats exactly. In so doing, they create an unlimited number of rationales for less-than-excellent results.

How can we learn how to achieve excellent results when we continually face new circumstances? Training programs with long approval, development and deployment cycles can't possibly predict and address all of these novel conditions and changing needs. But should we give up on traditional training? *Absolutely not.*

The challenge in such an environment is to focus on building skills around patterns of things that *do* repeat. This is the conclusion drawn by Dr. John Holland, who has spent a career thinking about how complex systems adapt in order to thrive in such perpetually novel environments.

Within those systems that succeed in perpetually novel environments, Holland observes, individuals focus on identifying a stable set of the most useful "building blocks" and becoming proficient in their use. Holland defines building blocks as familiar objects that we are able to parse from a previously unfamiliar situation (Holland, 1995). Part and parcel of learning to use language, for example, is learning to recognize letters and how to group them into meaningful words, and then learning the rules of syntax in order to string words into meaningful sentences.

Let us distinguish two kinds of building blocks that are needed to build capacity in operational environments:

1. Core skills
2. Common conditions

The task of building core skills is generally the focus of traditional training programs. The second type of building block, common conditions, is equally important in Holland's equation, but tends to be unrecognized in organizational learning. To be successful at adapting, individuals must also become skillful in recognizing patterns in their environment — elements of conditions that repeat.

In the example of learning to use language, letters, words and syntax are all core skills. But to become an effective writer, we need to learn to write in a different style when we write a personal letter to a friend, a research report for a scientific audience, or a memo intended to persuade a decision-maker. Some writing tasks even require breaking the rules of syntax (as in the incomplete sentences common in advertising copy).

When we put these two types of building blocks together, we get a complete definition of learning in a perpetually novel environment: one in which all of the individuals within the system are skilled at seeing patterns in their environment and applying a combination of core skills, often in innovative ways, to accomplish a goal around which they are aligned. Each situation may be unique, but understanding "learning" as a combination of these distinct skills makes the task manageable.

Adaptive Learning =
  (a) *Learning core skills +*
  (b) *Learning to recognize conditions +*
  (c) *Learning the rules for combining core skills in changing conditions to achieve goals*

In a perpetually novel environment, leaders cannot afford to align around specific business plans, but they can align around a vision, a passion for learning, and accountability for results.

General Electric is a case in point. Starting in the 1890's as an incandescent lamp manufacturer, the company innovated and morphed over the years from manufacturing lamps to toasters to turbine steam engines; from manufacturing medical diagnostics equipment to providing diagnostic services and consumer financing, and pioneering webcasting. During his tenure as CEO, while the company and its products morphed, Jack Welch maintained a common leadership vision for the leader of each business: Welch did not dictate which business a unit should pursue, but held a threshold that it would remain the first or second in that industry, or GE would discontinue its support of the business. This created a culture that was passionate about growth, but also about seeing changing conditions as a core ingredient in the success formula. Changing conditions represented a new opportunity, rather than a rationale for disappointing results.

In the formula above, clearly traditional training programs play an important role in accomplishing (a). But what is the nature of the rest of this equation and how do we go about doing it?

The early work of Gregory Bateson on "learning to learn" is useful here. While they never met, his solution presaged the work of John Holland by suggesting that the difference between "learning" about something and "learning to learn" about that thing has to do with learning about the context (situation or conditions) that affects how that "something" operates, and identifying effective *rules* about how the thing and its environment interact. Bateson talked about "sets of sets" to explain that the rules exist at a higher logical level than the set of things they describe. (Bateson, 1972). By introducing the idea that there are levels of learning, we can gain new insight into the learning process.

For example:

> To play American football, I must start by practicing over and over the core skills of running, tackling, throwing, receiving and kicking. I must memorize and practice the basic playbook. But to ultimately master the sport, I need to learn (1) how to factor in conditions (weather, the skill level and predicted strategies of the opposing team; the composition of the team on the field); (2) that there are some plays that work better in some conditions against some teams than others; and (3) how to modify a called play if my opponent does something unexpected after the ball leaves the line of scrimmage. I need to learn that what worked beautifully against one team one week may fail miserably against another team the very next week. *Learning to learn* is learning the *rules* that govern the use of the basic play book in a wide range of changing conditions. To master the game of American football, I need to spend as much time learning about the opposing team as I do learning how to throw the football. No amount of simulation will prepare me to win a league title game. The only way for me to master the sport of American football is on real football fields in real conditions against a worthy opponent.

Let us use Bateson's notion of levels of learning to think of the equation above. For purposes of this chapter, let us refer to (a) as Core Skills and (b) and (c) as Situational Skills:

> *Core Skills* are the "toolbox" of basic skills
> *Situational Skills* are knowing how to recognize common conditions and understanding the rules for how to combine those core skills to accomplish goals in those changing conditions.

Core skills are developed at the individual level, and are within the domain of training and development. Situational skills are best developed at the team level, during performance in real situations. We propose, therefore, that the ultimate responsibility for situational skill development rightly belongs to operational leaders.

EMERGENT LEARNING

Training departments and leadership development programs attempt to address situational skill development through action learning programs: creating scenarios or simulations that bring realistic conditions into the classroom. These action learning experiences are valuable inasmuch as they begin to help learners raise their awareness of the role of conditions in successfully using core skills, but they can never replicate all of the conditions a learner will face, and can never replicate the complexity of a team of people facing a complex situation. They are not a stand-in for situational skill development done in the context of real work.

To solve this problem, let us switch the foreground and background of "learning" and "action." Rather than relying solely on inserting action into the context of learning programs, let us find ways to insert learning into actual performance.

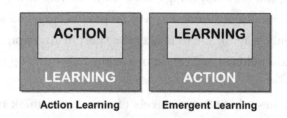

Action Learning   Emergent Learning

Emergent Learning is, quite simply, learning that emerges from the work itself, in the course of performing that work. There are many examples of Emergent Learning methods in the workplace today: reflection exercises, "postmortems," After Action Reviews or even just-in-time training tools. Some of these existing methods can be effective; others fail at their ultimate goal of building the capacity to achieve excellent results in dynamic environments. The goal of our work in Emergent Learning is to find the best ways to achieve this ultimate prize, without creating unnecessary overhead for operational leaders.

Emergent Learning happens in a cycle, which has been described in several different ways. For example, in *The Fifth Discipline Fieldbook*, Ross, Smith and Roberts describe it as "the wheel of learning":

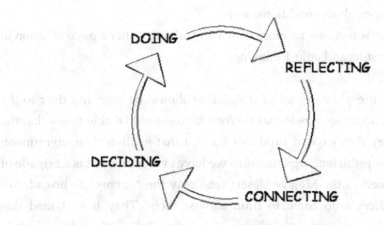

In their model, "connecting" is the process of "creating ideas and possibilities for action, and rearranging them into new forms....Scientists think of this stage as the time for generating hypotheses" (Senge, *et al.*, 1994).

In true learning organizations, operational leaders and their teams recognize that there are no "right" answers in dynamic environments; there are only hypotheses that need to be tested. Teams consciously predict what challenges they are likely to face in the next piece of action, and share their assumptions about what will make them successful. Having done that, each piece of action becomes a learning experiment. When they are done, they reflect on their immediate results. Performance and situational skill development happen at the same time. Over longer cycles, they reflect on results that take longer to see, or on the results of multiple "experiments," in order to develop a deeper understanding of the rules that produce excellent results consistently in widely ranging conditions.

This sounds more complicated than it is. In essence, what we are advocating is identifying another kind of building block: the repeating activities (critical meetings, project milestones, major decisions, emergency response, financial cycles, etc.) that are important to improve in order to build the capacity to achieve excellent results, and turning these recurring activities into conscious learning experiments by:

1. Having clear goals and metrics for them;
2. Doing sound planning that involves everyone in the team in some way, making predictions about conditions; and
3. Taking time (sometimes no more than a few minutes) after a piece of action to reflect on results and adjust thinking.

One principle of Emergent Learning that should be near and dear to the hearts of operational leaders is that *the team itself* should be able to see that the time and energy they expend produces a result that justifies their investment. One of the most proficient organizations we have ever witnessed is a brigade of soldiers stationed in the Mojave Desert who play the "enemy" to brigades of American soldiers who come to train against them. They have honed this process into a fine art that is "just how we do things." Give them a completely novel situation or an impossible objective, and they will work together to accomplish their goal in record time, all the while maintaining high operational standards that would be the envy of most civilian leaders (Darling, Parry & Moore, 2005).

Another principle of Emergent Learning is to employ the simplest, most widely applicable tools, so that teams can focus on the work challenge, not learning a new tool or arguing over how to apply a complicated tool to each new situation.

The Emergent Learning tools that we find to be simplest and best suited to accomplish the (b) and (c) part of the equation above in a wide range of situations are:

*   **After Action Reviews,** developed and evolved over the past 20 years by these soldiers described above, and well suited to fast-cycle learning in action; and
*   **EL Maps**™, a tool co-developed by one of the authors to enable the longer-cycle learning by studying results over longer time intervals and comparing results from multiple situations or pieces of action.

AFTER ACTION REVIEWS

After Action Reviews (AARs) allow a team of people who have just completed a piece of action to review it in a very simple but systematic way. First, they compare what they intended to accomplish and what they actually accomplished. Then they review what contributed to their results and why. Finally, they reflect on what learning they want to take forward: what worked that they will sustain; what needs to be improved.

In order to do this systematic review, the team needs to set the stage after planning, but before taking action, by making sure that (1) they all understand the intended result; (2) they have reviewed the situation to anticipate any glitches; and (3) they are prepared to deal with them. A simple way to begin to create this before and after pairing is to have the group conduct a "Before Action" and "After Action" Review (Darling, Parry & Moore, 2005):

Before Action Review	After Action Review
• What are our intended results and measures?	• What were our intended results?
• What challenges can we anticipate?	• What were our actual results?
• What have we/others learned from similar situations?	• What caused our results?
• What will make us successful this time?	• What will we sustain? Improve?

Many organizations use After Action Reviews to capture lessons learned at the end of a project or to assess operating strategy and plans at the end of the year, in preparation for the next year's business plan and budget. But waiting this long to conduct an AAR — as if it is a "post mortem" — is a mistake. Truly exceptional performance gains are made when AARs are applied to recurring activities, so that learning accumulates and, more importantly, learning impacts *current* results. Daily and weekly production plans, weekly sales campaigns, and monthly profit forecasting all present the opportunity to go around the learning circle, to: (1) declare intended results, (2) create an action plan that reflects previous learning, (3) execute the plan, (4) observe the results, and (5) seek to understand the cause of results and (6) adjust. By integrating the AAR into regular work cadence, an organization can quickly learn how to improve its performance at each and every cycle.

To use our American football example, a winning team would never consider waiting until the end of the game to reflect on why it lost a game. The team huddles in the locker room at halftime, on the sidelines when the offensive team leaves the field, on the field between plays, during time-outs. Huddle, huddle, huddle. After its post-game review, a winning team looks ahead to the next game, respectfully and humbly studying the next opponent, regardless of their standing. They suit up and play against each other, using the next opponent's anticipated tactics to refine their own strategy and prepare contingencies.

EL Maps

The EL Map is a visual tool that helps groups to reflect on multiple experiences, or on what is happening over longer time frames, by mapping out their experiences on a timeline and reflecting on the "defining moments" and patterns between stories that suggest insights into deeper causes. It helps the group to take insights and translate them into concrete learning experiments, using future work as the opportunity to test out new hypotheses in action:

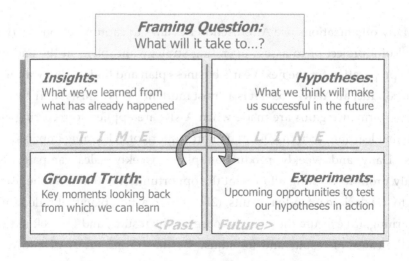

EL Maps can be done in groups of 2 to 20 or more people. They can be created in a few minutes or over the course of a multi-day annual planning retreat. Unlike traditional action planning, EL Maps keep the idea that conditions may change in the foreground and help teams set the expectation that they will need to track results and return to their Map to test out new hypotheses.

As with most simple tools, the art of both After Action Reviews and EL Maps is in their application. These are not mere facilitation techniques. Leaders have an important role to play to ensure that insights gained in learning meetings like these are translated into execution in the future.

What difference can it make when operational leaders build Emergent Learning into their work processes? Let us look at an example.

Most organizations have an annual budget process and do forecasts and report actual results on a monthly or quarterly basis. In far too many companies, the budget and forecast process is seen as a "finance exercise." The numbers are crunched, the variances are reported, but no real learning takes place, except possibly at year end, when, at best, managers try to tease out the thousands of factors that contributed to results over the year and, at worst, try hard to dodge blame.

If a leader is willing to build fast cycles of learning into the process, there is a huge opportunity to improve operating performance. As CEO of a transnational financial services company doing business in forty markets, one of the authors insisted that each business unit executive own the budget and forecast process. ("It's your plan. You figure out how to get there.") They were encouraged to shift their learning cycle from an annual to a monthly rhythm. At the end of each month, the finance and operating people sat together to understand what parts of the plan were working well and what needed to be upgraded, using monthly data as the foundation. They were expected to adjust. The results might show up as soon as next month's review. Over time, the team became more nimble: more able to see and address changing conditions more quickly; more able to separate the wheat from the chaff in terms of which products were truly competitive. Profits doubled in three years, as executives began to study environmental conditions that would formerly have been an excuse for poor performance, looking for ways to turn them into business opportunities.

WHAT CAN LEADERS DO?

What can leaders do to *own* the responsibility for learning in complex environments... without overburdening themselves with oversight and their teams with time spent away from performing?

1. *Build alignment around a vision and hold everyone — including yourself — accountable for getting there.*

Regardless of where in the organizational hierarchy they live, "leaders" are the people who focus our vision on the future and are driven to shape it. They are the ones who first challenge themselves, then challenge the rest of us who work for and with them, to go beyond common wisdom to set stretch goals. And they hold everyone — including themselves — accountable for achieving them, despite changing conditions. When results disappoint, they have little patience for rationalizations.

At General Electric, Jack Welch established his reputation by building an infrastructure for accountability. As described by Larry Bossidy and Ram Charan in their book, *Execution*, Welch held an annual "C Session" to review each business unit's talent pool and organizational priorities. Ninety days later, participants in the C Session would hold a 45-minute teleconference to track follow-through; to complete the learning cycle. "If people can't execute the plan because of changed circumstance, follow-through ensures they deal swiftly and creatively with new conditions." As with Before and After Action Reviews, the combination created the kind of "book end" for action that created accountability and set up the opportunity to learn and adjust (Bossidy & Charan, 2002).

2. *Be a role model for learning: be humble and curious, and take action on learning.*

Leaders can inspire organizational learning by being humble and curious themselves. Jim Collins described "Level 5" Leadership in his bestseller, *Good to Great*. Level 5 leaders build great companies through a paradoxical blend of humility and professional will. They shun the hubris that can come from spectacular success. As Collins described, they manage with a "window and a mirror." When they experience great success, they look out of a window to see how to apportion credit. When they experience failure, they look in a mirror (Collins, 2001). And they close the loop by ensuring that new insights that come from either success or failure become the basis of future action.

In the military example above, Lieutenant Colonel Bob Akam modeled personal accountability for learning simply by carrying a book with him everywhere he went and capturing his personal successes and failures and the lessons he was learning, referring to it often as he and his squadron planned their next campaign. His squadron leaders soon learned to do the same, setting the stage for a learning culture to emerge.

3. *Insist on learning through action: treat plans as hypotheses to be tested, and link lessons from the past to plans for the future.*

Leaders can inspire organizational learning by recognizing that new conditions will impact results, separating "what" (the goal) from "how" (the plan), and treating all plans and solutions as hypotheses. They can insist that they and their teams continue to learn *what* works, and *why*, and in *which* situations. Rather than creating new work or relying on special training events, operational leaders can search for the building blocks that will lead to their success. They can begin to recognize the kinds of activities that are the most important opportunities to learn and ask their teams to reflect, *briefly*, before and after the action, in order to make learning a conscious, emergent process.

CEO Mike Wooley took over the Detroit Institute for Children at a low point in its history, when rising health care costs and state budget cuts had put the institution's survival at risk. Rather than coming in to "save the day," Mike acknowledged that he did not have all of the answers and engaged his entire organization in a process of using Emergent Learning to turn the ship around. Eighteen months later, while economic conditions in the city are no better, the DIC has stabilized and the organization has built the capacity to learn in a dynamic environment in the process, which will help them expand their services to a larger number of needy children in the future.

While these three actions are not "free" in terms of the time and attention it requires from leaders to engage in them, they do not represent a trade-off between today's results and preparing for tomorrow. Investments made in these three actions take operational leaders *closer* to delivering today's results. They are a "twofer" (two for the price of one).

WHAT CAN HUMAN RESOURCES AND ORGANIZATIONAL LEARNING TEAMS DO?

It may seem counter-intuitive, but by expecting operational leaders to take responsibility for situational skill development, an organization actually strengthens the role of Human Resources, Organizational Learning and Training teams.

In the "shift-the-burden" model, HR, OL and Training organizations make their best effort to anticipate the needs of their line organization clients. But they suffer from long planning to execution cycles and competing demands from corporate and operational customers. As soon as they miss their target with a line organization, the frustration factor begins to rise; their client's trust in their capabilities begins to dissolve; lines of communication are broken; and, despite their best efforts to justify their contribution, the staff organization becomes marginalized and resources get reduced. It's a vicious cycle.

Shifting the responsibility and oversight for situational skills back to operational leaders, on the other hand, creates a virtuous cycle. It reinforces the importance of core skill development and strengthens the role of support organizations. A low level of a core skill will become a frustration to the whole group, because it makes it difficult to distinguish the cause of failure in new situations: Did we not recognize or respond to the conditions, or did we not apply our core skills well?

So what can HR and OL do?

1. *Act as a team coach, not as an expert.*

HR and OL leaders can shift how they think of themselves and their roles. Rather than thinking of themselves as experts whose job is to identify and address learning needs, they can instead think of themselves as partners — they can focus on helping their client teams build the capacity to do their own learning. They can co-facilitate, train and coach team members on how to conduct their own Emergent Learning activities around important operational challenges.

2. *Collaborate with leaders to identify and build training around core skills and common conditions.*

HR and OL partners can work with Operational Leaders to identify and build the team's core skill level. They can build scenarios into their training programs that introduce some common conditions, or provide workshops that help build awareness around common conditions participants may face. If the training and development plan does not include training in a critical skill, operational leaders will be in a position to help make a solid business case for the need to invest in these training programs.

3. *Coach leaders on how to create a learning climate.*

Operational leaders need to learn how to recognize which of their myriad projects and work processes represent the best opportunity to create value by focusing their team on learning through them. HR and OL leaders can help these operational leaders identify the best opportunities and learn what they can do before, during and after Emergent Learning sessions to create a climate that fosters candid reflection and taking action on lessons learned. HR and OL leaders can practice what they preach, embodying the same quality of humility and curiosity that they seek to promote in their client teams.

The more HR and OL teams know about what keeps their client leaders up at night and what tasks and challenges lie ahead, the better prepared they will be to recognize opportunities to help these teams embed learning into real work. HR and OL leaders who make a career choice to rotate back and forth between staff and operational roles are in an even stronger position to recognize their clients' needs and opportunities.

WHAT'S POSSIBLE?

Let us recall that our ultimate goal is to achieve excellent results in an environment full of unpredictable and interacting factors, and that we have proposed a formula for learning in that type of perpetually novel environment:

Adaptive Learning =
   (a) *Learning core skills +*
   (b) *Learning to recognize conditions +*
   (c) *Learning the rules for combining core skills in changing conditions to achieve goals*

If an organization is full of leaders who think of learning this way, and HR and OL coaches that support them, what does the organization look like and what is it capable of which other organizations can only hope to achieve?

Because these leaders of learning constantly strive to clarify goals and measures and work with their teams to conduct learning experiments, the learning cycles they create become a lever for changing the culture of the organization. Constantly comparing actual results against goals and plans at multiple levels helps separate the what from the how; it creates a natural drive for alignment of goals and measures, or "line of sight," up and down the hierarchy. It also has the happy consequence of building leadership bench strength.

The natural result is that leadership expectations get pushed down and out closer to the ground...the "learning surface," where teams develop a need to pay closer attention to recognizing conditions, combining core skills, and learning as they implement.

The leader of the military organization described above, the Opposing Force at the US Army's National Training Center, was given a mandate to make a major transformation, and given two years to do it. Using the principles and tools described in this chapter, the whole organization rolled up its sleeves and accomplished the transformation from top to bottom in six months. They spent the rest of their "allotted time" experimenting with new ideas and raising the bar on their own performance, winning Army-wide awards for their high standards. As their leader put it, "learning went vertical" (Darling, Parry & Moore, 2005).

In organizations like this, learning begins to emerge across the organization, without being directed from above, and without relying on functions to design expert solutions to challenges as they emerge. What previously needed to be "hand cranked" begins to happen of its own accord because it produces visible value for the teams themselves. When Emergent Learning happens at every level, it creates sustainable performance improvement and helps reduce the tension between time spent performing and time spent learning. Simply put, teams become agile, and the whole organization becomes *adaptive*.

REFERENCES

Bateson, G. (1972). *Steps to an Ecology of Mind*. New York: Ballantine Books.

Bossidy, L. & Charan, R. (2002). *Execution: The Discipline of Getting Things Done*. New York: Crown Business.

Collins, J. (2001). *Good to Great*. New York: Harper Business.

Darling, M., Parry, C., & Moore, J, Learning in the Thick of It. In *Harvard Business Review*, July–August, 2005

EL Map is a trademark of Signet Consulting Group.

Holland, J. H. (1995). *Hidden Order*. Cambridge, MA: Perseus Books.

Senge, P. (1990). *The Fifth Discipline*. New York: Doubleday/Currency.

Senge, P. *et al*. (1994). *The Fifth Discipline Fieldbook*. New York: Doubleday/Currency.

DOGGIE TREATS AND THE CORE GROUP

ART KLEINER

A manager at a Fortune 500 manufacturing company asked me, "How does the Core Group theory deal with doggie treats?"

I looked at her blankly. "The people I work with," she explained patiently, "aren't thinking about the Core Group. They aren't thinking about anything except the bonuses and points they receive at the end of every quarter." And then she mimicked them. "We *could* develop a new market or innovate new products. But my bonus depends on meeting quarterly targets." Or, "We *could* create a great laboratory here. But I only get bonus points for laying people off."

Oh. "Doggie treats." Incentives and rewards, based on measured performance according to numerical targets. Of course. She went on to say that there were plenty of messages coming down from the Core Group in her company: pronouncements, memos, conferences, and reports in the press, announcing a wide variety of aspirations and ideals. But people paid attention primarily to the incentives, targets and measurements. They didn't care about some metaphysical "needs or wants" of any Core Group; they were saving up for the downpayment on a house, or a car, or their kids' college tuitions. At some companies, a big bonus in a boom year, or a chance to flip stock-option shares during a temporary spike, can be an immense one-time bonanza worth thousands of dollars to employees of mutual consent. How can any Core Group perception compete with that?

Perhaps without realizing, the manager had touched on a richly complex problem that lies beneath the study of organizational change and effectiveness; a mixture of yearning and hopelessness which people struggle to express, yet which drives much of the behavior we see in modern organizations. The problem could be described as the deep sense of loss people feel for 'vernacular culture'.

We are most familiar with the word vernacular when it is used to untutored speech, but it originally came from the Latin word for "homegrown" — for anything that had its roots in the places where people lived. If you were to visit a pre-industrial village market you would find people living a vernacular life: trading goods that were locally grown and produced and doing so in a way that was characteristic of that particular place. People in the village engaged in business, yet the best things in life were free. Vernacular life involved a deep sense of belonging: they knew that they belonged to a particular community. And, as Arie de Geus, author of *The Living Company*, says, community gives peoples' lives identity, coherence and continuity.

Imagine doing business in this vernacular culture. In no way would you think to try to separate your work life from your private life. Your name might be derived from how you earn your living. Any transaction you undertook was an expression of your community's spirit.

While we may prize and appreciate the conveniences of modern life, people yearn for this lost way of life. It is the village life of our dreams, where work and life and family are all intermingled in a purposeful, complete and fulfilling tapestry. This yearning lies beneath the pleasure we take in television programs and movies that depict village or community life. Yet the situation seems hopeless; that this is a yearning that must remain unrequited.

Why? Because the world has changed, and the village life has made way for a world of business governed by the magic of "the numbers".

THE NUMBERS

It is said that "what is measured, matters." Measure something, and the modern organization moves to produce it — especially if you set up incentives accordingly. One of the most popular management theories of the past 20 years, the "Balanced Scorecard," is based directly on this premise. If you want to generate better results (the theory goes), then select more strategically-oriented incentives, targets and measurements. Be more attentive to the doggie treats, and you will develop an increasingly sophisticated body of employees — in the same way that a really good circus animal trainer, armed with the right kinds of food, can develop an increasingly sophisticated cadre of performing animals.

The "Balanced Scorecard" theory (or, if you prefer, the "doggie treats" theory) is a natural evolution in the history of modern management. Organizations as we know them started with the nascent railroading enterprises of the 1840s, which gained competence by comparing the measured speed and reliability of each railroad line against the others. The scientific management of Frederick Taylor, and the in-depth division management system developed by Alfred Sloan and Donaldson Brown at General Motors in the 1920s, both depended on innovative uses of financial measurements, incentives, and rewards. Modern finance is, itself, a kind of magic: it allows for the instant comparison, in objective terms, of the basic worth of human beings, the future risk of their endeavors, and the potential reward — the kinds of things that, previously, could only be talked about with vague terms like *karma* and *hubris*.

This power, or magic, was reinforced when behavioral psychologists entered the corporate consulting world in the middle of the 20th Century, showing managers how to use rewards and punishments much more effectively. Ever since, much of the power of the modern organization has stemmed literally from the use of incentives, targets and measurements to standardize and roll out technologies and practices. No wonder "doggie treats" work so well; they're the visible edge of the system of thought that gives organizations their power in the first place.

Within corporations, there is little room for the vernacular spirit: the whole point of the numbers is to free people from human ties, thus enabling them to be more productive.

There is, however, a dark side to the magic of the numbers. As well as overwhelming the vernacular life, pursuit of the numbers leads even the most thoughtful of manager tends to lose sight of what the numbers represent. Numbers may start out as a tool to enable people to pursue noble goals. Over time, tragically, the noble goal is sacrificed so that the desired numbers can be achieved.

Former MIT accounting professor (and current organizational learning theorist) Fred Kofman puts it this way: "When the numbers take on a life of their own, they sever their associations with us. They lose the memory of the process which created them. The accounting system then becomes like the Frankenstein monster: a human construct which turns on its creators."

Kofman quotes a manager at one of the companies he worked with: "I know how fuzzy my calculations were, how wide the margin of error in my measures was, how I had to combine the data to end up with a summary statement. But once my calculation is on paper, it becomes the truth and boy oh boy, you'd better not disturb it."

A SENSE OF VERNACULAR

While pursuit of numbers brought with it the destruction of vernacular life, many executives — believers in the magic of the numbers — have been well aware of the loss. They too, yearn for what has been lost and they recognize the yearning in others. They also see that recapturing what was lost might also be useful in their pursuit of numbers!

How can you make sure people are attracted to your corporation? Once there, what will make them stay? How do you ensure people feel safe enough to learn, to experiment and to deal with problems that are threatening or embarrassing? Vernacular life cared for these challenges; you 'belonged' to a village community, and this belonging provided what numbers could not.

The answer for many has been to try to create a 'sense' of community within the organization: establishing a unique character to the organization, so that people acted as though they were part of a village. A popular way to do this is to publish what the organization stands for, listing the "core values" that guide people in the organizational community.

While these values are meant to create a distinctive culture, often apparently diverse corporations end up with the same values. They typically declare that "The customer comes first", "Employees are our most important asset" and "We make our decisions on behalf of the shareholders".

The sameness of these values isn't their real problem. Worse than that, the statements simply aren't true. When we carefully observe how people actually make decisions, published values have little to do with their actions. Careful observation of actual behavior has given rise to Core Group Theory, an understanding of behavior in communities that applies everywhere, from village life to corporate life.

The actual objective of corporations is not pleasing customers or creating shareholder wealth. While these are clearly important for many organizations, what comes first in *every* organization is keeping the Core Group satisfied. The Core Group — normally most of the top executives — are the source of an organization's energy, drive and direction.

People naturally look to the Core Group of a community to see what is important. Of course, in complex communities where lots of things could be important a degree of guesswork is involved: what do members of the Core Group *really* want? What measures are they really interested in? What do they mean by the comments they make. Even small gestures of Core Group members are amplified by people in the community. And if there is a mismatch between published "core values" and the messages received from the Core Group, the Core Group's influence wins out in the end.

So, through processes of guesswork and amplification, the capabilities and interests of a small group determine the nature of an organization. This is not inherently bad or dysfunctional; rather, it is a natural process. The outcome of the process depends on the intentions of the Core Group and their skill at determining what messages people take from their actions.

THE PROBLEM OF BIGNESS

The nature of core group influence returns us to the problem that numbers pose for those wanting to generate a vernacular spirit in a modern corporation. Core Group Theory suggests that modern corporations can offer the quality of 'homegrownness' that we yearn for. A Core Group can, in the way its members work together to use their particular capabilities, generate a workplace that is distinctive and unique. How, though, to have that distinctive culture spread through a big corporation?

Of course, the organization still has to work, so the Core Group is obliged to communicate using numbers. A CEO of General Motors — or of Ringling Brothers, Barnum and Bailey Circus, for that matter — can't take each employee aside individually for an in-depth, trust-filled conversation. Nor can the organization rely on "cascading" that conversation down the hierarchy, because most middle-managers (who are not themselves members of the Core Group) will inevitably distort the message through self-interest and guesswork. So the Core Group members, particularly those at the top of the hierarchy, translate their goals into numerical targets and measures. These, at least, cannot be distorted. They are "objective." In fact (people tell themselves) the results will be better than they would be if the CEO *could* get to know each manager personally, because the results will be less influenced by the individual idiosyncrasies of the CEO's judgment.

Even the most well-intentioned Core Group, aiming to build a vernacular life for an organizational community pursuing noble goals, is operating in a larger culture in which people have been trained to treat numbers as doggie treats. Right through school, people will have learned to look beyond what the teacher is saying to work out what they must do to get the numbers working in their favor.

So, in the end, the numbers develop a life of their own. Nobody can quite discern who created them; it's as if they emerged, untouchable and irrefutable, out of the whole organization. Even the Core Group will shrink from criticizing them, and for good reason. If the incentives and measurements are questioned, then the Core Group will have to step in and replace them with something else, something much more (God forbid) qualitative and time-consuming.

But at the same time, these numbers do not address any of the ambiguities which decision-makers must resolve to earn their doggie treats. For example: Which performance targets must embraced wholeheartedly, and which can simply be fudged for the next quarterly review? Which "stretch targets" can be met simply by saying, "Well, we tried," and which require working all weekend and missing your kids' soccer games? To what extent must people work alone to meet our targets, and if they work collectively, how will the incentives recognize this? What are the acceptable and unacceptable ways of fudging the numbers, and how can people avoid embarrassing themselves or the organization? In short, what sort of response to the incentives and measurements is acceptable around here? And what is not?

As people come up with the answers to questions like these, and act accordingly, they turn once again to their perception of the Core Group. Two things happen simultaneously.

First, people assume that they should interpret the numbers according to the Core Group. They base their behavior (for instance, their willingness to fudge numbers) on whatever signals they get from (or about) the Core Group.

For example, at an insurance company I know, officers have long been rewarded for "volume:" the number and size of new policies and premiums. But several years ago, some Core Group members realized that profits depended far more on the speed, responsiveness, and efficiency with which claims were handled, because well-settled claims never went to court. Incentives and targets were adjusted to reflect profitability as well as volume. But which would matter most? Employees learned the answer in review meetings, where the first question that Core Group members asked was: "How much business do you expect to sign this year?"

Second, people assume that they should interpret the Core Group according to the numbers. If the incentives, targets, and measurements send a clear signal, then people assume that is where the Core Group wants the organization to go.

For example: during the cutbacks at AT&T in the mid-1990s, it suddenly became obvious that AT&T's Research Group might not continue to enjoy its exalted status as a cost center, or as an incubator of breakthrough technology. There was a scramble to come up with a key metric that would justify the research group's existence. They eventually settled on: The number of patents produced. The Vice President in charge of the labs was henceforth promoted or demoted based on that number of patents, regardless of whether or not these innovations could be used by customers. The Core Group understood that this was one key distinction among many, but that didn't matter: because this was the distinction they cared about most, it gave the innovators at the lab no incentive to think about potential customers or revenues.

THE CHALLENGE

For people interested in learning in organisations, doggie treats and the Core Group are a complex and on-going challenge. Learning requires that the link between measures and their real meaning be retained and strengthened. But many of the processes of the modern corporation seem determined to split them apart.

Essential to vernacular life is the integration of performance and learning. As well as expending capacity to get things done, successful communities systematically build their capacity for future work, maintaining the relationships on which the community run. For this to happen, numbers have to be truly meaningful, acting as useful feedback that contributes to learning, not just as a means of keeping score in a short-term performance oriented game.

What we really need around here, then, is a genuine conversation about the value of the measurements and incentives. Which ones truly matter? Why do they matter? Who put them in place, and what were they thinking of? How do they help the Core Group get what it needs? Did Core Group members ask for those particular measurements? Do we know why? How well do they serve the organization now, and how well might they serve it in the future? Do we even *need* measurements and metrics that go up the hierarchy, or should we reorient them so that the people conducting the work are the same ones who receive all the measurement reports, instead of melding them into aggregate figures that ring up on an abstract scoreboard? And, by the way, what are the appropriate incentives, targets, and measurements for Core Group members themselves? Can we construct and use the measurements to actually improve the organization, instead of to keep score?

If we start to answer those questions effectively, then the measurements are no longer "doggie treats." They are a necessary vehicle by which the organization learns.

ESSENCE OF STRATEGY: CONTROVERSIAL CHOICES

Chapter

7

ANEEL KARNANI

"The merger of HP and Compaq is the best way to strengthen our businesses and improve our market position, deliver more of what our customers need, enhance opportunities for our employees and increase the value of our share-owners' investments."

— HP CEO, Carly Fiorina, 2001
Letter to Shareholders

"We profoundly disagree with management's assertion that HP needs to make this large and very risky acquisition. It worsens the HP shareholders' portfolio of businesses. It does not solve any strategic problems."

— HP dissident Board Member, Walter Hewlett, 2001
Proxy Statement

The much publicized 2001 merger between Hewlett-Packard and Compaq was very controversial. The CEOs of the two companies campaigned vigorously for the merger while the most visible critic of the merger, Walter Hewlett, 14-year HP director and son of co-founder William Hewlett, heavily contested it. There were experts, including investment bankers, stock analysts and management consultants, arguing on both sides of the merger debate.

Strategy is always controversial; in fact, the very essence of strategy is controversial choices and trade-offs. In order for one firm to out-perform its competitors and gain a competitive advantage, it must act differently: make different choices and choose alternatives that are distinct from its competitors. Einstein is said to have defined insanity as doing the same thing and expecting a different result! The choices involved in strategy must be controversial and involve trade-offs; otherwise every company would choose the same alternatives and there would be no difference among companies. Moreover, equally smart managers could have very disparate views on the best strategy for the company, as seen in the case of the HP-Compaq merger.

Four years after the contentious HP-Compaq merger, and four years of disappointing results later, the board of directors fired Carly Fiorina. HP Chairwoman Patricia Dunn remarked that the company needs a leader who will better execute its existing strategy.[1] Sanford Robertson, founder of the investment bank, Robertson Stephens, Inc., differed in his view, "I always thought they executed pretty well [but I] was curious about the strategy." Even in hindsight, strategy is controversial!

Not only is strategy controversial, it is a critical driver of superior firm performance. Michael Porter, an influential strategy guru, argues that the root cause of poor firm performance is the failure to distinguish between operational effectiveness and strategy. While operational effectiveness is necessary, it is not sufficient for superior performance.[2]

Organizational learning is another significant driver of high performance. Much of the focus on learning has been on operational learning. But companies also need to engage in strategic learning to develop their capabilities at strategic planning and implementation. A cookie cutter approach that simply applies the latest management tool will not suffice. Because strategy has to be unique and differentiated, it cannot be easy; firms have to learn the tools to develop and implement strategy. Confronting and managing the controversies involved in strategy is a useful learning process. On a smaller scale, this is why business schools usually teach strategy using the Socratic method of case discussions.

CONTROVERSIAL CHOICES

In February 2005, The Wall Street Journal[3] sampled a range of industry veterans and management experts to ascertain their opinions on what HP should do next. Their responses highlight the problem: "turnaround experts offer a wide range of conflicting strategies." This is not an unusual, let alone a unique example.

Recently, Boeing announced its latest investment in its newest offering, the 787 Dreamliner, a mid-size, long range plane that seats between 200 and 300 passengers. Airbus, on the other hand, is betting on its A380, a super-jumbo, long range plane that seats between 550 and 800 passengers.[4] These two competitors are placing bets based on differing views of the future growth patterns in international air travel: point-to-point versus hub-and-spoke. Their wagers are not only controversial, but also substantial; Airbus has spent $16 billion developing its new A380 aircraft.

Blockbuster, the video-rental chain, has seen its business erode in past years as a result of new competition from a variety of sources: low-priced DVDs, online DVD rentals (e.g., Netflix), video-on-demand, and downloaded movies from the Internet. The company has invested money to expand its business in several different ways: selling and renting video games, offering used movies for sale, starting an online mail-order business, establishing a subscription service, and canceling late fees. Carl Icahn, the largest shareholder of the company, disagrees with many of Blockbuster's new strategies and feels that the company should significantly increase its dividend payout so that investors can better invest their money elsewhere. This situation is a familiar one: a once dominant business that generates plenty of cash sees its market slowly decline. So, should management use the cash to diversify the business into something new, but risky? Or, should they manage the business for cash and return it to shareholders? Other companies such as Kodak's film business and Time Warner's AOL business also are facing similar dilemmas.[5]

The examples discussed focus on large, well-known companies facing dramatic and challenging choices. Yet, all companies, regardless of size and industry, confront equally controversial choices in formulating their strategies. Why do some firms perform better than other firms? What can you do to be more successful, to gain a competitive advantage, and to create shareholder value? Strategy is a useful framework for answering these questions; the strategy framework can help you set your action agenda as a senior manager.

Strategy consists of a set of inter-related choices that have a major impact on a firm's performance. Strategy involves both formulation and execution, and the two are intricately intertwined and it is difficult, if not impossible, to separate the two steps. It is futile to argue about whether formulation is more important than execution or vice versa; they are both essential to achieving superior performance. Both strategy formulation and strategy implementation involve making controversial choices and trade-offs.

A VISION IS NOT A STRATEGY

In the lobby of many companies you will find a beautifully framed vision statement. However, if you take that vision statement and hang it in the lobby of a different company, most people would never notice the difference. These statements are often trite and full of platitudes. Besides, they are generic and exchangeable, not controversial and hence, not strategic!

Most vision statements are 'motherhood and apple pie' statements about being the best in terms of quality, service, growth, leadership, innovation, customers, employees, and/or shareholders. Both Nike, the athletic wear company, and Comerica, a banking organization, have vision statements that refer to "enriching people's lives."[6] Scott Adams, the author of the famous Dilbert comic strip, tells of a company that has the vision "Create effective partnerships with our customers that enable them to achieve excellence." That is not a bad vision even though it could apply to any company from IBM to organized crime.

Vision statements are useful for energizing people in a company and providing a common purpose and cohesive values. Instilling a vision in a company that significantly influences the corporate culture can be a source of superior performance — a vital aspect of strategy implementation. But, vision statements provide very little, if any, guidance for making complicated strategic choices. There is much more to formulating a strategy than devising a vision.

CAUSES OF CONTROVERSY

Strategy consists of a set of integrated choices: the domain in which the firm will compete, the sources of its competitive advantage, the value proposition it offers to its customers, and the organizational design required to execute its strategy. All of these choices are complicated and controversial; equally smart managers may have different opinions on these choices. Analyses alone do not yield the answers; managers have to make difficult judgments.

Strategic choices also are made in the context of considerable uncertainty. One source of uncertainty is that strategy deals with the long term outlook, and we can have many equally plausible forecasts of the future environment. Another source of uncertainty is the actions and reactions of competitors. Again, managers may advocate very different actions under such circumstances.

Strategy deals with complex issues and it is difficult to understand the trade-offs because of 'causal ambiguity'. We do not comprehend well the cause and effect relationships that underlie strategic decision making. For example, in trying to understand the drivers of demand, it may be hard to measure the relative importance of price and quality, and how quality is defined to begin with. In trying to ascertain the drivers of cost, it may be tricky to judge the effectiveness of automation in reducing cost. In designing compensation systems, it may be thorny to determine the appropriate mix of individual and group incentives.

Often the controversy in strategy resides not in a general statement of the firm's direction, but rather in its deliberate application: it is a matter of degrees. Choosing between black and white is not controversial, but choosing among the various shades of gray is — strategy lies in choosing the right shade. The exhortation that you should be customer-oriented and listen to your customers is not controversial — of course, you should. The strategic choice is to what extent should you listen to your customers? How much money should you spend on marketing research? How much of the CEO's time should be committed to customer contact? The more time the CEO spends with customers, the less time s/he spends with employees, suppliers, etc. Allocating scarce firm resources, both money and time, undeniably involves a choice and a trade-off. Listening to customers can include other trade-offs as well. If you cater too much to your current customers and align your organization solely to do so, you might be blind sided by a disruptive technology.[7] Paying excessive attention to customers also may reduce your ability to pursue technology driven innovations.

As another example, a large consumer products firm was considering its strategy for entering China. The issue was not whether to go to China or not; it was obvious to all the managers (and the competitors) that entering the Chinese market was critical to its growth. The controversy was the extent to which the firm should invest in China over the next three years: $15 million for a minor distribution presence or $100 million for a major presence that would include significant manufacturing and technology development.

THE PLANNING PROCESS

In a typical company, strategic planning is driven by the calendar. Managers initiate the process to analyze and formulate the company's strategy not because the firm faces a strategic choice, but because it is, say, June.[8] A better approach would be to have the strategic analysis triggered by the arrival of a strategic choice and not by dates on the calendar.

In the traditional strategic planning process, much effort is expended on analyzing the environment (political, economic, social and technological), the industry, the competitors, the customers, and the company. Several different frameworks may be used for these analyses: Porter's Five-Forces, SWOT, McKinsey's 7-S's, generic strategies, core competencies, balanced scorecard, and EVA (economic value added). Yet, the problem is that these analyses are not tied to a specific strategic choice the company faces and hence, the time and effort spent is scattershot and wasteful. Many of the analyses produced have no impact on the actual choices the company makes. No wonder that many firms are disillusioned with their strategic planning.

My favorite question to ask as a facilitator in a company's planning process is "So what are you going to do (or not do) as a result of your analyses?" Unfortunately, many managers do not have a good answer to this question. A better planning approach is to first, identify the major strategic choices the company faces and then, to focus the analyses on these choices. This way the planning process is much more directed and action oriented.

For example, a major US building products company began its planning process by identifying five key strategic choices: (1) whether to enter China; (2) what to do with current operations in Europe; (3) how to deal with consolidation of the distribution channel; (4) how to manage the shift from products to services; and (5) how to deal with large commercial customers. The rest of the planning process was then sharply focused around addressing these five issues. In the next planning cycle, the company may re-visit some of these issues and/or identify new strategic choices.

CONFRONTING DIFFERENCES

In order to make a strategic choice in an intelligent and effective manner, the firm must understand the pros and cons of each alternative and analyze the trade-offs involved — while in the context of much uncertainty and causal ambiguity. Managers may come to different conclusions based on their diverse perspectives, backgrounds, competencies, and access to information. The best way to deal with this issue is to make the strategic planning process as participative, explicit and transparent as possible. The firm needs all the managers to put their information, assumptions, and analysis on the table. Then, the managers can share, critique and understand each other's positions, and come to an honest resolution of their differences. This is an idealistic view of the process and reality will never be so perfect due to hidden assumptions and biases, vested interests, and organizational politics. But, the more you try to foster and encourage an honest and inclusive strategic decision making process, the more likely it is that the firm will make intelligent choices and develop strategies that create a competitive advantage.

Confronting differences is the key. We need to bring conflict out into the open. This is how wise trade-offs among competing alternatives can be made. Intellectual debate among managers with divergent views is a vital source of creative and innovative solutions within the company. Conflict is the source of creativity; dissent is the source of learning. We learn by talking with someone with whom we disagree. Managers must confront conflict rather than avoid it. Conflict, of course, needs to be managed such that it is constructive and intellectual.

Managers also need to be able to resolve their conflicts to arrive at a strategic choice. A firm is not a debating society and the process cannot end with the managers 'agreeing to disagree'. Once the firm has made a strategic choice, the managers who initially disagreed with the choice must work toward supporting the decision.

GENERATE CONFLICT

Strategic choices are inherently controversial. So, if right at the start of the strategic planning process all the managers seem to agree, this can be a symptom of organizational malaise. Lack of conflict is not the same as real agreement. Consensus can be a disguise for disengagement.

Do not settle for a premature consensus. The firm should explore different strategic alternatives and analyze the trade-offs involved, thoroughly. A quick decision on a particular option might mean that a better alternative is ignored. Even if the 'right' course of action was chosen, the managers may not fully understand the negative aspects of the chosen alternative well enough and risk running into problems implementing the strategy. A complete understanding of the various alternatives and their pros and cons, usually achieved through extensive debate, is essential to making a good choice and executing it well.

At a minimum, firms need to tolerate dissent. Yet, many managers do exactly the opposite and surround themselves with 'yes men' or people who think like them. If you penalize dissent among your staff a few times, subordinates quickly learn not to disagree with the boss. A sign of a healthy company is one where you have the ability to tell your boss that s/he is wrong and not have that be a 'career limiting' move.

It is not enough to merely tolerate dissent; firms must actively encourage dissent. Senior managers need to actively seek out opposing points of view and draw out people who are hesitant to volunteer negative or contrary opinions. It is important to keep in mind that as a senior manager, it is beneficial to not express your position too early in the discussion since it will intimidate some subordinates from voicing a differing opinion. An outside facilitator can help the company to bring forth different points of view during the strategic planning process. To avoid 'group think', diversity among the management team is also important. This is diversity in terms of education, functional expertise, work experiences, and business perspectives. You may invite someone who does not 'belong' there as well, such as a manager from a different division in the company, to your next task force or strategic planning meeting to gain his/her perspective.

Another alternative is to intentionally generate conflict, even if artificially. By assigning roles and positions to different managers, some in the role of the devil's advocate, ensures that all aspects of the strategic choices are thoroughly examined and is a good way to energize a debate. Recall the major US building products company, previously mentioned, that was faced with five strategic choices. On each of these five dimensions, top management identified two or three very different strategic responses and, arbitrarily, assigned a senior manager to make a case for each alternative at the company's upcoming retreat.

At the planning retreat, the top 25 managers in the company spent a one-half day session on each strategic choice. Each session started with two or three managers advocating their assigned alternative for 45 minutes. Each manager had devoted much time and effort gathering data and conducting analyses in support of his/her strategic alternative. After these presentations, the entire group debated the different alternatives and either made a strategic decision or agreed on specific steps for further analysis. Unlike planning retreats at other companies, the discussion at this company was focused on the strategic considerations at hand, was well informed by data and analyses, and was not based on unsupported opinions or hunches.

CONFLICT MANAGEMENT

Although the goal is to use debate to shed light on all sides of the strategic choice, conflict needs to be managed such that it does not degenerate into dysfunctional interpersonal conflict. Proper conflict management is vital so that the company benefits from the process in a manner that does not damage people's abilities to work together as a team afterwards. The strategic planning process is an intellectual debate and not a political fight. Hence, it should focus on ideas and decisions and not on personalities. We need to be mindful to de-personalize the debate. The underlying message is, "I disagree with your ideas, but I think you are smart and I enjoy working with you." If the underlying message becomes, "I disagree with you and I think you are dumb," then there will be an unproductive fight. The first requirement is that managers realize that they are on the same side with common goals; a team that does not compete with each other, but rather with external competitors. The conflict is but a means to greater collaboration.[9]

Unfortunately, debates can generate some heat in the conference room. You need to ensure that this tension is diffused quickly and harmlessly. Humor — even if it is contrived — is very effective at relieving tension and promoting a positive mood, thereby creating a collaborative esprit. A well-planned group social gathering over drinks or a meal can also go a long way towards smoothing ruffled feathers and creating a friendly tone. Yet, managing the tone is not enough; you have to be earnest about the role that accord plays in the conflict management process for it to be constructive.

Another way to steer the discussion away from the individual is to root the debate in facts and data. In the absence of good data, managers waste time in pointless debates over opinions.[10] People, and not issues, become the focus of the disagreement. Good data, defined as timely, relevant and objective, encourages managers to focus on the real issues and strategic choices. The problem is that many companies lack the quality of data required for a thorough examination of the strategic choice. The traditional planning process, which typically begins with analyses, requires extensive data collection, but much of this data and the analyses conducted go un-used. Starting with the strategic choices focuses managers and the data collection effort as well as ensures appropriate depth of analyses. More importantly, it equips the managers to begin formulating judgments and making decisions on strategic issues much faster.

Strategic choices always are complex given multiple trade-offs among several inter-dependent factors. One way to simplify the process is to break the complex problem down into sub-problems and then to identify the criteria for making each trade-off. Obviously, this method is not always possible, but it is worth considering. We highlight one method that can help you in the box titled, "Understanding Trade-offs".

UNDERSTANDING TRADE-OFFS

A company faced with competition from an emerging technology decided to invest in developing the capability of the new technology itself. The strategic issue was how to organizationally manage the development of the budding capability. The five identified strategic alternatives were:

- Ask the technology center at the corporate level (which is a cost center) to develop the new capability.
- Form a new division (which would be a profit center).
- Choose one of the current divisions to develop the new capability.
- Require each of the current divisions to simultaneously develop the new capability.
- Offer to each division the choice of developing the new capability.

Most managers realize that strategy formulation involves difficult choices, but often do not identify similarly sharp choices in strategy implementation. For this company, the strategy formulation choice — to invest in the emerging technology — was simple. The strategy implementation choice of organizational design was much more controversial. There is no easy answer to this problem; there are pros and cons for each of the above five strategic alternatives. The managers then identified six criteria for making the trade-offs among the strategic alternatives (see Fig. 1).

It was simpler for the managers to discuss the alternatives, one criterion at a time, after seeing the choices and trade-offs, more easily, in the matrix format. We did not assign weights to each criterion or numerical preferences to each alternative since this guide was not meant to be a mechanical tool for

Criteria Alternatives	Speed to market	Cost	Customer orientation	Standard platform	Radical change	Wide adoption
Technology center	Good	OK	Poor	Best	Best	OK
New division	Best	Good	Good	Good	Good	Poor
Champion division	Best	Good	Best	Good	Good	Poor
All divisions	Poor	Poor	Good	Poor	Poor	Best
Free choice	OK	OK	Good	Poor	Poor	Good

Figure 1.   Understanding trade-offs.

making decisions. The decision is much too complex to use such a structured approach. Rather, the managers used the matrix as a framework for initiating dialogue among the group and bringing out the salient points of each alternative. At the end, the managers still had to use their judgment and experience to choose among the alternatives. Yet, the matrix allows managers to be more focused on the components of their choices, to share their thoughts and ultimately, to be more comfortable with the final decision, which aids in the strategy process.

CONFLICT RESOLUTION

In order to de-personalize the conflict, it is essential to not tightly link the conflict to rewards. If the manager or the team that wins the debate stands to gain in terms of compensation, promotion, or the like, then everyone will fight too hard not to lose. But, if the conflict remains an intellectual debate, then it is easier for people to concede gracefully. In fact, it is useful (perhaps even critical) to have the person/team who opposed the 'winning' strategy to be involved in implementing it.

Another issue to be wary of in resolving conflicts is the desire to reach a unanimous decision. If the debate results in everyone seeing eye-to-eye, that is great — but, it is very uncommon. It is not necessary to arrive at a consensus, and you should not strive too hard or too long to achieve it and risk getting bogged down in an endless debate. Requiring unanimity implies giving everyone veto power which might force a decision with which no one is happy, a poor compromise. Besides, consensus is not necessarily a sign of harmony; it might very well be the result of fatigue and frustration.

Strategy development should be participative, but not democratic. The purpose of generating and managing conflict is to thoroughly analyze the strategic choices. Resolving the conflict, that is making the strategic decision, is the responsibility primarily of the senior managers.[11] It is important that senior managers retain the power to make the final decision, after hearing and carefully considering all the facts, data and perspectives surrounding the strategic choices. Senior managers should, however, also expect to and be prepared to explain the logic behind their final decisions since managers who disagreed with their decision will likely be more willing to accept it if they perceive the whole process as fair.

ASIAN CULTURE

Effective strategic planning and implementation requires that companies cultivate a culture that can deal well with conflict. As a broad generalization, many Asian companies are at a disadvantage in this regard because Asian cultures often handle conflict poorly. There are excellent companies in Asia, of course; and, all Asian cultures are not the same. Still, many Asian companies do not manage well the process for making controversial choices.

Asian societies can be characterized as collectivistic, where harmony and "knowing one's place", is not only valued but also expected. Collectivistic cultures view conflict negatively; conflict is avoided and even suppressed. Group cohesiveness is deemed to be very important. Asians have a strong sense of interdependence as their identity is embedded in their relationships. They are highly sensitive to losing social face in public; they avoid conflict which is seen as disrespectful and may lead to alienation. So, the first problem is that dissent is avoided or suppressed, let alone encouraged and generated. This is especially true of Chinese and Japanese cultures which have been influenced by the Confucian tradition of role appropriate behavior.[12]

The more direct, individualistic, confrontational style required of managers in the strategic planning process we have proposed here, hence, presents a challenge for Asian managers. Conflict avoiding behavior, in an effort to remain 'polite' and maintain false harmony, stalls the strategic planning process since participants cannot be relied upon to share their true views on issues, limiting the scope and innovativeness of the strategic debate. There may be an even worse consequence. Avoiding conflict does not mean that it disappears; the conflict later manifests in destructive, win-lose ways that undermine both performance and relationships.

The second step in our proposed process is to manage conflict. Since Asian managers are uncomfortable with conflict in the first place, they tend to seek a resolution too quickly. This action makes it difficult to thoroughly examine all sides of the controversial issue because too little time (and resources) are devoted to the debate.

Asian companies also often lack the appropriate facts and data to analyze strategic choices. This impediment is more of an institutional issue rather than a cultural one. There is a shortage of marketing research and information available in terms of customer needs, customer segmentation, market demographics and target psychographics due to lack of development. Little is known about competitors. Financial data is inadequate as a result of lack of transparency in financial capital markets. Even internal accounting data is often not suited for strategic analysis.

Additionally, Asian companies are typically more hierarchical than their Western counterparts (see Fig. 2).[13] The more rigid and tiered organizational structure results in conflict resolution being based more on formal power. The strategic planning process is thus more autocratic, rather than participative.

The issue, of course, is not to characterize Asian versus Western firms. Rather, firms characterized by conflict avoidance, lack of appropriate data, and rigid hierarchical organizations will find it difficult to develop good strategic management skills. Unfortunately, many Asian firms do suffer from these problems and need to devote extra efforts to strategic learning by embracing controversy and conflict.[14]

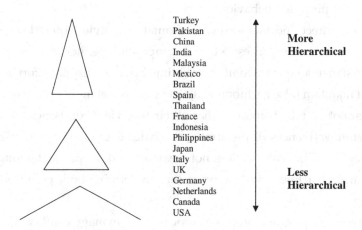

Figure 2.   Corporate hierarchial structures.

CONCULSION

The essence of strategy is to make controversial choices; this is the only way to gain a competitive advantage. Both strategy development and execution involve making controversial choices. Conflict is inherent in making strategic decisions. Therefore, an effective strategic management process requires managers to generate, manage, and resolve conflict.

REFERENCES

1. The Wall Street Journal, February 14, 2005.
2. What is Strategy, Michael Porter, *Harvard Business Review*, Nov.–Dec. 1996.
3. *ibid.*
4. Financial Times, May 4, 2005.
5. The Wall Street Journal, April 19, 2005.
6. *The Mission Statement Book*, Jeffrey Abrahams, Ten Speed Press, 1995.
7. *The Innovator's Dilemma*, Clay Christensen, 1997.
8. An alternative approach to making strategic choices, Jan Rivkin, *Harvard Business School Case*, 2002.
9. Want collaboration? Accept — and actively manage — conflict, Jeff Weiss, Jonathan Hughes. *Harvard Business Review*. March–April 2005. *83*, 3, 92.
10. How management teams can have a good fight, Kathleen Eisenhardt, Jean Kahwajy, and L. J. Bourgeois. *Harvard Business Review*, July–August, 1997.
11. *ibid.*
12. Michael W. Morris, Katherine Y. Williams, Kwok Leung, Richard Larrick, M. Teresa Mendoza, Deepti Bhatnagar, Jianfeng Li, Mari Kondo, Jin-Lian Luo, Jun-Chen Hu. (1998). Conflict Management Style: Accounting for Cross-National Differences, *Journal of International Business Studies*, 29, 4, 729–748.
13. *Riding the Waves of Culture*, Fons Trompenaars and Charles Hampden-Turner, 1998.
14. A similar comment could probably be made for companies from other emerging economies such as Brazil and Mexico.
15. Michael H. Bond & Sung-Hsing Wang, (1983). Aggressive behavior in Chinese society: The problem of maintaining order and harmony. In A. P. Goldstein & M. Segall, editors, *Global Perspectives on Aggression*, New York, NY: Pergamon.

16. Michael W. Morris, Katherine Y. Williams, Kwok Leung, Richard Larrick, M. Teresa Mendoza, Deepti Bhatnagar, Jianfeng Li, Mari Kondo, Jin-Lian Luo & Jun-Chen Hu. (1998). Conflict management style: Accounting for cross-national differences, *Journal of International Business Studies, 29, 4,* 729–748.

17. Steve K. Su, Chi-yue Chiu, Ying-yi Hong, Kwok Leung, Kaiping Peng & Michael W. Morris. (1998). Self organization and social organization: American and Chinese constructions. In T. R. Tyler, R. M. Kramer & O. P. John, editors, *Psychology of the Social Self.*

18. Deutsch, M. (1973) The resolution of conflict, New Haven, CT: Yale University Press, Fifty years of conflict, In L. Festinger, editor, *Retrospections on Social Psychology,* New York: Oxford University Press, 1980; Sixty years of conflict, *The International Journal of Conflict Management,* 1990.

19. Bond, M. H. & Lee, P. W. H. (1981) Face saving in Chinese culture: A discussion and experimental study of Hong Kong students, *Social Life and Development in Hong Kong,* Hong Kong: The Chinese University Press; Cocroft, B. A. K., & Ting-Toomey, S., Facework in Japan and the United States, *International Journal of Intercultural Relations,* Ting-Toomey, S. (1988) A face negotiation theory, *Theory and Intercultural Communication,* Thousand Oaks, CA: Sage.

20. Deutsch, M. (1973) The resolution of conflict. New Haven, CT: Yale University Press.

Applications

CREATING CONSULTING PARTNERSHIPS THAT FOSTER A DEPTH OF LEARNING

PETER BLYDE

When organizations are looking to bring about significant performance changes, they often engage the support of consulting organizations. In effect, organizations use consultants to build capacity.

Like many consultants, I aspire to work at deep levels of learning: working with clients so they build capacity in ways that affect them profoundly. That is, I hope to make a contribution that lasts; such that the organization is left with greater capacity to achieve important results. To do this, I need to focus on the depth at which learning occurs.

In part, the need for depth stems from the particular kind of consulting that I do. I work with individuals and teams concerned with issues like leadership, vision, collaboration and change. It is work that is at the edge of the learning — performance debate. Organizations may want improved performance in these areas and want it quickly, but there is no short cut. The way to get good leadership, for instance, is by building people's capacity for leadership through learning. This is a process that requires a depth of learning by those involved and thus takes time.

Associating the word 'depth' with learning is important. It has powerful connotations that signal the significance of the change involved in building capacity. When we speak of things done in depth we suggest that the work involves intensity, complexity, thoroughness, richness and insight. The term 'depth of learning' makes it clear that we are moving beyond the mundane.

How do you build consulting partnerships that deliver this level of learning? What has the biggest impact on the depth of learning conducted within organizations by consultants? In reflecting on these questions, I will explore two primary factors that impact the depth of learning and change. The first is the quality of the partnership between the client and the consultant, and the second is the quality of the underlying design of the development journey. In doing so, I will address what I have found gets in the way of, and those dynamics that enhance, the ability to create partnerships that foster a depth of learning.

ALL PARTNERSHIPS ARE NOT CREATED EQUAL

I'm aware that the nature of the partnership I have with my clients has a significant impact on the extent to which I am able to make a difference and truly build capacity for my clients. The higher the degree of trust, mutual co-operation and shared understanding, the more likely it is that desired outcomes can be achieved. In other words, to achieve a depth of learning, we need partnerships that are out of the ordinary.

Bill Isaacs, author of the book *Dialogue: the art of thinking together*,[1] makes the same point. The quality of our conversations depends on the relationships in which they are contained. Conversations associated with a depth of learning are filled with intense emotional and intellectual energy. Just as a strong container is needed to hold a highly energized liquid, intensely energized conversations require strong relationships as their containers. Without such relationships, these conversations either do not happen or result in people getting hurt in the process.

Partnership is one way of describing the quality of the relationship required. Partnership is defined as "A relationship between individuals or groups that is characterized by mutual cooperation and responsibility, as for the achievement of a specified goal."[2]

In a recent book,[3] Peter Senge and his colleagues have outlined 4 levels of relationship, and provide us with a framework for describing the quality of

---

[1] Published by Doubleday Currency, New York, 1999.

[2] The American Heritage® Dictionary of the English Language, Fourth Edition - Copyright © 2000 by Houghton Mifflin Company.

[3] Senge, P., Scharmer, O., Jaworshi, J. & Flowers, B. (2004). Presence: Human Purpose and the Field of the Future. Cambridge, MA: Society for Organizational Learning.

partnership that exists within a consulting relationship. Their model was originally created to describe doctor-patient relationships, and I have translated the language and context to fit the consultant-client relationship.

Level One: *Transactional.* At this level, the client comes to a consultant believing something is wrong, and needs to be fixed. The client has a problem and the consultant is a potential source of solutions. The nature of the partnership is mechanical, assuming the relationship or partnership has no affect on the outcomes achieved. The expectations are: "You have expertise in this area. Come and do your stuff and it will be fixed." Service consultant Ron Zemke, expressed the frustration this work has for many consultants when he described it as "throwing artificial pearls to real swine".

Level Two: *Changed Behaviour.* The second level relationship is one that focuses not on the broken part, but rather on how the issue/opportunity is related to behaviour. Here the client recognizes that the solution is not something that is done to them, but rather that some change in their behaviour is required for the outcome to be successful. Consultants and clients work together to explore what behaviour change is needed to really make a difference.

Level Three: *Assumptions.* At the third level, the consultant and client go beyond the behaviour. They work together to explore the reasons behind the behaviour. That is, they explore and challenge underlying assumptions, values and beliefs that shape what is happening in the client's system. This requires a stronger partnership because assumptions are not readily available. Assumptions exist beneath the level of conscious awareness and it takes time to bring them to the surface. When they do surface they contain elements that are contradictory and irrational — so the relationship has to assimilate the embarrassment and threat that is generated.

Level Four: *Identity.* The fourth level is where identities are changed. This is a consulting relationship where each is open to discovering themselves in the relationship, it is co-creation in the real sense of the word. The level of identity encourages each party in the relationship to consider who they want to be. In this relationship, the consultant is also altered as a result of the interaction — who they are, and how they see themselves are transformed in a relationship of mutual influence and vulnerability.

Level	Description	
1	Transaction	Surface
2	Behaviour	
3	Assumptions	
4	Identity	Deep

When I used this framework to reflect on my own experience, I was struck by several insights.

There are strong pressures on all parties to keep the relationship at surface levels. Every business that I have worked with or in has been affected by the time pressures and the need for tangible results. This can result in clients engaging in development to "be seen to be doing something", without really engaging serious effort for change, as well as consultants not thinking beyond past the solution they created to the last engagement they had.

I am convinced, however, that the more the relationship stays on the surface, the less likely depth of learning and real change will occur. To get the necessary results, both client and consulting organizations are going to need to expect more of each other, and invest more in the development of a partnership.

Using the word "partnership" to describe the relationship does not make it so. Even where clients and consultants understand the need for partnership, there is danger that the word will be used, but the spirit and reality of the partnership will not be achieved. In fact, some of the clients who have been the most vocal and explicit about the need for partnership have been those least likely to operate in the spirit of partnership. An experienced colleague once quipped, "When a client says 'partnership' what they usually mean is they want you to be *extra* attentive to doing *what they want, when they want it.*"

Recently, as part of a consulting team, I worked with a large, global organization. We spent just short of ten weeks working with the client to understand their needs and how we could contribute to the project team they were establishing.

We were interviewed at multiple levels to ensure "values fit." At the outset, it seemed that all involved strongly valued partnership. That was until, late in piece, the conversation turned to some needs we had as consultants: needs we considered critical if we were to deliver what the client expected. Despite clear verbal and written communication, within four days of raising our needs as part of the discussion for planning the project, we were dropped from the team (just prior to the final signing of the contract). The reason? According to the client, we lacked a "partnership mindset."

While there were many factors that contributed to this, what was startling to me was the speed at which conversations deteriorated once a conversation about our needs were included in the planning and scheduling.

Level Four relationships are rare.   A number of factors contribute to this. Forming deep relationships is time-consuming and difficult. Further, as a consultant, the focus is on bringing about change in the client therefore explicitly engaging in conversations about how to change consulting firm's *own* identities have been limited because they seem so self-serving. While it is counter-intuitive to think that conversations about one's own identity are in the best interests of the client, recent client reviews have shown me that clients can and do take an active interest in the consulting organization's operations and future. I am currently exploring different ways of having these conversations with clients.

The start of the relationship has a big impact on the ability to get real partnership. This is often expressed as a desire to have a good 'fit' with a consultant: a close match between the consultant's capabilities and values and their own culture and need.

Having started my life as a consultant in smaller consultancy firms, the issue of fit has always been very visible. In a very real sense, when you work as part of a smaller organization, the distinction between your own personality and the identity of the consulting organization is negligible. You know that you and your services are being assessed by the client. You feel you are being weighed in the balance.

When I worked for a large, global consulting organization, I assumed that this would be different; that the brand would give clients a sense of assurance that meant they were less concerned with the personality of particular consultants. I was wrong. Fit still mattered. If anything, clients are becoming more discerning and exercising more explicit choice regarding who takes part in a project team. Clients are increasingly recognizing that more than a technical exchange is required. A global brand with a well-validated approach and expertise does not in itself guarantee a successful engagement.

FALSE FIT

Both clients and consultants engage in behaviours that get in the road of establishing successful fit and forming sound relationships. Both can be tempted to shortcut the process of establishing a partnership by using surface level indicators of 'fit'.

Consultants, for instance, are often frustrated by clients' insistence on fit — complaining "we will not be dragged into a beauty parade with the client". This is especially so when a consulting firm has made a substantial investment in establishing processes that are 'tried and true' and has a need to ensure that work is spread around the consultants available (utilization). Further, internal decisions regarding fit are often based around comfort with working together, not necessarily the value they will add to clients.

The desire to "get the business" can often drive smaller firms to overlook problems they foresee with fit in the relationship. Consultants with fewer colleagues available may feel forced to ignore an evident mismatch of skills or values and present oneself as the best option to meet a client's need.[4]

Clients, on the other hand, may find that getting the consultant they want is not in their best interests. In the attempt to get best-fit, I have seen clients make poor judgments regarding who they will work with. Colleagues who I deemed to

---

[4] My personal approach to minimize the pressure for this has been two-fold. The first is to be honest about my own sense of fit. This takes a level of integrity and willingness to take some short-term financial "hits" that I trust will have a long-term benefit for me and the client. The second is to create a network of trusted associates so as to be able to provide a real sense of choice for clients, and a legitimate option between "yes I can do it" and "no I can't help you."

have a strong fit with the desired outcomes and values of the client have been rejected by clients in the early stages.

In part, this is because the notion of "fit" has strong elements of looking for similarity — a match between those being developed and those contributing to the development. Sometimes, however, to create the necessary growth and development, differences in personality and perspective are necessary. In part, it is because decisions regarding fit are made quickly and on superficial factors such as age, gender or 'presence' during the selling process e.g. is this person too old or too young relative to those being developed. This can result in, what we could call, "false fit," a poorer quality client-consultant partnership and consequently a reduced depth of learning.

I have found it valuable to reflect on my approach to the issue of fit. Take time to consider your own approach by reflecting on the questions in the box "Reflecting on Fit." Questions are provided for both parties to the consulting relationship, clients and consultants.

Reflecting on Fit

Questions for Clients

On what basis would you take advice on appropriateness of fit from a consulting firm?
What would tell you that the "fit" is not right, and to disengage?
What are the critical factors to pay attention to with regards to fit (beyond stereotypes)?

Consultants

What client work do you say 'no' to?
What would tell you that the "fit" is not right, and to disengage?
What are the critical factors to pay attention to with regards to fit (beyond stereotypes)?

The quality of the partnership (and the associated openness and trust) impacts the ability to have real conversations about the underlying factors contributing to change, and either supports or inhibits a depth of learning. Having explored some of the dynamics that enhance or reduce the quality of partnership, let's look at the second key factor for creating a depth of learning — the underlying design of the development approach.

DESIGN: THE UNDERVALUED ART

Who has the greatest impact on the successful operation of a cruise ship?[5] You might think the captain, the navigator, or the purser. The reality is that the designer of the ship plays a fundamental role in shaping everything that happens on board and what people in other roles are able to achieve. And just as the boat designer is the forgotten contributor to a cruise ship's success, in my experience the design of the process (and the design ability of the consultant) is often undervalued by client and consultant alike.

CEO Kevin Roberts has described his efforts to turn Saatchi and Saatchi from an "advertising agency" to an "ideas company". I believe this transition is needed in consulting. We ought not to be technical experts in the business of delivering programmes, but rather "people architects" who are able to design and co-create developmental journeys for organizations.

The consulting process involves four stages:

1. *Engagement*: where client and consultant agree to work together on a project of a particular scope.
2. *Design*: where the architecture of the approach is determined, with consideration given to the processes and activities that will deliver the outcomes the client is seeking.
3. *Delivery*: putting the design into action, working through the activities and processes.
4. *Evaluation*: reviewing what has been achieved by the process so that lessons learned can be captured, outcomes identified and so the parties can agree on when to stop.

The design stage is critical to the success of the entire process as it informs and impacts everything that happens with the client. Which raises the question, why is this stage so often neglected?

---

[5] Peter Senge posed this question in his article "The Leaders New Work: building learning organisations" (Sloan Management Review, 31, 1, Fall, pp. 7–22, 1990).

Many wrongly assume that a design that has worked in one place can be readily transplanted to another. They underestimate the need to learn during the process of design: to learn about an organization's culture, its core group, its history, its business and so on.

Design is also costly. Engagement and Delivery are far more visible to clients and the costs associated with them are easy to justify. Clients may be dubious, even cynical about the need for customization of a consultant's products or process when they believe they have already made the effort to identify an expert: someone who should already know what will and will not work.

Part of this cynicism I can understand. Many consultants claim a high level of customization when the reality is that few actually provide it. Clients are rightly frustrated when they pay for something that is not delivered.

In working to make customization real for clients, I use a matrix, shown in the table "Levels of Customization" which highlights the options available. Rather than being an exhaustive list of options, it is meant to be illustrative of the different levels of customization that are possible, so that my clients can choose the appropriate level of customization for their needs. It also encourages clients — and me — to use processes appropriate to the level of customization for which we are aiming. It makes little sense, for instance, to use highly customized evaluation for processes that were 'off the shelf'.

DESIGNING TO ACHIEVE A DEPTH OF LEARNING

If design is a critical factor for creating a depth of learning and achieving real change — what needs to be done to ensure good design? In my experience, five key principles help with the design process. Let's consider them.

Design with multiple stakeholder input

In a consulting partnership, design needs to be a collaborative process. The key question is, "collaboration with whom?" Reflecting on development initiatives I have been involved in, it is clear to me that often as consultants, we find

Level of Customisation	Off the Shelf		Fully Customisable
Design Process: Extent of Design Collaboration	Consultant and Senior Line or HR Manager	Consultant, Senior Line or HR Managers, and cross-section of participants	Consultant and Senior Line or HR Manager, and full team of participants
Development Process: Content	Pre-determined content areas	Customised selection of content based on needs analysis	Customised selection of content areas, and development of unique examples, exercises, and simulations from the organisation itself

(Continued)

128

(Continued)

Level of Customisation	Off the Shelf				Fully Customisable
Depth of Skill Building in Workshops	Presentation of ideas and tools	Think about issues, apply to own situation	Practice of skills/tools with peer feedback	Practice of skills/tools with expert facilitator feedback	Video practice and feedback with peers and expert
Development Experiences in Workshop	Presentations Videos	Group discussion	Case studies. Simulations	Self or 360-degree assessment	Actor role plays with current, real work situations. Real time strategic facilitation
Development Process: Skill Building and Development Experiences Beyond Workshops	Discuss lessons and next steps with manager, peers, or staff	Individualised development planning. Use of movies, literature, music to stimulate and reinforce learning.	Community service projects. Shadowing other executives or peers	Coaching and mentoring (internal and external)	Job rotations Special projects Internal alignment of people systems to match development outcomes

(Continued)

129

(*Continued*)

Level of Customisation	Off the Shelf	→	Fully Customisable
Facilitation	Facilitators contracted who have not been involved in discussions regarding organisation's future and needs	Facilitators fully involved (from initial needs analysis, design, and delivery)	Facilitators fully involved AND internal leaders actively used to develop others (recognised role models who can provide relevant examples)
Materials: Depth of Content	Key principles and workshop exercises only	Full reference manual with background notes and self paced exercises	Full reference manual and on-line development materials
Measurement	Workshop Evaluations	Pre and post 360 assessment	Tracking key behaviours and business results over 3–5 years

ourselves marketing to, and therefore designing solutions based upon, information provided by either senior line or HR managers. Further, it is not uncommon to find that the development needs and agenda described by these managers are based on untested assumptions about the needs of the target audience.

One simple habit I have found effective has been to solicit input into the design of the programme from participants. Rather than talk to everyone involved, I ask to speak to a sample of the group being developed. I typically ask for someone enthusiastic, someone typical of the group, and someone likely to be most cynical about the process. In discussing the business situation, the team dynamics, and their own personal expectations, I find that the final design of the programme is often significantly different from what I originally envisioned, or have been briefed to provide.

It has been my experience that taking the time to do this, in itself, sends a signal about the seriousness of your intent to make a difference. One senior executive from a global financial organization said at the start of programme on developing emotional intelligence, "I was heartened by the fact that you called beforehand to find out what was going on with our business and the team. It signaled to me that this wasn't just going to be another course where you get put through a set process like some sort of sausage factory."

Design a development journey, not a development programme

The metaphor of a development journey is more appropriate than the use of words like project, intervention, or programme.

Sustained behaviour change takes time. Yet despite overwhelming evidence that this is the case, most development programmes still fall in the 1–5 day category. While the notion that development should be an 'on-going process of life-long learning' is widely espoused in development circles, in my experience, the development journey is not a mindset or practice taken by many clients or consultants. Instead, organizations lurch from one initiative to another, and consultants provide options that are difficult to integrate with past development efforts.

By thinking of development as a journey, both client and consultant remain open to the idea that lessons learned and insight gained on one leg of the trip can provoke what will be incorporated into the next leg. It also encourages the parties to think of themselves as travelling companions who can get to know each other better as the journey progresses.

Design with the future destination in mind

All development is an investment in the future. To that end, effective design depends on those involved having clarity and commitment to the future they are endeavoring to create. While this is easy to say, in practice, it is often very difficult to achieve.

In part, difficulty arises because individuals often struggle to articulate what they are committed to creating. With teams and organizations, this lack of clarity is compounded and a shared vision can be elusive. It doesn't help that the world-view and language of the two parties (client and consultants) are often very different. While this difference is what allows value to be exchanged, in the early stages of development it makes conversations about desired outcomes and futures difficult.

Difficulties aside, one of the practical actions that I have found helps shape the design with the future destination in mind is to have discussions with the client regarding what success would look like in 2–3 years time (not just at the end of our contracted arrangement). By getting the executive team to identify what success would look like in 2–3 years time, everybody learns to focus on the factors that will determine on-going success. This prompts both the consultant and the client to make decisions that maximize the long-term benefit, not just short-term.

Design in ways that integrate with past initiatives

Many organizations have a history of lurching from one development initiative to another. For example, a client I have worked with recently has, in the past two years, put people through a 2-day personality type workshop, a 2-day personal leadership styles workshop, an organizational culture assessment and debrief, a 2-day emotional intelligence workshop and is planning another 2-day leadership approach. Each initiative has its own language, set of diagnostic tools and perspectives on how leaders and staff add value.

While the organization sees this series of development events as a commitment to the development of its people, my impression is that the impact on staff is a growing sense that the organization is pursuing fads. In this case the whole development journey is less than the sum of the parts: and each new initiative takes greater effort for fewer gains.

With growing awareness of this phenomenon, a habit I have developed is to find out as much as possible about the previous development experiences the organization has undertaken, and explicitly work to link language and frameworks to work that has been done before.

In doing so, I have found that people recall little from previous sessions, and that few people are actively using the tools/frameworks from previous development to inform their practice. It seems evident that the sustainable way to get a depth of learning and behaviour change is for an organization to commit to a particular framework (and related assessment tool), and use this as the primary language for the development journey.

This is not to say the organization should be locked in to one consultant. Rather, there is a commitment to a coherent and consistent journey. If a particular language or approach is only going to be relevant for a few days, people will not bother investing time and energy in really understanding the framework being used.

Consultants act in ways that make this type of commitment difficult by insisting (overtly or covertly) that their frameworks are the only way. I have my own strong preferences and struggle at times with putting these preferences aside, but I do so knowing that frameworks are a means to having meaningful conversations which can catalyze action and engagement. Insisting that your model is the only sound way of moving forward does little to build on the investments made by the organization or contribute to a journey of shared development.

Ensure strong connections between marketers, designers and deliverers

When marketers and designers are disconnected, sometimes the solutions sold are either not the best possible option for delivering the desired outcomes, or that expectations created are difficult to deliver in the agreed process. When designers and facilitators are disconnected, often part of the passion for the idea (the "know-why" and "care-why" regarding the design) is lost, as is the ability to be flexible in the delivery of the material to meet the real-time needs of the people in the development process. At its worst, this disconnect results in facilitators who take an "off the shelf" product and faithfully work at delivering a scripted process.

In my experience, the real advantage of many of the smaller, boutique consulting firms, is that the marketer, designer and facilitator are often the same person. This gives a greater flexibility to the design and facilitation, as well as a stronger commitment to the ideas and learning environment one is working to create. Larger consulting firms need to work harder to ensure that strong connections exist. Because, whenever the connections are weak, explicit and tacit information that can inform the facilitation and design of the development journey gets lost.

CREATING PARTNERSHIPS FOR A DEPTH OF LEARNING

The expanding use of consultants as capacity builders shows the executives are well aware of the need for learning in their organizations. This awareness also needs to be matched by an understanding of the conditions necessary to create a depth of learning that will really make a difference.

Both parties must go beyond surface relationships and develop partnerships that address underlying assumptions and identity. This requires going beyond superficial issues of fit to allow quality conversations that ensure quality design and real change. Lessons learned about creating partnerships are highly personal and difficult to test, so in your own client-consulting relationships make it your resolve to have conversations that allow you to learn about the depth of your relationship and thereby have actions that increase the quality of your partnership.

Further, if we are serious about achieving a depth of learning, we must increase our attention on the design process itself. Rather than rely on packaged solutions to issues and short-term interventions, we should focus on development journeys that begin with the final destination in mind, and build strongly on past development. The more we are able to do this, the greater our chances of achieving our desired outcomes.

Exploring Performance Versus Learning in Teams: A Situation Approach

D. CHRISTOPHER KAYES

INTRODUCTION

Mountain climbers recognize the difference between following an existing route and blazing a new one. Similarly, the ability to distinguish and respond to a task that requires performance versus one that requires learning may be the difference between an effective team and one that fails. This chapter suggests that how a team interprets its task and its subsequent response forms the basis of team effectiveness. Implications for goal-setting, behaviors, and shared beliefs in teams that lead to effectiveness are presented.

CONVENTIONAL WISDOM AND TEAM EFFECTIVENESS

Contrary to conventional wisdom, effective teamwork follows anything but a rational path. Conventional wisdom tends to define effective teamwork in terms of performance outcomes, such as improving efficiency or achieving a measurable goal on a predetermined task. As the first American to summit the world's tallest 14 mountains and one of five people to do so without supplementary oxygen, Ed Viesturs has experienced some of the potential consequences of focusing solely on performance.

> *When you're up there, you've spent years of training, months of preparation, and weeks of climbing and you're within view of the summit, and you know, you have — in the back of your mind you're telling yourself, "We should turn around 'cause we're late, we're gonna run out of oxygen," but you see*

the summit, and it draws you there. And a lot of people—it's so magnetic that they tend to break their rules and they go to the summit—and, on a good day, you can get away with it. And on a bad day, you'll die.

Viesturs' experience helps expose some of the limitations of conventional wisdom on team effectiveness. These limitations include the following:

- When teams focus on performance, they tend to lean on prior learned behavior rather than learn new behavior ("years of training, months of preparation, and weeks of climbing").
- Effective teamwork requires attention to managing emotions (the summit "draws you there"; it's "magnetic").
- Effectiveness relies on balancing tired strategies of action with contingencies and adjustments ("On a good day, you can get away with it. And on a bad day, you'll die").

Learning and performance in teams

The experience of Viesturs and other mountain climbers provides a metaphor for team effectiveness. More than that, it echoes one of the most important findings I have come to after observing, consulting for, and training hundreds of groups: the best teams manage their environment by attending to both performance and learning demands. Team effectiveness requires that teams successfully interpret the nature of the task they face and the behaviors that follow.

This chapter outlines a situational framework that describes the conditions under which teams should focus on learning- versus performance-directed behaviors. I argue that effective teamwork relies on learning as much as performance, especially when teams face novel tasks. Ultimately, this chapter seeks to provide new insights into the different conditions that require learning versus performance in teams by suggesting a "task epistemology." Chapter conclusions lead to a better understanding of the relationship between learning and performance, the role of team emotions, and the challenge of learning in the face of narrow goals.

THE PROBLEM WITH PERFORMANCE

Over the last few years, I have learned that mountain climbers, like Ed Viesturs and his colleagues, are not the only teams that must balance learning and performance demands. Teams of all sorts need to develop behaviors that promote learning and performance. Mountain-climbing conjures images of a lone individual conquering the untamed mountain. However, mountaineering is most of all a social process that requires learning, problem solving, cooperating on distinct parts of a task, and coordinating different kinds of expertise and experience.

A growing body of research and theory on team learning suggests that teams should act with caution when adopting outcomes that are purely performance driven. Performance behaviors drive success when teams face problems — such as assembly production, sales goals, or operational improvement — that have clear parameters. When teams face novel situations, however, the problem-solving activity that normally leads to effective outcomes often leads to failure. The problem with performance emerges because the behaviors that enhance performance in some situations may prove disastrous when teams need to learn new skills, develop capacity, or respond to crisis. Teams that focus primarily on performance-related behaviors often do so at the expense of learning. This leads to a number of problems:

- Leaning too heavily on prior learned behavior rather than developing new behavior.
- Failing to develop shared beliefs about the importance of responding to changes in the environment.
- Focusing on predictable strategies for completing tasks at the expense of contingencies and adjustments required for learning.

TASK EPISTEMOLOGY

The distinction between learning and performance is a matter of how a team interprets the knowledge requirements of its task. I call this interpretation process "task epistemology" because the team develops a theory about the kind of knowledge that is required to perform its task effectively. Said simply, a team's task epistemology and the team's subsequent response form the basis of its effectiveness.

The distinction between learning and performance began to emerge as a colleague and I observed teams in a manufacturing environment. The teams were working on a continuous, highly interdependent task. Essentially, the team worked on an assembly line. Our objective in this research focused on determining which team-level behaviors, what we called team-level competencies, improved performance. We believed in a general set of competencies that existed across teams of all types. Our research revealed a more complex picture of team competencies than we imagined. We developed a picture of team behaviors that were dependent on the particular task performed by the team. We quickly found evidence for what others had been saying about team effectiveness: task mattered.

Our research led us to consider the special interaction between knowledge and task. Successful task completion involves gathering and processing knowledge. Further study confirmed this initial finding but led us to believe that conceptualizations of team task based simply on task interdependencies failed to tell the whole story. Tasks also carry knowledge demands. In other words, certain tasks require different kinds of knowledge than other tasks. Tasks have their own epistemology, in the sense that certain tasks demand different types of thinking for successful completion.

TASK KNOWLEDGE DEMANDS

This task epistemology can be illustrated by the process of climbing a mountain, a kind of short-term project. The first ascent of a mountain requires climbers to use a host of behaviors, including deciphering a new situation, identifying routes, trying out the routes and knowing when to abandon them, and establishing new techniques and then applying them in novel situations. On the other hand, once climbers successfully summit a peak, they must enlist another set of behaviors in their pursuit. The new strategy might include following a predefined route, clocking estimated ascent and turnaround times, identifying weather patterns, and following stop rules that specify when to abandon the pursuit. The first ascent requires learning-directed behaviors, while subsequent ascents, assuming other factors remain relatively stable and that processes have been determined, likely require performance-directed behaviors.

This distinction between learning- and performance-related task conditions forms the basis for a task epistemology. A task epistemology rests on at least three considerations:

- *Problem.* An ill-structured problem can be contrasted to a well-structured one by at least two characteristics. First, an ill-structured problem has no clear outcome; experts will disagree as to what answer is correct. Second, the solution necessary to achieve the outcome is not clear, and experts will disagree as to the correct method. The complexity of the problem is another consideration. Complexity is the degree to which the task requires integration and differentiation of knowledge, as well as the technical knowledge required to complete the task. Integration requires the ability to see connections between seemingly unrelated concepts or the ability to create a holistic framework from seemingly diverse and disparate variables. In contrast, differentiation requires noticing slight differences and recognizing uniqueness in seemingly related or similar concepts.
- *Context.* Environmental factors impact how the team accomplishes its task and measures its outcome. One example of a contextual factor impacting task epistemology can be found in the nature of the organization's goals. For example, an organization that has multiple goals will put different demands on a team than one that has a single well-defined goal.
- *Work processes.* One important consideration is whether or not the team has an established process or strategy to accomplish its task and whether or not the work process can be maintained until task completion. A second consideration is whether the team has established stop rules. Stop rules consist of a specified time table or set of work processes that trigger different actions. For example, a mountain-climbing team will abandon its pursuit of the summit if certain weather patterns are detected, and a manufacturing process will be shut down if certain quality infractions are detected.

Taken together, problem, context, and process factors provide the basis for understanding task epistemology. The epistemology of task becomes the basis for understanding the different conditions under which teams need to focus on learning versus performance. Simply stated, when teams face a complex and shifting problem, then learning processes are most likely to enhance teamwork. On the other hand, when teams face more clearly defined and linear problems, performance processes are likely to enhance teamwork. I suggest a more detailed explanation of the distinction between performance and learning epistemology by integrating various streams of research on knowledge into two categories: those conditions that require performance and those that require learning.

PERFORMANCE CONDITIONS

When performance conditions prevail, a team's goal becomes clear and teamwork entails developing a relatively stable set of goal-directed strategies. Once a team has developed effective goal-directed strategies, the team can then develop means to improve efficiency and effectiveness by slight modifications in reaction to new information or changes. A performance strategy works when several conditions exist based on the problem, context, and process factors related to task.

Problem factors

The problem is pre-existing

A pre-existing problem exists when a team faces a problem that has been seen before and for which a clear and effective solution has been developed. In some cases, the team itself has faced the problem before; in other cases, another team has faced the problem and developed a clearly defined strategy to accomplish the task. Examples of teams with pre-existing procedures include an airline cockpit crew on a routine flight and an assembly line production team working on a continuous process.

The task is well structured

A task is well structured when it can be completed by following a simple formula, such as a team of chefs working at a restaurant. A well-structured task involves a minimal number of steps to complete, and each step requires no special skill beyond the current expertise of the team members. Typically, a task will be considered well structured if the process necessary to achieve the goal can be agreed upon by experts. For example, some types of medical surgery qualify as a well-structured tasks because they seldom produce any difficulties and the steps necessary to successfully complete the procedure require no new skills.

The task is low complexity

A task can be considered low complexity if it requires little integration or differentiation of knowledge, such as when a sports team plays a game.

Context factors

The environment is stable

An environment is stable when it produces few anomalies and only routine change. Examples of a stable environment include a team of students working on a class project and a construction crew building a highway.

The goals are narrowly defined

A narrowly defined goal usually has a single measure of success, and success is easily measurable. The more easily defined a goal, the more likely the problem will be narrowly defined. Examples include a mountain-climbing team summiting a mountain, a sales team seeking to increase revenue, and a mutual fund invest-ment committee seeking to increase the value of a fund.

Process factors

Clear stop rules have been established

Clear stop rules exist when the team clearly understands when to abandon pur-suit of its outcome and seek additional help. A good example of clear stop rules exists in the case of an airline cockpit crew that cannot take off for flight until it receives a go-ahead signal from air traffic control or a chemical safety team that evacuates a plant during specific conditions.

Work processes are established

Under conditions requiring performance, teams typically rely on past strategies, processes, and problem-solving abilities to perform the task. The team does not require new skills or abilities for effectiveness.

In summary, performance conditions describe a situation in which existing processes prevail, with a relatively low need for new knowledge or innovative uses of old knowledge. We might call these conditions routine in the sense that a team's extant beliefs and behaviors provide the raw material for effectiveness. Task knowledge demands remain relatively low because the situation requires lit-tle knowledge creation. When all or most of these conditions exist, a team focus on performance-related behaviors becomes more likely to produce effectiveness. In contrast, learning leads to effectiveness when different conditions prevail.

LEARNING CONDITIONS

Team learning leads to effectiveness when situations are novel, adaptive, and complex. The conditions for learning have several characteristics related to the problem, context, and process of the task factors.

Problem factors

The problem is ill structured

The definition of the problem itself as well the solution to solve the problem is difficult to identify. This means that even if a resolution to the problem is reached, there will be little agreement as to the "correct" solution. Consider, for example, a feature film that costs millions to produce and achieves critical acclaim yet fails miserably at the box office. Little consensus exists as to the success of such an outcome.

The problem is highly complex

When learning demands emerge, the team will probably need to reconfigure knowledge in such a way as to make it useful. This knowledge reconfiguration requires synthesis or integration of existing disparate knowledge into a new whole or dissection of knowledge to find new essence or application. Examples include a research and development team that needs to identify a new approach to manufacturing an existing product.

Context factors

Environmental stability is low

When environmental stability is low, the team works under conditions in which external forces are constantly changing. An example is a military expedition faced with guerilla warfare, where both the nature of the attacks and the nature of the enemy are constantly changing.

Multiple competing goals exist

Another condition consists of facing multiple and often conflicting goals. Such is the case in many foreign policy decisions, where the goal is to remain in good standing with allies while at the same time exerting pressure to make an unpopular decision.

Process

Ambiguous stop rules exist

The rules or procedures to determine when to abandon a project or goal are not clear, as in an expedition team that sets no turnaround time and no criteria for when it should abandon its exploration and return home.

Work processes are difficult to maintain

This situation occurs when a team faces a problem that is constantly evolving, changing, and developing with new information or events, such as a television production team that is constantly trying to respond to the changing tastes of viewers.

Taken together, the above conditions for team learning require adaptation and demand new knowledge or reconfiguration of existing knowledge. Extant knowledge, team beliefs, and behaviors remain inadequate for effective task performance. Demands for problem solving are high. Under these conditions, knowledge demands are relatively high because teams require new knowledge for effective teamwork.

Table 1 summarizes the conditions that support learning versus performance in teams. These distinctions provide the first step in building a knowledge-based approach to tasks.

SITUATION APPROACH

When teams can distinguish between performance and learning conditions, they can choose the behaviors necessary for effectiveness. In the model presented in Fig. 1, task knowledge demands and solution complexity are classified as high

Table 1. Conditions for learning versus performance

Condition	Performance	Learning
Problem		
Nature of problem	Preexisting	New
Structure of problem	Well-structured	Ill-structured
Complexity of problem	Low	High
Context		
Environmental stability	High	Low
Definition of goal	Narrow	Broad
Process		
Stop rules	Clear and established	Ambiguous and underdeveloped
Work processes	Established	Difficult to maintain

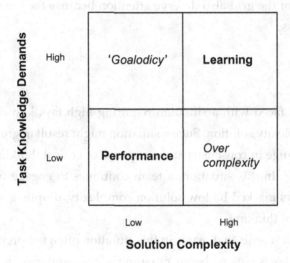

Figure 1. A situational model of learning versus performance in team effectiveness.

or low. Learning and performance occupy distinct, opposing positions in the model. The model provides a useful way for teams to determine whether a performance or learning focus is appropriate based on task knowledge demands.

Teams are more effective when they engage in behaviors appropriate for the task. When task knowledge demands are high and the solution complexity is high, then conditions for learning exist. When task knowledge demands are low and the solution complexity is low, then conditions for performance exist. Surely, understanding the basis of teamwork requires a more detailed explanation than can be explained using a simple 2 × 2 matrix. However, depicting teamwork in this way provides a useful and theoretically viable framework to understand the distinction between team learning and performance conditions. Indeed, learning and performance behaviors exist to some degree or another under all conditions, but the degree of focus can be determined more specifically through adherence to this model.

I suggest that team effectiveness begins when teams match the complexity of their solution with the "correct" interpretation of task knowledge demands. Team effectiveness emerges based on either learning or performance behaviors and shared beliefs. While the main focus of this chapter is the relationship between learning and performance as they are related to task effectiveness, the remaining two quadrants of the grid also deserve attention because they may result in limited effectiveness.

"Goalodicy"

Imagine a team faced with a situation requiring high task knowledge demands and a low-complexity solution. Such a situation might result in groupthink, where groups overindulge in consensus at the expense of critical thinking and complex decision making. In this situation, a team continues to engage in performance-related behaviors marked by low solution complexity, despite a situation calling for complexity of thinking.

My research reveals that teams in this situation often fall prey to the destructive pursuit of goals. Teams begin pursuing a goal under performance-related conditions. When the situation shifts and begins to call for more complex goal-setting processes, the team continues to develop relatively low-level solutions. When this shift happens, the normally helpful process of team goal setting begins to go awry.

I have developed the term "goalodicy" to describe how the normally useful process of goal setting actually drives failure. *Goalodicy* describes the processes in which group members and leaders closely identify with a future as yet unachieved goal. The term is a conflation of the ancient Greek word for "justification" or "judgment" *(dikee)* with the Anglo-Saxon word "goal" *(gal)*.

"Goalodicy," or goal justification, describes how teams and their leaders justify the pursuit of goals.

As shown in the figure, goalodicy seems more likely when the combination of high task knowledge demands and low solution complexity emerge. Problems that might result from this condition include the sacrifice of long-term objectives for short-term successes, the unforeseen consequences that actually undermine teamwork, and even unethical behavior driven by single-mindedness inappropriate for the task.

Overcomplexity

Working diagonally down and across the grid is a situation requiring low complexity which is met by a team response of high complexity. Examples are an organization that adopts complex legal procedures to regulate behavior between its members or a government program designed to improve transportation that requires decades to implement. Academics are fond of making complex solutions out of simple tasks as well. One problem with overcomplexity lies in its inability to integrate and differentiate knowledge appropriate for the task so that the problem becomes too complex to solve effectively.

The situational approach describes effective teamwork as a function of team task and solution. Effective teamwork is a function of being able to engage the right behaviors with the ensuing situational demand. Teamwork becomes ineffective when solution and task are out of sync. The situational approach takes the first step in developing the conceptual distinction between learning and performance based on task and solution complexity. The next section highlights some of the insights that might be gained from this idea and explores some of the future directions for study and implications for practice.

DIRECTIONS FOR LEARNING AND PERFORMANCE

Remember the mountain climbers I mentioned in the beginning of the chapter? I suggested that they provided a unique illustration of the distinction between learning and performance. I want to return to the theme of mountain climbing by looking at three key insights to be gained from my studies. These insights center on diverse learning competencies, psychological and emotional dynamics, the usefulness of goal-setting, and the relationship between learning and performance in teams.

Learning competencies

Team learning implies a variety of processes that may lead to team effectiveness. My observations suggest that mountain climbers must engage in a variety of learning activities from problem solving to cooperative learning and adaptation to changing circumstances. For example, one team of climbers I studied found themselves trapped in a blinding storm with no compass; they were unable to identify the path home. The team tried several different strategies to learn their way out. They suggested various solutions (problem-solving) and discussed potential solutions (cooperation). Finally, a short clearing in the clouds provided a view of the stars that allowed the leader to navigate back to camp (adaptation). When climbers talk about "years of training, months of preparation, and weeks of climbing," they imply developing a variety of learning competencies.

The different methods of learning demonstrated by the mountain-climbing team suggest that learning entails a diversity of behaviors. The research on team learning is diverse, emerging from fields such as education, organization and management sciences, psychology, and child development. This diversity provides a rich basis to further the study of team learning; however, it also poses a challenge. For example, the research has yet to result in a comprehensive model of team learning. Further research might seek to integrate across these fields and propose a multidimensional model of team learning and the shared beliefs that support learning.

Psychological and emotional factors

The growing interest in the cognitive aspects of team learning implies that learning rests on a rational or strategic foundation aimed at achieving rational outputs such as detecting and responding to errors, improving effectiveness, or achieving predefined goals. However, when mountain climbers talk about a summit that "draws you there," of a goal that has a "magnetic" quality, these climbers imply that emotions account for an important part of the effectiveness equation. One study I conducted revealed that climbers often fail to heed pre-established stop rules in the form of turnaround times. Over time, climbing teams establish turn-around times that estimate the last possible time to abandon a push for the sum-mit and return down. Many times, however, climbers ignore the turnaround times and continue to the summit. This explains, in part, what happened in the 1996 Mount Everest climbing disaster, in which eight climbers died, attracting world-wide attention. Lulled by the magnetic force of the summit, climbers allowed emotions to take over and continued to the summit, despite the rational rules standing between life and death.

Usefulness of goal setting

The climbers also highlight the importance of goals. After all, summiting a moun-tain serves as a platitude for goal achievement. Managers and scholars alike read-ily recognize that effective teamwork involves presenting multifaceted solutions, requires complex thinking, and mandates the balance of multiple, if not conflict-ing, goals. When advocates of goal-setting, such as Seijts and Latham, propose goal-setting as a way to help improve effectiveness, they ignore the unintended consequences that often result from setting and pursuing difficult goals. As a growing body of research and theory on learning suggests, teams should act with caution when adopting something called "learning goals."

Learning versus performance goals

Learning goals rest on the assumption that most teams face well-defined problems emblematic of performance conditions. Goals, whether they are learning or per-formance in nature, work best when tasks and desired outcomes are easily defined. Goals provide managers with an important tool to enhance performance when organizations face clear parameters such as changes in production, sales, or revenue but often prove disastrous when organizations need to learn, develop, or respond to crisis.

For teams to realize the benefits of Seijts and Latham's recommendations, a number of additional considerations become essential. First, research suggests that, contrary to Seijts and Latham's characterization, learning follows anything but a rational path. Second, learning requires a number of interrelated psychological processes, often involving hidden defenses, ego-preservation mechanisms, and self-deception. Third, the goal-setting approach to learning fails to consider the distinction between learning and development. Learning describes an iterative process that results in development — a qualitative change in how people learn over time. The failure to distinguish between learning and development misses the distinction between the process and the outcome of task performance. Fourth, research shows that fundamental differences exist between which goals predict performance and which goals predict learning, seriously challenging the generalizations made about the benefits of goals in improving team effectiveness. Goals may improve task performance, but the impact of goals on task learning remains unclear. Fifth, research reveals that learning requires an organizational culture that supports psychological safety among members of the organization. A culture lacking in such psychological safety may not support team learning, even when conditions demand it. In short, the relationship between learning and performance in goal setting deserves further attention, and the setting of something called "learning goals" should be approached with caution.

Relationship between learning and performance

Effective teamwork emerges from the ability to respond to changing situations. Learning and performance occupy a distinct but interrelated territory of the task demand equation. The best mountain climbers, for example, demonstrate the ability to understand contingency and shifting of circumstances. These climbers understand that when they take certain actions, "on a good day you can get away with it. And on a bad day, you'll die." This ability to understand contingency may explain why it took American Ed Viesturs 16 years to achieve his goal of summiting the world's highest peaks. The 16 years of effort hint at the need for both learning- and performance-directed behaviors in many circumstances. My research has revealed two specific insights into the relationship between learning and performance.

Team learning and performance are related

Most tasks faced by teams involve both learning and performance outcomes. Some aspects of a task are familiar, while other aspects are novel. Effective team-work requires balancing the unique demands of learning and performance. Some of the team processes that support both learning and performance include inter-personal understanding and proactivity in problem solving.

Interpersonal understanding. Interpersonal understanding is team members' awareness of other members as well as themselves. Teams that share a high degree of interpersonal understanding possess an accurate understanding of the prefer-ences, moods, and emotional states of other team members. Unlike some other shared beliefs, such as team cohesion, interpersonal understanding does not nec-essarily create positive feelings towards other group members. Rather, the empha-sis lies in greater knowledge of team members' current states and preferences. A strong sense of interpersonal understanding in teams seems to lead to learning because it allows team members to gauge and, therefore, respond to or compen-sate for other members of a team at any given moment. Interpersonal under-standing makes tacit knowledge more explicit by surfacing hidden aspects of knowledge that may not be readily visible.

Interpersonal understanding can be built in a team by setting aside some time during each team meeting for members to "check in" with each other. During the check-in session, team members briefly talk about their current state, includ-ing demands faced and recent challenges faced outside the team environment.

Proactivity in problem solving. Proactivity in problem solving involves antici-pating and working to head off potential problems before they occur. Proactivity in problem solving can be thought of as a form of learning in which teams develop strategies that allow it to adapt to changes in the nature of the task as they arise. Teams that develop behaviors related to proactivity in problem solv-ing create the ability to respond to changes in the environment—which is an essential skill for learning since it allows teams to acquire new knowledge about the task as it develops.

CONCLUSION

This chapter explores the relationship between learning and performance in teams. Learning and performance describe two distinct approaches to teamwork, each of which leads to team effectiveness under different circumstances. Team performance leads to effectiveness when teams face a task that consists of low knowledge demands and a solution that requires low complexity. Team learning leads to effectiveness when teams face a task that consists of high knowledge demands and a solution that requires high complexity. The distinction between learning and performance becomes particularly relevant with short-term project teams and in situations involving knowledge work. Several problems can arise when teams fail to adequately manage this distinction. New directions for understanding the distinction between learning and performance require a greater elaboration of the differences between the two approaches to teamwork and a better understanding of the behaviors associated with learning and performance outcomes.

Like the mountain climbers who recognize the difference between following an existing route and blazing a new one, successful teams can distinguish and respond to a task that requires learning versus one that requires performance.

REFERENCES

Druskat, V. U. & Kayes, D. C. (2000). Learning versus performance in short term project teams. *Small Group Research, 31,* 3, 328–353.

Kayes, A. B., Kayes, D. C., & Kolb, D. A. (In press, September 2005). Experiential learning in teams. *Simulation & Gaming.*

Kayes, D. C. (In press, 2005). The destructive pursuit of idealized goals. *Organizational Dynamics.*

Kayes, D. C. (2004). The limits and consequences of experience-absent reflection: Implications for learning and organizing. In M. Reynolds & R. Vince (Eds.), *Organizing Reflection*. Aldershot, Hampshire, UK: Ashgate Publishing.

Kayes, D. C. (2004). The 1996 Mt. Everest climbing disaster: The breakdown of learning in teams. *Human Relations, 57*, 10, 1236–1284.

Kayes, D. C. (2003). Proximal team learning: Lessons from United Flight 93 on 9/11. *Organizational Dynamics, 32*, 1, 80–92.

Kayes, D. C. & Raelin, J. (In press). Goalsetting. In J. Bailey & S. Clegg (Eds.), *International Encyclopedia of Organization Studies*. Thousand Oaks, CA: Sage Publications.

Mitchell, R. (1983). *Mountain experience: The psychology and sociology of adventure*. Chicago: University of Chicago Press.

Perrow, C. (1984). *Normal accidents*. New York: Basic Books.

Seijts, G. H. & Latham, G. P. (2005). Learning versus performance goals: When should each be used? *The Academy of Management Executive, 19*, 1.

Vaughan, D. (1996). *The Challenger launch decision: Risky technology, culture, and deviance at NASA*. Chicago: University of Chicago Press.

Viesturs, E., quoted on the Charlie Rose Show (1998, March 23). *Climbers describe expedition to Everest as "triumph"* [broadcast transcript #2122]. New York: Rose Communications.

Weick, K. E. (1993). The collapse of sensemaking in organizations: The Mann Gulch disaster. *Administrative Science Quarterly, 38*, 628–652.

EVALUATION BY MEANS

PHIL RAMSEY, BETH TOOTELL AND ROBYN MASON

INTRODUCTION

Whether to evaluate training is a vexed question for HRD practitioners. For most, the logic of evaluation is almost self-evident. Feedback is an essential component of any learning process. In designing training courses, professional standards dictate the need to ensure participants will have opportunity to practice skills and receive feedback on their performance.

It makes sense that HRD practitioners — people who value learning — would want to "practice what they preach"; that they would use evaluation to generate feedback for themselves and use it to improve their training efforts. Yet, in depth evaluation of training rarely takes place.

Most HRD practitioners are familiar with Donald Kirkpatrick's four levels of evaluation. Kirkpatrick[1] suggested that training efforts could be evaluated in the following terms:

Level One: Reaction. The extent to which participants respond favourably to various aspects of the training experience: to the trainer, the content, the venue and so forth.

Level Two: Learning. The extent to which the training produces a change in the knowledge or skill of participants. What can participants do differently as a result of the instruction?

---

[1] See Donald Kirkpatrick's book *Evaluating Training Programs: the four levels* (San Francisco: Berrett-Koehler, 1998).

Level Three: Behaviour. The extent to which skills learned by participants produce a change in behaviour on the job. Do newly learned behaviours get transferred from the learning environment to the workplace?

Level Four: Results. The extent to which training contributes to the attainment
of organisational objectives. Did the changed behaviour in the workplace make a
positive contribution to results that are important to the organisation?

Kirkpatrick's levels make good sense to most people. It is evident that each
level is important: as the levels ascend, the value to the organisation increases. It
is important that learners find training a positive experience, but our purpose in
training is to achieve more — we want people to learn useful skills. While we
want them to learn skills, our purpose is to achieve even more than that — that
these skills are put to use in the workplace. Further, we want our skills to do more
yet — to make a difference to the organisation's results. As the levels increase,
evaluation addresses issues closer to our ultimate purpose.

Given that the significance of evaluation grows as we move toward Level
Four, you might expect that people interested in making real improvements to
training would concentrate their efforts at the higher levels. Yet, what is the case
in practice? If you are a training practitioner, likely you realise that when evaluation is done at all, typically it is limited to Level One. Trainers may survey learners' reactions, but rarely address issues of learning, behaviour or results.

Why is this? What prevents professional trainers from acting in an apparently
professional manner? And what might be done to make evaluation more practically relevant to people within the profession?

MENTAL MODELS

Gregory Bateson is credited with the rule of thumb, that the cause of any problem
is the gap between how we are thinking and how nature works. In other words,
things might appear to be paradoxical because of a mismatch between our mental models of the world how the world really works. It seems that such a mismatch
exists in the way we typically think about evaluation. Trainers are torn: they may
espouse the need for evaluation, but act as if it is not really worth the effort.

Is it reasonable that otherwise professional trainers should be so consistently unprofessional when it comes to evaluation? Surely there is something wrong with the way we think about evaluation that leads to the current state of professional ambivalence.

Tom Johnson's[2] work on 'Management by Means' provides an insight into what may be going wrong with the way we think about evaluation. Johnson explains that in most organisations, people are used to managing by results: a practice and mindset that is out of step with natural processes, and which leads to a variety of undesirable consequences.

Managing by results is a "command and control" oriented approach to management, that involves specifying — or commanding — the results that you want from a system, and then using measures to identify variance from these targets.

What's wrong with this approach? According to Johnson, it gives the misleading impression that a manager can command an organisational system to achieve any arbitrary target as long as it can be measured. Further, it suggests that managers do not need to understand the forces involved in creating the results they desire; rather they simply need to be skilled at applying measurement techniques associated with command and control.

How does this mental model affect the way we approach evaluation? Rather than seeing Kirkpatrick's levels as steps in a process designed to produce results, levels are seen as potential targets; points at which desired results might be defined. People contemplating evaluation may tend to think of these as disconnected areas of interest. Consequently, evaluation leaves them perplexed. The thinking of an HRD practitioner might go along these lines:

"I want the training to produce results in all these areas, so which do I measure? Should I measure them all? But really, only 'reaction' and 'learning' are directly related to what happens during the training. All manner of other variables — the nature of the workplace, relationships with management, changes to the job — are going to affect whether there are changes to behaviour and results. Given that people will use the evaluation report as the basis

---

[2] See *Profit Beyond Measure: Extraordinary results through attention to work and people* by H. Thomas Johnson and Anders Broms (New York: The Free Press, 2000).

for managing (i.e. controlling) me, what is the point of measuring 'behaviour'
or 'results'? Won't my training get blamed for the failure of others to use
it properly?"

Further, practitioners are aware that learning is complex, and involve dynamics that can be confusing. Prior to training, a participant might self-assess their
level of knowledge on a subject as 'moderate'. Following the training, having
learned a great deal, the participant might realise how much more is involved in
the subject than was originally apparent, and may self-assess their knowledge as
'below average'. As well as learning skills, some participants may experience personal transformation: the training is involved in a fundamental shift in the way
they approach an important part of their lives. Yet this profound change — one
that is typically highly valued both by participants and HRD practitioners — is
more easily seen though qualitative rather than quantitative methods, thus treated
with suspicion by people enamoured with command and control.

Little wonder that practitioners find themselves in a bind. Evaluation
might seem like a good idea, in that it fits within prevailing beliefs and models
of management — many of which practitioners teach on their Management
Development programmes. At the same time, there are clear dangers associated
with applying measurement processes to learning. For many practitioners
the answer seems to be to restrict evaluation to measurement of participant
reaction.

But is there a better way? We believe there is, and recently we have been
exploring the use of an approach to evaluation based on collecting information
on the relationships within the learning process that give rise to the results
we want.

FOCUS ON MEANS

How do training results get produced? It is evident that a rich web of relationships
is involved in even the simplest instructional process. Results depend on the
interplay of learners, instructors, subject matter, organisational context and the
learners' co-workers, managers and clients. Evaluation by means shifts the focus

away from the measurement of results produced by the system. Instead, we aim to generate information that tells us about the quality of the relationships making up the system.

Why make such a shift? Results may be a snapshot of a situation that tells us little about what is really going on. They may reflect the efforts of past players who are no longer involved. They may have been manipulated in a variety of ways to appear healthy. By paying attention to relationships in the system we address whether the system as a whole is designed so that it is able to produce, *in a sustained way*, organisational well being.

How do we assess relationships? While an attempt to do so might sound hopelessly diffuse, Johnson has described how it can be done in imitation of the way natural systems operate. Firstly, we need to map out the process — the means — by which results are produced in the system. If the process of training is designed to produce changed behaviour in the organisation, our map will indicate what each person in the system must produce in order for the next in line to make their contribution. At each point in the process, information on the quality of relationships lies with whoever is next in line: have they received what they need to receive in order to make their contribution to system-wide results?

Using this approach, we have adapted a similarly means-focused model used by Zeithaml, Parasuraman and Berry[3] to evaluate the quality of customer-service systems. The model is shown in Fig. 1. We have built the model around the behaviours the system is designed to produce. Behaviours act as the *lingua franca* of training: a common means of expressing what we want from others and what we contribute. By collecting information at the points indicated, we aim to highlight gaps — discontinuities — in the system, rather than arbitrary targets at each point. The model thus allows professional HRD practitioners to bring their knowledge of learning to bear on discontinuities. Why do they exist? What might be done to put them right? By removing discontinuities in the system, the evaluation process endeavours to produce an optimal level of functioning, with knowledge and energy flowing between the parts of the system.

---

[3] See *Delivering Quality Service: Balancing customer perceptions and expectations* by Valarie Zeithaml, A. Parasuraman and Leonard Berry (New York: The Free Press, 1990).

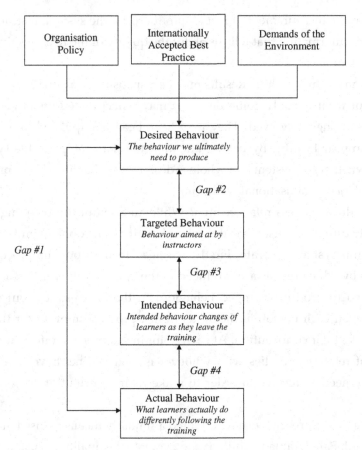

Figure 1. Model for training evaluation.

THE BEHAVIOUR GAP MODEL

As its name suggests, this evaluation model is based on gaps associated with changed behaviour. The Behaviour Gap Model is shown below. We have based the model on a series of gaps. Why? It has been well established by HRD practitioners and theorists like Robert Blake, Jane Mouton and Robert Fritz that a gap between what we want and current reality has a powerful affect on people, motivating and directing their efforts.

Gap One represents our key concern: the gap between the behaviour desired by the organisation and the actual behaviour of people in the workplace following the training. The purpose of evaluation — and the purpose of efforts to improve training — is to minimise this gap. The more that we can do that, the better our training system will be in producing the behaviours we care about.

It might seem that the existence of a gap is a bad thing. It is not. We need to take the realistic view that there will always be a gap between what we desire and what our training is delivering. Being able to clearly understand the nature of this gap is the basis for improvement. As Chris Argyris has said, learning is the process of identifying and correcting such gaps: the existence of Gap One is a *good* thing to the extent that it mobilises our efforts to improve our training system.

Because Gap One is so crucial, it is important that we can define it clearly. That depends, to a large extent, on how clear we are about the behaviour we desire. Often training takes place without people having a clear vision of what they want learners to do as a result. It can be that the vision is murky because there are mixed message about what constitutes desirable behaviour.

As the model shows, our understanding of desired behaviour is influenced by organisational policy, internationally accepted models and the demands the workplace puts on those practising in the workplace. In combination these factors all influence the behaviour that is desired. The model suggests that evaluation should start by examining the degree to which these influences are aligned. Is there agreement about what constitutes desired behaviour? Or is work needed to clarify the vision?

Gap Two indicates that those delivering the training may aim for outcomes other than those desired. This may happen because the training has existed for some time and has not been revised. Or, within a group of instructors there may be differences regarding the outcomes to be targeted. In many instances instructors think primarily about the subject they want to cover rather than the behaviour they are attempting to produce.

Gap Three indicates that learners on a course may leave having intentions different to those teaching the course. Identifying the intentions that learners have formed provides valuable insights for instructors into the true impact of their training. The messages received may be very different from those instructors thought they were sending.

Finally, factors in the workplace may mean that people do not put into practice what they intend to do at the end of the training. The work context may result in learners shifting their priorities or in sticking with their pre-training behaviour. Gap Four is a measure of the extent to which the work context has impacted on behaviour.

While HRD practitioners are primarily interested in reducing the magnitude of Gap One, understanding this gap as the sum of Gaps Two, Three and Four enables those involved in evaluation to gain insight into how Gap One is created: where the relationships in the system need to be strengthened.

METHODS

A variety of activities can be involved in the evaluation process. These can be selected or designed to suit the particular situation in which the evaluation is taking place. Activities might be selected on the basis of the nature of the programme, the resources available and access to the people involved. Evaluation activities focus on the issues displayed in the boxes of the model. Measuring these allows us to determine the nature of gaps that are of interest.

Establishing the Desired Behaviour: Typically, a number of issues shape desired behaviour. We have identified three in our model: behaviours suggested by Organisational Policy, by Best Practice, and by the demands of the work environment. Appropriate processes at this stage include: reviewing the Policy using relevant documents and interviewing key managers; reviewing internationally accepted model of work practice using relevant publications; and discussion of ways in which workplace demands modify the expectations of those responsible for carrying the work. This discussion can be facilitated through use of focus groups with incumbent employees, particularly those responsible for balancing implementation of policy with other work demands.

Establishing the Intended Training Outcomes Aimed for by Teaching Staff: As is the case with a great deal of training activity, those involved often think in terms of the subjects they teach rather than intended behavioural outcomes. A list of intended behavioural outcomes can be often derived from the course curriculum through a guided discussion with Course Director. If more than one instructor is involved, each can be asked or guided in producing a set of behavioural outcomes. These can then be compared to assess the level of agreement as to intended behaviour.

Establishing Intended Behaviour Changes of Participants Leaving the Course: It is important to differentiate between what the participants have learned, and what their intended behaviour changes would be. There can often be a substantive difference in the practices identified by the participants that could be implemented and those they perceive they actually will implement. Participants are often well positioned to note the barriers they perceive to the wholesale introduction of the techniques they have learnt.

Establishing Actual Behaviour in the Workplace: We have used two processes — survey and work samples — to establish a measure of changed behaviour. The survey asks employees, their managers, and a subordinate of their choosing to report on behaviour of the employee. With both surveys and work sample a comparison can be made between: (a) employees who had completed all aspects of the course, (b) employees who had attended the formal face-to-face programme but had not completed subsequent project work, and (c) employees who were yet to attend the course.

THE MODEL IN USE

A recent application of the model was with the evaluation of a cross-cultural training programme at Massey University in New Zealand — the Massey Kiwi Friend Programme (MKFP). The MKFP primarily endeavours to help international students adjust to life in New Zealand and at Massey University. In particular, it aims to introduce students to aspects of "Kiwi" life and culture, language, and the processes and expectations at University. The programme encourages students to open themselves to new ideas and experiences in pursuit of integration, in order to adjust successfully to their new academic and socio-cultural environments. The

MKFP is a voluntary programme offered to new international students studying in the College of Business.

The programme aims to help international students develop skills associated with successful integration into the New Zealand culture. Students meet in small groups for one hour each week with a senior New Zealand ('Kiwi') student, who coordinates and facilitates the workshops as part of the course requirements of the Cross-Cultural Management paper in which they are enrolled. Six workshops are offered as the formal part of the programme, and begin in week 2 of each new semester. Additionally, students are encouraged to attend a Conversation Hour on Fridays' throughout the semester to learn about and discuss current events in the local and national news, and to practice their English conversation skills. Other activities such as bush walks, social sports and farm visits are also arranged.

Since the programme began in July 2002 it has experienced considerable growth, with between 40–50 students consistently participating each semester. Because of the potentially significant impact the programme can have on students' adjustment, an evaluation was needed to gauge its effectiveness and to determine what changes or improvements were necessary.

An initial evaluation was conducted during the third offering of the programme. Using the Behaviour Gap Model focussed on the behaviours associated with successful adjustment to a new culture. More specifically, evaluation using this model involved identification of gaps between: ideal behaviours associated with adjustment; the outcomes intended by those providing instruction, which included academics and New Zealand students; intentions of international students completing the programme; and actual outcomes, that is, specific behaviours of participants.

The first challenge was to establish a clear picture of desired behaviour. Our model emphasises the need for a standard or 'ideal', against which to compare outcomes for the training system. A review of cross-cultural psychology, expatriation and cross-cultural training literature revealed numerous studies that focussed on establishing and describing various dimensions of culture, dimensions and processes of adjustment, and the design and delivery of training. However, these studies did not provide a framework that enables behaviours expected as a result of training to be determined: the basis sound training design.

Use of the Behaviour Gap Model highlighted this confusion, and prompted the development of our own behaviourally-based model of student behaviour, which became known as the Balanced Adjustment Model. The Balanced Adjustment Model was the first outcome of the evaluation process: a clear picture of ideal behaviour that eliminated much of the confusion as to what the MKFP hoped to achieve.

We used interviews, focus groups and questionnaires to collect data from trainers and student participants. Results of the evaluation showed that gaps existed in several parts of the system; the one of primary concern lay between the intended outcomes of trainers and the intentions of students to engage in the expected behaviours.

Gap Two: The first level of analysis compared the intentions of trainers to the ideal behaviours described in the Balanced Adjustment model. This gap indicates whether or not trainers have clear understanding of outcomes the training seeks. In the case of the MKFP, a high level of continuity was found: trainers' intentions were closely matched with the behavioural outcomes described in the Balanced Adjustment Model. This is despite the fact that the Balanced Adjustment Model was constructed *after* the MKFP had been running for several semesters. Evidently the model fitted with the tacit model used by trainers involved in the programme.

Gap Three: The second level of analysis was to measure any gap between the behaviour the trainers intended to produce and the behaviour students on the programme intended to display as a result of their participation. An important gap was found to exist at this level of the evaluation: some students indicated the intention to engage in the full range of behaviours dealt with in the programme, while other students were very vague as to their intentions. Some students, for example, were enthusiastic about initiating conversations with domestic students, learning more about local culture, joining clubs and participating more actively in class discussion. Others were uncertain about what they would do.

What might account for this variation? It may be that the result was very dependent on the particular student. Some students naturally think in terms of specific actions. Others do not make the link between the training received and the action needed. Given the range of instructors involved in the MKFP, it may also be that different groups were given messages of varying clarity. Whatever the case, those involved with the MKFP have seen the need to include more specific direction for students on actions they should take both during and after the programme.

Gap Four: The evaluation project for the MKFP had difficulty in assessing the final gap of interest: that between student intentions at the end of the programme and their actual behaviour in their work environment. A number of factors contributed to this difficulty. Firstly the MKFP was run over a six-week period, during which time participants were also engaged in their primary 'work': studying at the University. There was no clear demarcation between the programme and the students' work. Access to students following the programme for the purpose of evaluation was also difficult. These and other reasons made it difficult to get a final picture of how behaviour had changed following the programme.

That difficulty meant that Gap One of the model did not contain all the error that was possible. Nevertheless, the evaluation process highlighted a rich variety of areas in which the MKFP could be improved and at the same time justified the College's investment in the programme by indicating the significant impact it was having a student intentions.

CONCLUSION

Evaluation poses real challenges to HRD practitioners. It is a process that promises gains that typically fail to be realised in practice. We have endeavoured to develop a approach that builds on the practical insight inherent in 'Management by Means'.

The Behaviour Gap Model enables us to focus on the quality of relationships in a training system, rather than giving attention only to the results produced. This shift in mind is consistent with many of the principles associated with

Learning Organisations: the importance of strengthening relationships, clarifying one's vision, and detecting and correcting error.

While the Behaviour Gap Model has been used in a limited number of evaluation projects, each time we have used it we have gained valuable insights into the quality of training being done and how it might be improved. It is has strengthened our confidence in the usefulness of evaluation processes and in the value of using learning principles as the foundation for learning processes.

LEARNING TO BE AN EXPERT: THE PLACE OF VOCATIONAL EDUCATION

PETER JARVIS

An expert is one who 'has extensive skill or knowledge in a particular field' or someone who is 'skilful or knowledgeable' (Collins English Dictionary). Perhaps the dictionary should also have offered the possibility that an expert is both skilful and knowledgeable. Yet it would be true to say that for a number of years the word 'expert' has fallen into something like disrepute as terms like 'competency' dominated the vocabulary of political correctness. But we have all been witnesses to deskilling as the world of technology has intruded into the worlds of production and service. It has changed the nature of work and, therefore, of work preparation. Even Lyotard (1984, p. 48) wrote about higher education and the higher professions:

> In the context of delegitimation, universities and institutions of higher learning are called upon to create skills, and no longer ideals — so many doctors, so many teachers in a given discipline, so many engineers, so many administrators, etc. The transmission of knowledge is no longer designed to train an elite capable of guiding the nation towards its emancipation, but to supply the system with players capable of acceptably fulfilling their roles at the pragmatic posts required by its institutions.

But, despite this emphasis, we have not destroyed the need for experts, although we have wrongly downplayed it in recent years, as I want to argue here. If we carefully examine the new work force, we can see that there are many who have been deskilled, those whom Reich (1991) called the routine production workers, whose employment involves operating technology that has removed the skill from the production processes; they can be trained to operate the machinery and with every new piece of technology they can be updated and once they have learned it, then they go and operate it. They are the flexible work force since they can be trained to operate almost any piece of machinery. In addition, there are those who do the routine manual and service but non-technological jobs also need to be competent and can be trained to be so. But there are still other types of workers who have just as great a need of expertise (both knowledge and skill) as they have ever had, and there are at least three types of workers who fall into this category: the professionals, the crafts and trades people and those who work with people (managers and sales people). This is not a matter of dividing the work force into those who need knowledge and those who need skill — it is about dividing it between those who need expertise and those who need competency. My concern in this paper is with those who need expertise and I want to focus on three aspects underlying the process of becoming an expert — the nature of knowledge, practice and learning — and in the final section I want to examine the implications of this for vocational education.

THE NATURE OF KNOWLEDGE

Knowledge has been traditionally regarded as theoretical, objective and an unchanging truth, but in recent years this has been recognised as misleading.

Objectively, there are data and information but they are not necessarily unchanging. They are objective in as much as they can exist outside of and beyond the knowledge of those people who do not know. Data and information are the knowledge of those who propound them but they only become other people's knowledge when they have been learned subjectively. Then they become knowledge and as knowledge develops so it might assume the form of wisdom — knowledge and wisdom are learned. We will return to the nature of learning below — but in the first instance, we see that the transmission of data and information are part of the curriculum of vocational education but knowledge and wisdom cannot be taught only learned. This distinction between objective and subjective knowledge is fairly recent and traditionally scholars have not separated objective and subjective knowledge in this way but rather just referred to it all as knowledge — but not all knowledge carries equal status or significance.

But as early as 1926 the German sociologist Max Scheler (Stikkers, 1980, p. 76) began to classify knowledge into seven types based upon their speed of change:

- myth and legend — undifferentiated religious, metaphysical, natural and historical;
- knowledge implicit in everyday language — as opposed to learned, poetic or technical;
- religious — from pious to dogmatic;
- mystical;
- philosophic-metaphysical;
- positive knowledge — mathematics, the natural sciences and the humanities;
- technological.

Scheler regarded his final two forms of knowledge as the most artificial because they changed so rapidly, whereas the other five are more embedded in culture. Whilst his analysis was a little over-simple, he does make the point clearly that many forms of positive and technological knowledge change rapidly — he suggested 'hour by hour' — but that was in 1926! Not all scientific knowledge changes rapidly — the speed of light, for instance, has not changed, whereas our understanding of the nature of light has changed. Hence, Scheler's typology, whilst useful for our discussion only represents some aspects of our understanding of the complex nature of knowledge itself. We might also dispute with Scheler that the humanities should be coupled with mathematics and the natural sciences — indeed, I would place them in the same category as philosophical and metaphysical knowledge. While Scheler was not totally correct, his artificial forms of knowledge are related to the dominant forms of knowledge in the knowledge economy.

It is those societies at the centre of economic globalisation that might be seen as knowledge societies: it is these that Daniel Bell (1973) first called the post-industrial societies. For him, knowledge is the fundamental resource for such societies, especially theoretical knowledge (Bell, 1973, p. 14), and as

Stehr (1994, p. 10) pointed out that when these societies emerge they signal a fundamental shift in the structure of the economy, since the primacy of manufacturing is replaced by knowledge. It is not knowledge *per se* that is significant to the knowledge society but scientific — including social scientific — knowledge (Stehr, 1994, pp. 99–103) since it underlies production of new commodities and services and, consequently, has economic value. Knowledge in itself has no intrinsic value; it is only its use-value as a scarce resource which is significant. Indeed, new knowledge is a scarce resource. Every marginal addition to the body of scientific knowledge is potentially valuable in the knowledge economy.

If some forms of knowledge are changing so rapidly, the question needs to be asked as to how do we know that they are true? It was Lyotard (1984) who answered this question when he referred to performativity — that is that useful knowledge works — it has use-value. Knowledge then is not just something that exists in the mind, it has got to work in practice. Practical knowledge has become a dominant form of knowledge in the work place — and this again is something that is learned rather than taught, although teaching can play some part in the process. Since there is a great emphasis on practical knowledge, curricula have to be more practical than in previous years, although universities especially have not traditionally concentrated on the practical aspects of the knowledge that they have taught, and so when they are teaching practical subjects they need to recognise that they should teach not only *knowledge that* but also *knowledge how.* But even *knowledge how* is not the same as *being able to.*

However, Stehr's assertion about the knowledge economy utilising artificial, or rapidly changing, knowledge is correct and it has at least two implications that concern us here: firstly, these artificial forms of knowledge soon become out of date so that initial vocation preparation must focus on the short-term and, secondly, there is a tendency to omit those other cultural forms of knowledge, such as moral knowledge, from our considerations as insignificant for vocational preparation since they apparently have no use-value. We will return to both of these points, but before move on we can see that each of these three types of workers needs a practical knowledge base in order to enter practice, even though the new worker remains a novice at the outset. However, it must be emphasised that the knowledge economy demands, even if it does not need such, highly qualified novices when they embark upon their careers (Livingstone, 2002). I do not want to discuss this point here, but it is one of the un-debated discourses of the knowledge economy that requires more consideration.

THE NATURE OF PRACTICE

Traditionally, it was assumed that the knowledge learned in the classroom could be applied to practice and we used to talk about practice being the application of theory. But gradually over the past two decades we have learned that there is a major gap between theory and practice and when I wrote *The Practitioner Researcher* (Jarvis, 1999), I assumed that practice preceded the practitioners' own theory — or rather their own practical knowledge. Practice is the process of transforming *knowledge that* and *knowledge how* into *being able to* — this is a process of learning.

However, the process of learning to be able is a much more complicated process that merely applying theory to practice as Nyiri (1988, pp. 20–21) made clear:

> One becomes an expert not simply by absorbing explicit knowledge of the type found in text-books, but through experience, that is, through repeated trials, 'failing, succeeding, wasting time and effort...getting a feel for the problem, learning when to go by the book and when to break the rules'. Human experts gradually absorb 'a repertory of working rules of thumb, or "heuristics", that combined with book knowledge, make them expert practitioners. This practical, heuristic knowledge, as attempts to simulate it on the machine have shown, is 'hardest to get at because experts — or anyone else — rarely have the self-awareness to recognize what it is. So it must be mined out of their heads painstakingly, one jewel at a time.

(All quotations from Feigenbaum and McCorduck, 1984)

As the years go by the experts not only gain knowledge and skills, they gain wisdom, which can be regarded as:

the ego's increasing capacity to tolerate paradox. This same capacity characterizes the mature defenses, which can maintain a creative and flexible tension between irreconcilables and allow conscience, impulse, reality, and attachment all to have places at the center stage.

(Vaillant, 1993, p. 328)

But this process of gaining expertise and wisdom is not something that happens in a short period of time. Through these complex learning experiences, novices might move gradually towards the status of expert, a process which was first discussed by Dreyfus and Dreyfus (1980). They posited that a learner goes through five stages in becoming an expert: novice, advanced beginner, competent, proficient and expert (cited from Benner, 1984, p. 13 — see also Tuomi, 1999, pp. 285–340). But it was Aristotle who focused on this practical knowledge — which he called practical wisdom — something that could only be learned with the passing of years. In precisely the same way, more experienced workers might continue to learn and continue to develop new knowledge through the process of practice. But there is no short time scale on this process — Benner (1984, p. 25) suggests that competency in nursing (the field of her own research) might come after two or three years of practice and proficiency between three and five years (p. 31). However, this raises quite major questions when we recognise the speed of change of artificial knowledge — some of the knowledge learned in the classroom might already be out of date before the practitioner has become an expert. Indeed, practice itself is not static but rapidly changing so that practitioners are not simply using knowledge gained in the classroom or in any form of initial vocational education. Indeed, they may reach a stage where they have to innovate within their own practice or, in other words, where they create new knowledge and new ways of doing things and their expertise means that they also need to be creative — they become experts. But we have to be aware, not every practitioner moves through this progression — for some, each procedure is the mere repetition of the previous one so that we can say that some practitioners have twenty five years of experience whilst others have one year of experience twenty five times.

Practitioners also have to gain that wisdom — the ability to 'maintain a creative and flexible tension between irreconcilables and allow conscience, impulse, reality, and attachment all to have places at the center stage' of practice, since these go with expertise. Immediately we see that practice is no longer just a matter of knowledge and skill, it is about the practitioner being confident, creative, having the right impulses, commitment, and so on. But more than this — in practice, practitioners work with others — patients, clients, colleagues and so on. It is a social activity and while expertise is very important, Maister (cited in Daloz *et al.* 1996, p. 25) wrote that 'Your clients don't care how much you know until they know how much you care'. In other words, practice is a moral undertaking; it is about trust and respect for others. Practice is ultimately about the nature of the practitioners themselves. Practice is about the person — as practitioner. This points us to a broader understanding of vocational education since it is about developing the person as well as teaching knowledge and skills. But before we examine this, we see one other thing — *being able to* is not something that can be taught, it has to be learned but it is even more than this — *being able to* is about *being* itself, but before we turn to this we now need to look at the nature of human learning.

THE NATURE OF HUMAN LEARNING

Being able to is not something that can be taught, neither is expertise nor wisdom — but they can be learned and learning is not something that is restricted to the classroom or the lecture theatre — learning is something that can happen anywhere and at any time. Consequently, at the heart of our concern lies in understanding the learning process, which is itself a very complex process — but one that we take for granted. Learning is *the combination of processes whereby the whole person — body (genetic, physical and biological) and mind (knowledge, skills, attitudes, values, emotions, beliefs and senses) — experiences a social situation, the perceived content of which is then transformed cognitively, emotively or practically (or through any combination) and integrated into the person's individual biography resulting in a changed (or more experienced) person.*

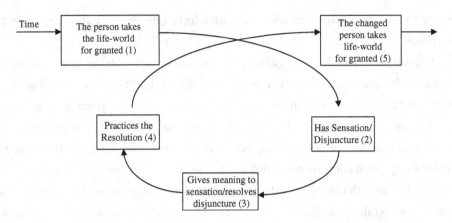

Figure 1. The transformation of sensations in learning.

This is a much more complex definition of learning than usually suggested and more complex than the one that I posed when I originally sought to understand the learning process (Jarvis, 1987) and which I have argued for much more fully elsewhere (Jarvis, 2006), and so I do not want to rehearse that argument here. Basically, however, four things happen during the learning process: a sensation (physical, emotional, attitudinal, etc) is changed into 'brain language', the experience that the person has on receiving the stimulus is transformed, the person is changed from one state to another and the person's relationship with the life-world is changed from harmony to disjuncture and gradually back to a new harmony provided the external world does not change (which is debatable). I have tried to depict this process in two diagrams.

Following Schutz and Luckmann (1974), we take our life-world for granted (box 1), and we live in the flow of time (what Bergson called durée) but when we cannot take our world for granted we experience disjuncture or have some sensation or stimulus that causes us to experience disjuncture (box 2). Through the learning process we transform the sensations (box 3) and then we seek to practise the resolution (box 4) which may be much more than just performance since we are not mindless individuals, and this may, after many attempts, lead us to a new harmony with our life world — provided other factors in the life world have not altered.

When we move from the classroom to the field of practice we actually move from the taken for granted to a new situation (box 2) which is disjunctural and it is here that we try to resolve the disjuncture by utilising the *knowledge that* and the *knowledge how* that we have learned as we begin *to be able to*. Through practice (box 4), we gradually learn to take our practice situation for granted (box 5). This is where the danger occurs in practice — we can then just take our practice situation for granted and perform our practice unthinkingly, or else we can see each situation as unique, each differing slightly from the last, and so we make each one disjunctural and we adapt our practice accordingly, or as Nyiri says "through repeated trials, 'failing, succeeding, wasting time and effort...getting a feel for the problem, learning when to go by the book and when to break the rules'" we learn to perfect our practice, even to innovate upon it and produce that new knowledge and skill that we discussed earlier.

Learning, however, is still more complicated than this first diagram suggests, as the second diagram illustrates, because it involves the person of the learner.

In this second diagram, we can see the other aspect of the learning process that occurs simultaneously with the first — the learner is transformed: the learners in

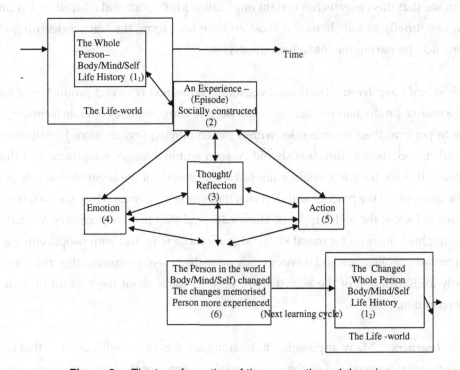

Figure 2. The transformation of the person through learning.

the life-world (box 1_1) have an experience (box 2) — that can occur in the class-room or the work-place, or elsewhere — which is constructed as a result of our perception of the situation and our previous learning, and it is the content of this experience which is transformed through our thinking, our doing and our emotions (boxes 3,4,5) and through this learning that the whole person (body, mind, self, life-history — box 6) is changed. It is this changed person (box 1_2) who has future experiences and continues to be changed as the practitioner gradually becomes an expert . But the significant point is that it is the whole person — body and mind — who is changed and who acquires expertise and wisdom as a result of all that trial and error learning in practice, especially if it is coupled with continuing vocational education.

SOME IMPLICATIONS FOR VOCATIONAL EDUCATION

Thus far we have looked at the nature of knowledge, practice and learning and we can see that this analysis has certain implications for vocational education. I want to look briefly at four here: the short and the long term; the learner; learning in practice; preparing the manager/supervisor.

Short and Long Term: Traditional vocational education is an end-product only for the routine production workers who can acquire competence to operate technology or to perform their routine roles within the employing organisation. For all other workers, vocational education should be seen within a longer time frame and this means that we have to recognise not just the demands of the occupational role but the demands of the practice within which that role is performed. Once we do this we have to look at the wider types of knowledge and skill that are necessary. We have highlighted the need for moral knowledge for those who deal with people either as clients or as colleagues and this demands more than mere instrumentality. But this is only an illustration of the way that we need to think about the breadth of initial preparation.

The Learners: Many approaches to learning are concerned with the way that the information is processed or the behavioural outcomes of the learning process, but in the model of learning that I have suggested I have focused on the learners themselves. Most theories of learning are, I believe, quite deficient in this in a number of different ways, as I have argued in my new book *Towards a Comprehensive Theory of Human Learning* (Jarvis, 2006) and I have focused on the person of the learner. The learner is both mind and body and in learning and in practice the one does not operate without the other. This also calls into question the emphasis on the concept of competency with its behavioural implications and also information processing with its emphasis on the brain as a glorified computer. The expert is more than a functionary responding to the demands of the system — the expert is a significant person in society using expertise and knowledge to enrich the lives of all who live in society. We need to understand the nature of personhood and learning if we are to be of service to those with whom we work; we need to value the person of the learner and this is more than human resource development — it is about personal growth and development. At the heart of our concern is respect for the personhood of people as we help them develop all of their abilities. Ultimately, we are all involved in *learning to be* as well as *learning to do* and *learning to know* — this presentation is about *learning to be an expert*.

Learning in Practice: We have to recognise that if we want experts, and wise ones at that, we have to prepare workers to understand that the practice into which they are going is a constantly changing one where new demands are being made on them all the time so that they have to be prepared to learn new practices, and so on. They have to learn how to learn, which means that new types of teaching and learning techniques have to be incorporated into the vocational training programme. New knowledge, new skill, new teaching and learning techniques — this points to the fact that vocational education needs itself to be undergoing continuous change and the importance of work-based learning needs to be recognised and. In addition, we have to help educational institutions to recognise and accredit such work-based learning programmes. However, programmes of this nature require higher educational institutions to adapt their understanding to accreditation. We have to recognise the complex process of learning in practice and help those who are undertaking it.

Preparing Managers and Supervisors: Since the work place is a site of learning, those who supervise need to be involved in the workers' learning. Consequently, managers and supervisors should to be taught how to be mentors of work-placed learning. This then is part of their continuing professional development and the concept of management needs to undergo some transformation as we develop teams who need to learn to work together.

CONCLUSION

Vocational education is now is far removed from training and the old debates about knowledge and skill, and the policy implications of these changes have to be taken into account from the outset. In this depersonalised society, we need to re-emphasise the place of the person and we need to re-conceptualise learning away from the rather sterile debates about lifelong learning that occur in policy documents and learn what it really means to learn. Perhaps the focus of our vocational education needs to come from the UNESCO report *Learning: the treasure within* (Delors, 1996) in which there are four pillars of learning — to be, to do, to know and to live together. Here we really begin to grasp what it means for people to learn: primarily learning *to be so* that we can also learn *to know, to do* and *to live together wisely* and with expertise.

REFERENCES

Aristotle (1925). *Nichomachean Ethics* (trans David Ross) Oxford: Oxford University Press

Bell, D. (1973). *The Coming of Post-Industrial Society*. New York: Basic Books.

Benner, P. (1984). *From Novice to Expert*. Menlo Park, Calif: Addison Wesley.

Daloz, L., Keen, C., Keen, J. and Parks, S. (1996). *Common Fire* Boston: Beacon

Delors J. (1996) *Learning: the Treasure Within* Paris: UNESCO.

Dreyfus, Se and Dreyfus, H. L. (1980). *A Five Stage Model of the Mental Activities Involved in Directed Skill Acquisition*. Unpublished Report: University of California at Berkeley.

Feigenbaum, E. A., and McCorduck, P. (1984). *The Fifth Generation*, New York: Signet.

Jarvis, P. (1987). *Adult Learning in the Social Context*, London: Croom Helm.

Jarvis, P. (1999). *The Practioner-Researcher*, San Francisco: Jossey Bass.

Jarvis, P. (2006) *Towards a Comprehensive Theory of Human Learning*, London: Routledge

Livingstone, D. (2002) Lifelong Learning in the Knowledge Society: A NorthAmerican Perspective reprinted in Edwards R, Miller N, Small N and Tait A (eds.) *Making Knowledge Work: Supporting Lifelong Learning*, (Vol. 3) London: RoutledgeFalmer.

Lyotard, J.-F. (1984). *The Post-Modern Condition: A Report on Knowledge*, Manchester: Manchester University Press.

Nyiri, J. C. (1988) Tradition and Practical Knowledge in Nyiri J. C. and Smith B. (eds.) *Practical Knowledge: Outlines of a Theory of Traditions and Skills*, London: Croom Helm.

Reich, R. (1991). *The Work of Nations*, London: Simon Schuster.

Schutz, A., and Luckmann, T. (1974). *The Structure of the Life World*, London: Heinemann.

Stikkers, K. (1980). (ed.) Scheler M. ([1926]1980) *Problems of a Sociology of Knowledge*, London: Routledge and Kegan Paul.

Stehr, N. (1994). *Knowledge Societies*, London: Sage.

Tuomi, I. (1999). *Corporate Knowledge; Theory and Practice of Intelligent Organizations*, Helsinki: Metaxis.

Vaillant, G. E. (1993). *The Wisdom of the Ego*. Cambridge Mass: Harvard University Press.

Performance — Learning Dysfunctions

WORKPLACE BULLYING: THEFT OF THE CAPACITY FOR LEARNING

ANDREA NEEDHAM

INTRODUCTION

Steve has been systematically destroying his organisation. To satisfy some deep-seated dysfunctional urges he has robbed the company of some of its most precious assets. Others know of the damage he is causing, yet do nothing. What is going on?

The law is simple: If Steve, a senior manager, embezzles the company he works for, the CEO can terminate the employment immediately. Theft is against the law in most civilised countries.

However, Steve has not been robbing the company of its financial assets. Rather, he has consistently humiliated, undermined and psychologically terrorised a succession of management and professional employees over fifteen years, causing a series of talented people to leave. Because he has been destroying *human* assets, the CEO felt he could not be terminated. The CEO determined that Steve needed to be disciplined — involving minimal action — and provided with a developmental plan which required him to show improvement. He would remain in place, with the same people reporting to and working with him including some who have previously been terrorised by him.

Grounds for instant termination were slim despite the fact that he had trampled on people's self-esteem, undermined their well-being and destroyed their reputations to feed his addiction to control. The impact of these behaviours and the resulting uncertainty and fear directly and indirectly impacted the productivity of his team. It seemed there was a succession of Targets; all good people who were ground down and forced out of the company, largely because they tried to perform well.

What could the CEO expect if the organisation tried to terminate Steve 'for cause'? Based on similar cases in New Zealand, it is likely that Steve would respond with swift legal action and the company would be forced to negotiate a substantial settlement package. Worse, Steve might demand to be reinstated and a naïve Employment Court judge might concur.

What really happened? Steve intimidated the CEO and Board Chair to such an extent that they too were afraid of him and, therefore, did little to ensure the emotional safety of the employees. It was easier to ignore the issue and leave him in his role with a development plan where he could terrorise some more.

The truth is that Steve is a chronic Workplace Bully. This diagnosis can be supported using criteria established by international researchers working in the area. Sadly, cases like this one are common. They challenge executives attempting to build robust organisations; they also challenge us to think about assumptions we make about the assets of our organisations.

In the eyes of the law, loss of a human being's self-esteem, self-worth and productivity is not seen as valuable as losing cash. This creates a situation that is disastrous for those wanting to create workplaces in which people can learn. At what point did we decide that this is okay? What will it take for self-worth to be considered an asset in a workplace? If we are to truly value people and their self-worth we need to understand the nature of workplace Bullying: what bullying is and how it can be effectively addressed.

BULLIES AND TARGETS

Bullying is a process that centres on people in two roles: the Bully and the Target. Because Workplace Bullies typically act with stealth, they are best identified by the impact their actions have on their targets. We can identify bullying when a pattern emerges, where several individuals perceive that they have been on the receiving end of behaviour intended to cause harm, and where they have difficulty defending themselves.

Examples of what Targets might experience include unwarranted or invalid criticism; having important information withheld; being publicly or privately humiliated; being subjected to excessive monitoring or micro-management;

isolation from colleagues; being shouted at; and being excluded from important social networks. These behaviours are instrumental in Targets feeling unsupported, isolated and exposed. It seems that the typical Workplace Bully focuses their threatening behaviours on one person at a time. And when the Workplace Bully succeeds in running that person off the job, another Target will be subjected to the bullying behaviour.

Workplace Bullying is about a Bully's addiction to control and what he or she does to feed that addiction. Research indicates that chronic Workplace Bullies — sometimes called 'serial' or 'recidivist' bullies — have been psychologically contaminated from an early age and their behaviour has become second nature. Their need for control is such that, once they have succeeded in driving a target out of the organisation, it typically only takes between 4 and 21 days for them to identify a new target and begin the bullying process again. The chronic Workplace Bully has behaviour patterns that often stem from psychological or other power- and control-based dysfunctions. Intervention with chronic Workplace Bullies is seldom effective: typically, no significant improvement is noticed subsequent to the intervention.

Not all bullying, however, is carried out by chronic Workplace Bullies. Sometimes people take up bullying because they are modelling their behaviour on the lead given by others. These 'situational' bullies, when confronted about their inappropriate conduct, are more likely to stop or significantly reduce the bullying behaviour. Of course, a situational Workplace Bully who is allowed to persist in damaging behaviour for an extended period will become as entrenched in their addiction as a chronic bully.

The difference between situational and chronic bullies is important to organisations. If we treat all bullying as chronic we might believe that there is no point in attempting to intervene where there is inappropriate conduct. And if we treat all bullying as situational we may expect chronic bullies to respond rationally and reasonably to interventions that have been successful with others. The distinction, however, makes little difference to the person on the receiving end of Workplace Bullying, the Target.

Targets are innocent. They do not deserve or participate in the Workplace Bullying process. They tend to be the competent, consistently well-performing members of teams. Typically it is their competence that makes them attractive targets to a bully. While competent, Targets are not perfect; they have weaknesses and strengths like everyone else.

Because they are capable and diligent workers, the bullying tactic of criticising their performance works well for the Workplace Bully: Targets are welcoming of feedback because they desire to remain productive team members. It is through this 'feedback' — most of which is unfair and undeserved — that the Workplace Bully establishes an initial hold on the Target. Once that hold is in place it is easy for the Workplace Bully to close the grip, moving on to more abusive strategies.

It may seem strange that Workplace Bullies target potentially high achievers. Yet these individuals are often identified and recruited by the Workplace Bully on the basis of their outstanding abilities or potential. Many targets are considered 'favourites' prior to being targeted by the Workplace Bully. Until the Workplace Bullying takes place, it is not usual to see evidence of concern over poor performance of a Target. If anything, the opposite is true. The Target's consistently high performance level and good feedback from others is a major reason for being targeted. The chronic Workplace Bully, addicted to the abuse of power, gets greater satisfaction from exercising control over capable people.

THE WORKPLACE BULLYING PROCESS

Workplace Bullying is not the obvious "beating up" that is associated with school children in playgrounds or brutal school teachers. Physical violence in the workplace is typically rare in the twenty-first century developed world.

Workplace Bullying is much more subtle. Each incident is trivial. Each incident, looked at in isolation, has minor impact. In chronic Workplace Bullying, each incident is targeted at one person, while others are treated well. With a situational Workplace Bully, he/she may 'bully' more than one at a time but it is not necessarily pre-meditated as with the chronic Workplace Bully. It is the stream of seemingly trivial incidents over a period of time and focused on one individual that constitutes a determined, targeted undermining of an individual's self-worth. Bullying is the psychological equivalent of the 'dripping tap' method of torture.

Bullying develops progressively. Incidents will initially be focused on performance-related issues and may have some basis in fact. The undermining will eventually become blatantly personal, initially during one-on-one interactions where there are no witnesses; later it becomes more public. By the time attacks are public, however, the Target's performance will have begun to slip and others may think the attacks by the Workplace Bully are justified.

Workplace Bullies are politically astute. As well as identifying targets, they work out who is likely to support targets, who can be manipulated to help in the bullying, and who in the organisation provides control functions that might prove to be obstacles. Depending on the position of the Target, some time might be spent influencing this network of people before attacks on the Target are made directly.

In a brief description like this, it is difficult to capture the vicious, destructive nature of Workplace Bullying. It is a cruel process that creates lasting damage both to Targets and the organisations in which Workplace Bullies operate. Bullying is repulsive. A natural reaction is to try to avoid the company of Workplace Bullies or to have as little to do with them as possible. Interestingly, the subject of Workplace Bullying is largely avoided by textbooks on management, perhaps because they prefer to deal with organisational processes that are more pleasant and rational. Sadly, the prevalence and costs of bullying require executives to learn about the subject. Bullying is a threat to healthy, productive work environments; to workplaces in which learning can flourish.

WHAT IS THE COST?

Research by Griffith University, Australia, suggests that Workplace Bullying costs Australia $12 billion annually, with one person in four affected in some way. There is little doubt that other countries are similarly affected. Why are the costs so high?

Workplace Bullying, while it is an equal employment opportunity concern and does exist on the shop floor and in clerical work environments, is primarily found in management and professional groups. According to UK and US research, between 70% and 80% of Workplace Bullying is top down. Some bullying is carried out by peers and relatively little is directed from bottom up. If Workplace Bullying was primarily an obvious, 'shop floor' issue, it might be dealt with through disciplinary action and incidents of bullying could be relatively contained within an organisation. Because it is primarily managerial and subtle, however, dealing with Workplace Bullying is complex and time-consuming. Workplace Bullying can have a pervasive impact on managerial action and decision-making, the effect of which is felt throughout an organisation. Consider two forms of cost: the direct costs to an organisation and the impact on learning.

Direct Costs: The case of Steve provides an excellent example of how costs can soar without an organisation realising what is happening. Sadly, only the financial impact can be calculated — the most crucial cost of Workplace Bullying is the emotional damage and permanent loss of self-worth and potential loss of income to the Targets, as well as their colleagues and family.

Steve worked for the national organisation for fifteen years. He was a senior manager for the last ten of those. He had people reporting to him at all times — he began with two direct reports and ended up with ten. He had internal relationships with many others. While it is not possible to estimate the loss of people and productivity from those who indirectly worked with him, it is possible to calculate the cost of the devastation he caused over fifteen years just within his team.

The last team he led consisted of ten professionals, each of whom received an annual base salary of $50,000. The first twelve months of a team member's role involves a training and orientation period that is necessary to ensure a competent level of skill. HR professionals usually estimate 30% of the first year's annual salary as a management recruitment expenses (15% for non-managers). These costs typically include fees, management and human resources time and an orientation period where the newcomer will not perform at the expected productivity level. As Steve's team consists of highly and specifically trained professionals, it is safe to assume that 20% of the first year's pay is the cost of replacement.

Over a period of five years there was a 20% annual turnover (two people per year) within the team, so the cost becomes $20,000 per annum and $100,000 over five years. This cost does not include the absenteeism, medical leave from stress, legal fees, management and human resources time.

Productivity was a greater loss and one that is harder to quantify. Estimating the cost to an organisation of people figuratively barricading themselves against 'attack' is difficult. How do you put a price on copying all and sundry emails, spending more time over coffee or at the water cooler, with the smokers outside or in the bathrooms furtively discussing the latest casualty and new Target?

If we assume that the productivity loss was 30% per team member, this provides another cost of $150,000 per annum or $750,000 over five years. This cost never shows directly on the financials; neither does it indicate the hidden expense such as lost opportunities, services, sales and profit and customer dissatisfaction.

The bottom line on Steve: his Workplace Bullying cost his employer a minimum of $850,000 over a period of five years. Over his fifteen year career with them, the cost was well in excess of one million dollars even without the cost of fixing the damage he caused.

Impact on Learning Environments: A growing body of literature records the value of social capital and trust to organisations. Fukuyama,[1] for instance, has described the link between prosperity and the level of trust in organisations. Prosperity requires that people work together; that they are spontaneously sociable and ready to undertake collective effort. A high level of trust cannot be purchased by an organisation; rather it must be built over time as people learn to work together. This can happen where people have cultivated social virtues: honesty, duty, self-sacrifice and politeness. Decades of work on organisational learning has highlighted how the ability of teams to tackle difficult, threatening issues without descending into self-defeating patterns of defensiveness, depends on the quality of the relationships in which their conversations take place.

Workplace Bullying systematically undermines relationships and social virtues within an organisation. Bullies deliberately set out to disrupt social networks so that they can more readily attack their Targets. Tragically, Workplace Bullies are often skilled at taking advantage of crises that they have been instrumental in creating. In the context of a lack of trust, they are often able to convince others of the need for 'tough management' and thereby justify their attacks on Targets as a drive for improved performance.

Bullying is thus a hidden element in the neglect of learning within organisations. It destroys learning environments: the social context in which learning most readily occurs. It forces people to focus their efforts on protecting themselves through attention to performance issues and to political game-playing. Workplace

---

[1] See Fukuyama, F. (1995). Trust: the social virtues and the creation of prosperity. New York: The Free Press.

Bullies need to mask their destructive activity by framing it as valuable behaviour their organisations need. For this reason, Bullies thrive on confusion. The next section of the chapter deals with confusing issues that make Bullying difficult to deal with.

SORTING THROUGH CONFUSION

As we have discussed, Workplace Bullying is typically subtle, and bullies are skilled at creating confusion as they undermine relationships and feed their dysfunctional need for control over others. People who might otherwise take action to protect their work environments are sometimes immobilised because of confusion. They get confused about the difference between Targets and 'chronic victims'; between bullying and 'tough management'; and over the role of the Human Resource function in dealing with the issue. Let's consider each of these issues in turn.

Issue #1: Genuine Targets versus Chronic Victims: A troubling consequence of labelling the Workplace Bully phenomenon and educating people about it, is the emergence of 'chronic victims'. Chronic victims detract attention from harmful Workplace Bullies and can damage the career of a strong manager. The chronic victim blames his or her manager for anything and everything, and blames senior management for the wrongs of the world. Chronic victims claim they are never listened to; that management does not care; that they are being picked on; that their poor performance is always someone else's fault. They will be known to all for their ramblings, false accusations and whining. They often create chaos and become known as an organisational troublemaker.

Unfortunately, when genuine Targets find the courage to speak out in organisations where chronic victims reside, the Targets are mistaken for victims: they are labelled troublemakers and their concerns are trivialised. The existence of chronic victims contributes to Targets becoming isolated and marginalised. Bullies contribute to this confusion by labelling their Targets as victims.

The following table identifies some of the specific characteristics of a genuine Target as opposed to the chronic victim. The Target is easy to identify if one knows what to look for.

The Genuine Target	The Chronic Victim
Is genuinely bewildered — 'why me? I have an excellent performance & work history'	Knows exactly why he/she was 'targeted'; has a constant refrain of 'everyone hates me' & 'I am always being picked on'
Confused about why senior management does nothing — 'do they not care enough about us'; can't they see what is going on?'	Does not go to senior management or human resources; keeps saying to anyone who will listen — 'typical, they always do this to me'
Is very weepy; cannot hold a conversation, focus or concentrate. This continues long after Workplace Bully is past unless Target seeks professional help	Continues the blame game — will use tears only at strategic points of discussion
Will often defend the Workplace Bully's actions especially at first; Target just wants him/her to stop'; does not necessarily want them fired.	Wants the alleged Workplace Bully fired
Blames themselves, reluctant to blame Workplace Bully. Thinks "I'm going crazy"	Blames everyone except him/herself for the hard luck
Can give three to five detailed examples of the Workplace Bullying behaviours; can readily describe subtle context	Cannot give detail examples of Workplace Bullying behaviours; uses broad brush statements and sweeping allegations which do not describe the subtlety
Talks about double messages; is confused at varying behaviours	Is not confused at all; does not identify double messages
Historically high performer	Historically achieves minimum standards or is an inconsistent performer
Is very reluctant to complain; he/she does not like to cause 'trouble'	Complains about everything; will often have a long history of being a 'troublemaker'

Source: © 2004 Andrea W Needham, www.beyondbullying.co.nz.

The issue of identifying genuine Targets from chronic victims is one that needs to be resolved so that organisational and societal support and resources can be provided to Targets.

Issue #2: The Tough Manager versus the Workplace Bully: Jim, a high prospect for a senior management role, felt disadvantaged. He had been doing extremely well in

ABC Ltd. and had an enviable track record for his achievements. He had built a good team — half of whom he had recruited and the rest of whom were there when he began work. He was a natural. His people respected him — some were not so sure they liked him, primarily because they did not know him. Jim kept his personal and professional lives separate. He had never bought into the 'my colleagues are my best friends' concept.

Jim was condemned by some colleagues for being tough. A chronic victim in his team laid a complaint alleging that Jim had 'bullied' him. Jim was eventually investigated and cleared. However, the stress and unfairness of the accusations resulted in him reacting in a similar way to a Target. In effect, Jim was the Target of situational bullying; in this case carried out by a chronic victim who was one of his employees.

In order to understand the differences, the following table summaries key criteria to distinguish the strong manager from the Workplace Bully.

The Tough Manager	The Workplace Bully
Has low turnover — people very loyal	Has a succession of Targets — all with good reasons for leaving
Clear about goals and expectations. Does not play favourites	Plays favourites — rewards sycophants — the 'yes' men/ women in the organisation
Is not known to exhibit a nasty side.	Is known to exhibit a nasty side — Is forgiven because s/he is so important to organisation
Is known to be fair and reasonable	Is known for being super charming and a nice guy
Provides and demands direct, timely honest communications	Inconsistent communication style; sometimes communicates very well; at other times is very obtuse or ambiguous
Builds relationships only when has to through respect/necessity — too busy	Has excellent relationship with superiors/ important people — politically savvy
Promotes and reinforces team and partnership 'think'	Divides and conquers
Employees respect him/her — some are not sure whether they like him/her	Employees have either love or hate relationship
Completes minimum paperwork necessary; dislikes too many policies, preferring efficiency and effectiveness over 'cover your butt' mentality	Uses organisational systems to corner Targets and reduce them to poor performers; knows how to ensure his/her 'butt' is always covered

Source: © 2004 Andrea W Needham, www.beyondbullying.co.nz.

Issue #3: Human Resources as Protector, Perpetrator or Bait: Executives might hope that any problem involving Workplace Bullying can be dealt with through the Human Resource function of the organisation: that they can leave it to professional HR people, who are better able to deal with the challenge. However, the Human Resource function is placed in an awkward position with a Workplace Bully. If the Bully is vital in a particular role or HR is unable to arrange a change of assignment, they will feel the need to collude with the Workplace Bully even when he or she is known to be lying and developing fantasy 'facts' about a Target. HR professionals who confront a Workplace Bully are likely to become the next bait. Once the current Target is out of the way, the HR professional becomes the Target.

Human Resource professionals should be as wary of the Workplace Bully as anyone else. If HR does not do the Workplace Bully's bidding, the Bully will make trouble for them, particularly if the Workplace Bully is a senior manager. A Head of HR brave enough to tackle a Workplace Bully in senior management will often end up leaving in anguish: it is a no-win situation if the CEO and Board Chair are not willing to take the lead in dealing with the situation.

CEOs and senior management place their HR function in an untenable role for the most part. It is often demanded that they protect management individuals unconditionally, even when managers are wrong or acting illegally or unethically. HR people are often torn between doing what is right and the needs to (1) protect the interests of the company, and the need to (2) protect their own jobs.

PREVENTING BULLYING

The values of organisations mirror the behaviours of the senior management team. When senior managers fail to act on Workplace Bullying — perhaps minimising the seriousness of bullying or denying its existence all together — they condone destructive behaviours that jeopardise their organisations. Workplace Bullies take advantage of inaction, seeing it as a clear message that abuse is acceptable, even encouraged. If a senior manager — for instance, the board chair or the CEO — is the perpetrator of psychological harm in the company, then the organisational culture becomes accepting of destructive behaviours and power plays. Action to prevent Bullying is imperative. What does it involve?

Leadership is fundamental to prevention. Leaders need to have a clear vision of the environment they want to create within their organisations. They also need a willingness to see things as they are, accepting that bullying is real, then having the courage to act.[2] Organisational leaders must take responsibility for creating the psychological security people need to learn and to work at their best.

This will involve establishing policy and systems that protect the organisation from destructive actions of emotionally damaged individuals. This includes establishing principles of governance that preserve the self-worth of organisation members. It also means giving attention to systems for the selection, promotion and development of people who are emotionally sound and capable of building trusting relationships.

Employees and clients or customers need to know that there is zero tolerance for Workplace Bullying. This needs to be regularly and well publicised and updated though various communication vehicles. The prevalence of Workplace Bullying requires that a clear message be sent throughout the organisation that these behaviours are neither desirable nor acceptable. Managers and staff who are not capable of treating others with respect and dignity should be identified, assessed and developed. If the desired results are not achieved, redeployment or redundancy will be of benefit to all concerned. The outcomes of complaints need to be monitored to evaluate success in addressing the issue.

It is important to spread the message that all allegations pertaining to abuse, Workplace Bullying, harassment, intimidation and humiliation will be taken seriously. The purpose of this message is to deter individuals from filing false and unfounded complaints, as well as sending a clear message that undesirable behaviour will not be tolerated. And complaints and allegations should be acted on in ways that recognise the complexity of abusive behaviour, the damage that it causes and the need to create a healthy and safe Workplace.

Of course, Workplace Bullying behaviour also needs to be confronted when it occurs. This is no easy task; as you might imagine, Workplace Bullies will actively resist such efforts. They might admit to some undesirable behaviour, but

---

[2] A full range of leadership activity is described in Peter Koestenbaum's 'Leadership Diamond' model. See Koestenbaum, P. (1991). Leadership: the inner side of greatness. San Francisco CA: Jossey-Bass.

are likely to suggest that Targets have over-reacted. And when Bullies deny behaviours they do so without the signs of a stricken conscience people might expect; in other words, they are highly believable.

Prevention is the only strategy for dealing effectively with Workplace Bullies. Prevention is most effective at recruitment, through screening processes. Prevention also involves permanently removing Workplace Bullies from the environment. Permanent removal is the most appropriate option to prevent re-occurrence of the undesirable behaviour and is in the best interest of all. Chronic Workplace Bullies are not strong candidates for interventions, because they are rarely treated or managed successfully. Redeployment simply shifts the problem to another part of the organisation. Half measures, such as redeployment or coaching can quickly reinforce a culture of acceptance and denial that makes the organisation a breeding ground for situational bullying.

Because some people — the situational bullies — may respond to interventions, one-on-one coaching can produce results.[3] Such coaching, however, needs to operate with a strict time line outlining in detail the required behaviour change, and rigorous monitoring to ensure change is happening.

CONCLUSION

People involved with learning in organisations are often idealistic. They seek what is best for their organisations and the development of others. They often care deeply about the self-worth of those with whom they work. Workplace Bullying challenges all of us because it is antithetical to so much of what really matters to us.

The first challenge of bullying is that it operates to destroy what learning seeks to build. It undermines the competence and confidence of Targets. Further, it destroys social capital within our organisations, attacking the networks and trust that are needed for on-going learning.

---

[3] This is not to be confused with mediation between a Workplace Bully and a Target. Mediation does not work. Rather it creates opportunities for further bullying.

The second challenge is that bullying calls for a different kind of response from normal. We may be used to assuming that undesirable behaviour is best dealt with rationally and developmentally. We are interested in learning because we prefer to see and develop the best in people. Yet the behaviour of many Workplace Bullies is immune to our standard ways of acting. It calls for a determined, confrontative approach pursued with courage. Denial or 'hoping for the best' simply leads to more of the same and to organisational crises. Workplace Bullying requires us to go into battle for the kinds of organisations we want to see.

PERFECTIONISM AND LEARNING

DEB RAMSEY AND PHIL RAMSEY

"Excellence" is a term often used in relation to organisational aspirations. We want our products to be excellent. We want customers to experience excellent service. We want to employ excellent people. Most companies have quality programs to ensure excellence and ongoing performance improvement. Excellence shows up repeatedly in the Vision Statements of organisations; perhaps it is in yours.

This aspiration to excellence feels compelling. It might seem difficult to argue with the value of excellence. And yet, the urge to consistently attain standards of excellence can be destructive to both individuals and organisations. This happens when a healthy striving for excellence is replaced with the dysfunctional world view known as 'perfectionism'.

What is perfectionism? How does it develop and what problems does it create? What can be done about it? In this chapter we will look closely at this disposition and the impact it has on learning.

PERFECTIONISM — A DISTORTED WORLD VIEW

Most people appreciate when something is done well. And we know what can result when we strive to do something to the best of our ability. People who consistently strive for excellence make a tremendous contribution to organisations, challenging themselves and others to learn, grow and find better ways of meeting the real needs of stakeholders. These people are motivated by a desire to succeed and they take pleasure in their accomplishments.

For some people, however, striving for outstanding performance is not a healthy pursuit of excellence. On the surface their behaviour may look healthy, but their striving is driven by fear of failure and worthlessness. Rigid thinking, self-deception and image maintenance all contribute to what is, essentially, a learning disability. Perfectionism is the term used to describe this pattern of self-defeating attitudes.

Perfectionists believe that unless one is perfect, one is worthless as a person (Greenspon, 1999). Living according to this principle means that perfectionists' self-esteem depends on their attainment of perfection. Since perfect performance is unlikely, the opportunities for perfectionists to feel good about themselves are severely reduced. This link between performance and perceived self-worth is captured in the following definition by cognitive psychologist David Burns (1980 p.34):

> "... perfectionists... are those whose standards are high beyond reach or reason, people who strain compulsively and unremittingly toward impossible goals and who measure their own worth entirely in terms of productivity and accomplishment. For these people, the drive to excel can only be self-defeating."

In addition to highlighting how perfect performance becomes fused with identity and self-worth, this definition stresses that the standards set by the perfectionist are inappropriately high. Not only are these standards unjustifiable, but the perfectionist pursues them relentlessly in the face of adverse consequences. Such a pursuit is not fuelled by positive qualities of 'tenacity' and 'resilience'. Rather, the perfectionist doggedly sticks to a course beyond the point when it is prudent to do so. The cost of the pursuit (emotional, financial, physical or social) might outweigh any benefit to either the individual or their organisation, yet the perfectionist is unable to pull out of the pursuit, to 'cut their losses', and refocus on another more important task.

What are some of the self-defeating attitudes that maintain perfectionism? One of the most common is 'all-or-nothing thinking' whereby perfectionists evaluate experience as either all-black or all-white. Shades of grey do not exist. This kind of inflexible thinking leads a perfectionist to consider anything other than first place as a total failure. As a result, perfectionists may experience a roller-coaster effect on their mood and feelings of self-worth.

Occasionally perfectionists meet their self-imposed stringent standards, but they are unable to savour the fruits of their accomplishment. Even when successful, they experience little or no satisfaction, since they have only done what was expected. Instead, they minimize their achievements in what has been called 'telescopic thinking' (Adderholdt & Goldberg, 1999). It is as if the perfectionist views successes through the 'minifying' end of a telescope, which makes them appear minute and insignificant. Failures, on the other hand, are viewed through the 'magnifying' end and appear enormous and overwhelming. Oscar winning film director, Peter Jackson, renowned for his pursuit of excellence, was asked whether he was a perfectionist in his work. He admitted to a certain 'pernickety-ness' and a belief that the longer you spend on tasks the more you can improve them. Jackson showed an understanding of the true nature of perfectionism when he said that what separates him from perfectionists is that for him 'work has always been such a joy'.

A further distorted thought process of the perfectionist is the tyranny of "should" statements. This refers to the harsh and unforgiving attitude of perfectionists toward their own short-comings. At these times, they find it difficult to treat themselves with compassion and self-acceptance. Instead they harangue themselves with 'shoulds', such as: should have done it differently, should have studied harder, should have been kinder.

These self-defeating attitudes result in perfectionists fearing new challenges and living in a state of constant anxiety about making mistakes. For perfectionists, a mistake is not simply a mistake; it is evidence of a character flaw. So, many perfectionists avoid healthy risks that will help them grow, procrastinating or refusing outright from fear of failure (Adderholt & Goldberg, 1999).

HOW DOES PERFECTIONISM DEVELOP?

There is no definitive answer to this question. It is probable that perfectionism begins as primarily positive and rewarding (as perceived by the perfectionist) with apparently minor negative consequences. It is relatively easy to 'be perfect' in one's early school years by gaining a perfect score in a test and consequently receiving adulation from well-meaning adults. Such attention and praise become powerful payoffs for error-free performance (McGee-Cooper, 2000). Over time and given the 'right' enabling conditions, the pursuit of perfection becomes excessive with negative and destructive consequences overwhelming any positive outcome (Shafran and Mansell, 2001). For example, when circumstances change, a previously accessible standard may become unattainable. This may happen when a person moves from high school to university and struggles to maintain a pattern of straight 'A' grades. Persisting with perfectionistic expectations and behaviour is now unrealistic and will likely have negative consequences such as exhaustion and repeated exposure to failure.

There seems to be little doubt that perfectionism, as we have described, undermines learning, and that something needs to be done to help perfectionists. The complexity of the phenomenon, however, makes it difficult to know what to do. A significant challenge for anyone wanting to take thoughtful action is to develop a model of perfectionism that integrates existing knowledge into a complete picture. We have generated such a model based on application of Systems Thinking, a tool for understanding complexity (Senge, 1990).

The nature of perfectionism, along with the learning challenges it presents, can be charted using a Causal Loop Diagram, shown below as Fig. 1: "Striving for Consistency". This diagram can give us clues about what drives perfectionism and offers ideas for ways to break the cycle of negativity that it can lead to.

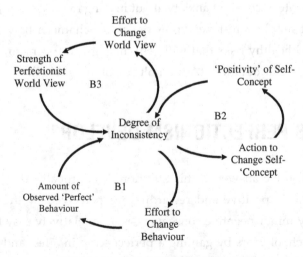

Figure 1. Striving for Consistency.

People strive to establish consistency in their lives. Each of us desires that our behaviour (what we see ourselves doing) and our self-concept (the assessment we make of ourselves) align with the deeply held beliefs that make up our World View. Perfectionism involves a distorted World View that over time makes it harder and harder to achieve this alignment or consistency.

By World View we mean a set of beliefs that are typically held at a 'tacit' level. While people might find it difficult to put into words the underlying assumptions and beliefs making up their World View, these beliefs shape the way they react to situations that arise in their lives. Perfectionists share some crucial attitudes which, were they expressed, might include the following:

- It is important to be a worthwhile person;
- To be worthwhile, a person must do everything perfectly;
- Worthwhile people do not lower their standards.

Imagine you are six years old, intelligent and hardworking and you have just scored 100% on a mathematics test at school. You can hold on to these perfectionist beliefs without experiencing any great inconsistency. You can believe yourself to be worthwhile and observe that your performance is perfect. What happens, though, if you sit another test and you 'only' score 90%?

This score, while acceptable for most people, is inconsistent with the perfectionist's World View and self concept. As the CLD shows, the cognitive inconsistency could be brought back into balance in one of three ways: changing behaviour to make it perfect (Loop B1), changing one's self concept to "I am not worthwhile" (Loop B2), or changing the World View (Loop B3). If you were a six-year-old, you would not give much thought to your World View; it is most likely you would decide to work harder at being perfect, thereby activating Loop B1. And for bright six-year-olds, perfect performance on tests is possible so the effort will be rewarded.

As a child gets older 'perfect' performance becomes more elusive — eventually unattainable — as tests get harder and competition gets tougher. Efforts to change or improve behaviour do not deliver the reduced inconsistency; they just leave the perfectionist exhausted. With growing exhaustion, perfectionists seek consistency in a different way: by reassessing self-worth.

Deciding "I am not worthwhile" is more consistent with the perfectionist World View and the observation that perfect performance has not been achieved. So instead of cycling around B1 the perfectionist flips over to B2 and adopts a negative self-concept.

Time spent in Loop B2 is time off from the rigors of B1, so over time the exhaustion will subside. However, even with the new negative self-concept, there is still inconsistency, since part of the perfectionist World View is that it is important to be worthwhile. The perfectionist feels compelled to try to be worthwhile. A new pattern emerges: striving for perfect performance (B1) until reaching a state of exhaustion, flipping into B2 and a more negative self-concept, then as one's energy allows, returning to the grind of B1 with efforts to improve behaviour. Consequently, perfectionists oscillate between determined action to be perfect and misery based on deeply negative self-assessments.

Both of these approaches (changing behaviour and altering self-concept) are quick-fixes that cannot last. They do not address deeply held destructive beliefs that are at the heart of perfectionism. We suggest that leverage lies in proposing changes to perfectionists' World View in terms that do not attack their underlying beliefs, in particular the belief that worthwhile people do not lower their standards (B3).

How this might be possible will be discussed in a later section. Before considering this fundamental change, we will look more closely at some of the actions perfectionists take to achieve 'quick-fix' consistency, and how this is likely to affect them at work.

PERFECTIONISM AT WORK

Perfectionists often adopt strategies that enable them to perform without learning. They focus exclusively on end results, and in the process they sacrifice creativity, learning and enjoyment. Such an approach might be described as a performance orientation (Fritz, 1991). What are the consequences of such an orientation in the workplace?

Individuals with a performance orientation act defensively, with all their efforts directed toward how to avoid making a mistake, being rejected or given criticism. Jule (2000) described the difference between judo students with a performance orientation and those with a learning orientation. Those with what he terms a 'performance paradigm' try to avoid being thrown by their opponent. When they do get thrown they are very hard on themselves, call themselves derogatory names, get more and more frustrated and generally aren't fun to be around. Ultimately, the students who have a performance paradigm tend to drop out because the frustration is too high.

Those with a learning paradigm, he says, act offensively, trying to learn what is necessary in order to be successful (to throw an opponent). These students understand that learning how to be successful will involve being thrown by others many times. But when thrown they respond quite differently to those with a performance paradigm. They are less judgmental of themselves, asking useful learning questions to find out "What did my opponent do? What could I do differently?" They listen to the answers and experiment with new behaviours. Most importantly, Jule concludes, these students tend to develop skills more rapidly and are most likely to remain with judo.

Lastly, a performance paradigm or orientation is convergent, limiting one's field of vision to options that already exist. Dag Hammarskjold, Secretary General of the United Nations from 1953 to 1961 points to this limitation in these words: "Compulsive perfectionism polishes the past when bold new skills are needed to unlock the future." How might this conservative approach impact on the workplace?

Perfectionists may decline challenging assignments, or fail to complete designated projects by procrastinating. In this way, they protect themselves against possible failure. Their negative self-talk runs something like: *"If I never [write that report/make that presentation/develop that programme], I don't have to risk rejection or criticism"* (Adderholt & Goldberg, 1999, p.28). So, lowered expectations and 'opting out' are strategies for reducing risk of failure but the impact on the workplace is non-performance and underachievement.

Another related risk-avoidance strategy is chronic indecision. Perfectionists constantly worry about making the wrong decision. They toss around all options and their possible consequences until they are paralysed by indecision. Nachmanovitch (1990) says it is as if they append a little superscription "but on the other hand, maybe not" to every impulse. If the decision is delayed long enough it may be made by default (Basco, 1999), so the perfectionist avoids responsibility and the threat of failure. What is the likely impact of an indecisive manager? Have you been on the receiving end of a manager's indecision and reluctance to manage? This approach to work is deeply frustrating both to perfectionist managers and those impacted by their work.

McGee–Cooper (2000) observes that perfectionists may devote disproportionate amounts of effort to less important tasks — those which can be perfected — leaving little time for tackling the big challenges. For example, when someone labours over the visual presentation of a report at the expense of meeting the deadline and covering the salient issues, they have lost their ability to match effort to importance. In a report to colleagues, presentation is important but the critical factor is the quality of the analysis. With more and more demands on managers' time we need to be able to match effort on a task to its overall importance, to demand of ourselves and others a standard of performance relevant to the situation.

Another learning disability related to perfectionism is rigidity of thought. Truly creative people become adept at shifting gear, changing direction and yielding to the suggestions of others. But the rigidity of perfectionistic thinking leads to an avoidance of healthy risks that might teach them new ways of doing things. Instead, perfectionists live in constant anxiety about 'getting it wrong'. For perfectionists, there is usually one 'correct' response and they are driven to find it. They have little tolerance for uncertainty and ambiguity, preferring to plan aspects of their lives well in advance. This scripted approach reduces uncertainty, but it also reduces opportunities for perfectionists to shine. Outstanding performance arises from flexible and creative responses to new circumstances, rather than the rolling out of standard and premeditated responses.

Related to rigidity is the perfectionistic characteristic of 'trying hard'. Perfectionists try hard to do well. They interpret the feelings of struggle and striving as a sign they are doing what is right. Yet, in the 'trying' they attempt to control the process and thereby create a distance between themselves and what they are aiming for, taking themselves out of the moment and reducing responsiveness. Nachmanovitch (2002) likens 'trying hard' to looking this way and that for your own head, and he claims that the key to true creative success lies in surrendering control, to stop 'trying'.

One of the occasions when others are likely to encounter the perfectionism of work colleagues is when giving them feedback. A debilitating fear of failure along with all-or-nothing thinking renders perfectionists exquisitely sensitive to criticism. A single mistake can be sufficient to cause the perfectionist to experience a dramatic loss of self-esteem. To protect themselves from this painful process, perfectionists use several defensive strategies. Firstly, they do not actively seek feedback, and they strenuously avoid opportunities to receive any from their colleagues. If feedback is unavoidable, they may react defensively with self justification, rationalisations, minimisations or angry accusations aimed at their critic.

Perfectionists tend to avoid working with other people even though this might provide a rich learning environment for them. When working in groups they do not feel they are in control of the performance of the group as a whole, and often feel compelled to either double-check or actually redo all the work of the group, to ensure it meets their standards.

Perfectionists are prepared to drive themselves mercilessly through stressful conditions in order to maximise performance. They may go without sleep and deny themselves leisure periods. They may try to motivate themselves by refusing to get satisfaction from work that contains any flaws. If they begin to expect these same exacting standards from others, what they may also achieve is the alienation of fellow workers or of those they manage.

Perfectionists may experience some success as a result, or in spite of, their short-term strategies, but ultimately these lead to burnout and non-performance. Not surprisingly, the anti-learning behaviours of perfectionists do not go forever unnoticed by work colleagues. What have concerned friends and colleagues tried in order to encourage perfectionists to have a more balanced approach?

MANAGING THE PERFECTIONIST

How can people working with perfectionists help them break free from their punishing beliefs? Some have tried to bolster the self-assessment of perfectionists, encouraging them to feel better about themselves. While there might be an immediate positive impact, the circular causality of the Causal Loop Diagram suggests that this approach is unlikely to bring about a long-term solution. The dictates of the perfectionist World View still insist that worthwhile people produce perfect work and the perfectionist can readily observe the yawning gap between perfection and their own flawed efforts.

Well-meaning friends, parents and colleagues may offer advice like "Just do your best", but for perfectionists 'their best' is a limitless striving for the impossible. Their inability to match effort to importance means they give 'their best' to almost everything. Hearing 'just do your best' is an invitation for perfectionists to obsess and lose perspective. Rather than providing relief for perfectionists, this comment likely reinforces the belief that worthwhile people do everything to 'their best', that is, perfectly.

Others may recommend "Don't be so hard on yourself", "Lighten up" and "Be happy with 90%". Such advice would be fine for someone who was not a perfectionist. But these exhortations require perfectionists to act on a set of beliefs to which they are strongly opposed. If they could apply this advice, they would not be perfectionists; compromising their standards is not something perfectionists do. Perfectionist beliefs, therefore, become a self-perpetuating trap that prevents people from taking the one action that will bring about fundamental relief from the inconsistencies in their lives.

So, encouraging perfectionists to lower their standards is self-defeating. But perfectionists are usually eager to raise their standards; that is, to believe that they are not doing enough. How might a change in World View be framed as a 'raising of standards'?

FUNDAMENTAL CHANGE

Research into sustainable work suggests that balance is needed between performance, learning and experience (Gallwey, 2000). Performance involves using present capacity, learning grows capacity for future demands and experience refers to the quality of life as people engage in work. Perfectionism does not seek this balance. Rather, as we have discussed, perfectionists consistently give priority to performing. They sacrifice opportunities to learn and the quality of their experience in a vain attempt to achieve perfect performance.

It is possible to frame a new World View for perfectionists as a raising of standards by demonstrating that existing beliefs are incomplete. Truly worthwhile people not only perform outstandingly, but they also ensure that they are learning and having a high-quality experience. Presenting change in this way may overcome the unwillingness of perfectionists to lower their standards and modify their world view.

Suggest to perfectionists that they are currently delivering in just one of three critical areas. You might say "It is important to us that you not only perform, but that your performance is sustainable. At the moment you are concentrating your effort on delivering performance now. I need you to also give attention to what you are learning and to the quality of your work experience. You need to deliver in each of these areas, not just one".

Arrange for measurement of the learning and experience aspects of the perfectionist's work. Measures of their performance are likely to already be in place. These measures are externally-derived. Measuring learning and experience requires an internal measure; the perfectionist needs to give their own rating of how a piece of work compares to previous work in terms of the amount they learned and how much they valued the experience (Ramsey, Franklin, Ramsey & Wells, 2002). Initially providing such ratings will be difficult. Assure the perfectionist that rating themselves in these areas is necessary and becomes easier once they have established their own internal benchmarks.

Help perfectionists to match effort to importance; help them to save their 'best' efforts for when it really matters. If you are managing or working with a perfectionist be sure to prioritize tasks. Be explicit about which tasks are critical and which are not so important. If you are the perfectionist, ask a trusted work colleague to give you feedback when you are 'obsessing' over non-essential tasks rather than getting on with whatever really needs your attention (McGee-Cooper, 2000).

Along with prioritising, perfectionists need help figuring out how to vary the effort they devote to each task. It may be useful to determine parameters for the amount of effort that will be invested in various tasks (effort in time, money, number of revisions allowed etc). An externally imposed limitation such as "This report can only be revised twice" can provide a welcome respite for perfectionists, giving them permission to interrupt their obsessive behaviours.

Build regular feedback into work processes in order to lower the stakes associated with receiving criticism. Perfectionists will try to avoid sharing unfinished work, preferring to save it all until the end when it is, hopefully, perfect. So, it is important that someone else take responsibility for ensuring there is on-going feedback throughout a project.

Stress developmental and learning goals in performance appraisal processes. Reward effort and creativity as well as outputs. Encourage risk-taking and forays by perfectionists into areas where they are not already experts. Make it safe to fail.

Perfectionism, with its emphasis on hard work and excellence, can appear to be highly desirable. Don't be fooled. The dynamics revealed in "Striving for Consistency" take a heavy toll on the people involved, their colleagues, friends and families. And this behaviour cannot be indefinitely sustained; it ultimately leads to burnout in one form or another. Look for ways to help perfectionists understand these dynamics and address the World View behind them.

REFERENCES

Adderholdt, M., & Goldberg. J. (1999). *Perfectionism: What's Bad About Being Too Good?* Minneapolis: Free Spirit Publishing Inc.

Basco, M.R. (1999). *Never Good Enough: Freeing Yourself from the Chains of Perfectionism.* New York: The Free Press.

Burns, D.D. (1980). The perfectionist's script for self-defeat. *Psychology Today*, November 34–52.

Fritz, R. (1991). *Creating*. New York: Fawcett-Columbine.

Gallwey, T. (2000). *The Inner Game of Work*. New York: Random House.

Greenspon, T. S. (1999). *Perfectionism*. Annual Meeting, National Association for Gifted Children Atlanta. November.

Jule, W. (2000). Learning and performing. *The Systems Thinker*, 11, 6, p. 11.

McGee-Cooper, A. (2000). Quality vs perfectionism: when does our push for excellence become dysfunctional. *The Systems Thinker*, 11, 5, p. 9.

Nachmanovitch, S. (1990). *Free Play: Improvisation in Life and Art*. New York: Penguin Putnam Inc.

Ramsey, P., Franklin, T., Ramsey, D. & Wells, R. (2002). Rethinking grades for sustainable learning. *Innovations in Education and Teaching International*, 39, 117–123.

Senge, P. (1990). *The Fifth Discipline: The Art and Practice of the Learning Organisation*. New York: Doubleday Currency.

Shafran, R., & Mansell, W. (2001). Perfectionism and psychopathology: a review of research and treatment. *Clinical Psychology Review*, 21, 6, 879–906.

Looking to the Future

SINGAPORE: MOVING AHEAD OF CHANGE

PREM KUMAR

INTRODUCTION

The Singapore, Inc. 'brand' is associated with performance. Singapore is a place where things work; it is well-organised and yet highly vulnerable to changes in the external environment. It has to constantly manage the delicate balance of what to conserve versus change and navigate successfully through the known and the unknown. One of the knowns is the quality of its governance. Constantly reviewing, remaking, and refreshing itself are imperatives for remaining relevant in a vibrantly competitive, 24/7 globalised world. This is Singapore's unique value proposition. Sustaining superb performance requires superb learning!

Will this be sufficient for Singapore's long-term survival and continued growth and prosperity? Singapore — an immigrant society and without any natural resource — did not fight for independence in a one-off struggle. Rather, Singapore has approached the work of establishing its own nationhood as an unending challenge of survival. In this way, Singapore resembles many of today's major corporations, and it strives to be a 'learning country' that successfully balances learning and performing.

The learning and performance debate in not new. Swanson and Halton (2001) mention that performance has focused on practical applications rather than viewing it from a philosophical perspective. From the performance paradigm it could be seen as a natural result of what we do; one that is require for economic output and as a tool of coercion Learning on the other hand is viewed as a natural part of human endeavour; where information is transferred in a 'value-neutral' way; and a means of oppression use by societies.

Reflecting on Swanson and Holton's definition, it is evident that people have remarkably varied experiences of both performance and learning. Singapore needs both, yet there are inherent dangers if the quest for either is mismanaged. Clearly the country faces some challenging questions: What does Singapore need to do to continue to stay relevant and succeed? Is she able to learn important lessons from exemplary performers? How easily can such lessons be transferred? What is involved in making the transfer? How does Singapore, a small city state of about 700 square kilometres build on its successes?

Organisational learning alerts us to important overlapping issues that will need to be considered in addressing these questions. In this chapter we will consider three: (1) the role of mental models; (2) the dynamics of change; and (3) the architecture of performance and learning.

ROLE OF MENTAL MODELS

Mental models are powerful structures that influence our thoughts and actions and ultimately our performance. In 1943 Kenneth Craik referred to them as 'small-scale' models of the mind that construct reality to anticipate events, to reason and to underlie explanation. Recent work at MIT viewed them as assumptions, generalisations, and images that influence how we understand the world and how we take action (Wind and Crook, 2005).

Mental models do not change easily: they have been shaped by our experience during our formative years. Individuals, teams, organisations, and countries could be prisoners of their own thoughts and actions if they do not frequently revisit assumptions and beliefs that may need to be changed in light of the emerging new data and information produced by constant changes taking place in the environment. Changing mental models is a particular challenge for Singapore because of its past success; it is natural to want to stick with the assumptions and beliefs that have apparently generated prosperity up until now.

It is difficult to disassociate the link between the message and the messenger. The 'father knows best' adage — closely linked to Singapore's recent history and culture — conflicts with the notion that nobody has a monopoly of ideas and solutions can come from anyone if the people are involved, engaged and given the opportunity to do so. However, in the Asian context there may be an increased lack of tolerance for disagreements and loss of the skills associated with the effective handling of conflicts. Singapore needs disagreements and the conflict of ideas as a spark for dialogue. This means that we must develop patience and the ability to slow down in order to reflect on the impact our thinking and actions have on ourselves and others. Our thoughts ultimately guide our behaviour and actions.

Bohm (1994), a noted physicist, suggested that the source of all the problems that exist in the world lies primarily in thoughts that are disconnected or fractured. We need to see the world as a whole or interconnected. In his book on *Thought as a System* he discusses among other things the notion of fragmentation and the difficulty of human beings have accepting its' effect. He draws examples where:

Nations fight each other and people kill each other. You are told that for the nation you must sacrific everything. Or you sacrifice everything for your religious differences. They split into racial groups and say that's important. Inside every nation there are various splits…You can see that nations are established by thought. The boundary of the nation is invented by thought. If you go to the edge of the nation, there's nothing to tell you that it is a boundary, unless somebody makes a wall or something. It's the same land; the people may often be not very different. But what is one side or the other seems all important. It's thought that 'makes it so'….what we are doing is establishing boundaries where really there is a close connection — that's what is wrong with fragmentation (pg. 3–4).

Bohm contends that "the meaning — which our thought gives it — is that no dialogue is necessary, that we can all go on as individuals doing whatever we like, that the highest form of civilisation is every individual doing something just for himself and not consulting anybody else. And that's what almost everybody is saying" (pg. 197).

Getting to common meaning is a challenge because there are:

...vast numbers of thoughts which have come in, and they enter into the perception of the meaning. People are seeing the meaning differently, which is why we can't get together...They all have different meanings as to what should be done, and they can fight each other and cancel out each other's efforts... I'm trying to say that we have to see the meaning of dialogue, the significance and the value of dialogue, if we are going to sustain the work needed to make it happen. It won't happen in just five minutes. You have to sustain the dialogue week after week, because there are all these resistances that are going to come up. So people will need to have a firm perception of the meaning of dialogue, of the meaning of the whole situation (Bohm, 1994: 198–199).

He points to the need for dialogue - a disciplined process of group conversation that involves inquiry into the thought processes behind our words. Embarking on this journey requires organisations and teams to embed in their organisational system and structures a way of working that needs a deeper more open communication and building closer, stronger relationships. The challenge lies in how the principles of dialogue and the process are implemented and sustained given the practical realities of staff turnover, authority and power structures that exist in organisations. A number of authors have shared examples of the process and how dialogue has helped organisations and individuals improve on their learning and performance capability (Ellinor and Gerrard, 1998; Isaacs, 1999)

The issue of missing the answers or seeing what may be obviously in front of us is one of the shortcomings of human beings. Simons and Chabris (1999) conducted an experiment on the phenomenon of sustained inattentional blindness for dynamic situations where unexpected events are frequently overlooked. The findings suggest that we perceive and remember only those objects and details that receive focused attention. The brain does not appear to trigger consciousness, even to dangers that may be obvious and organisations — and countries like Singapore — can miss opportunities to resolve conflicts, expand businesses, and solve problems.

Another challenge to shifting mental models is the role of the media and internet. What we learn during our formative years, which nowadays means what is shown in the media and the internet, has a profound effect in shaping our beliefs and assumptions. The ability of the internet and media to surface multiple perspectives and realities puts pressure on those in authority to learn how to manage them effectively. Telling the truth and thinking through consequences has become increasingly important: doing otherwise creates a jaundiced view of authority with long-term negative consequences for performance.

A recent example in Singapore demonstrates the kind of governance that I believe is needed. A student blog caused a buzz when the junior college student took issue with the views of a Second Permanent Secretary (PS) of the Ministry of Foreign Affairs. The issue in question was on how outsourcing had impacted the local population. She called his response to her question 'callous' in her blog. 'Her blog was visited by 2,000 readers over the next two days, after it was recommended as an engaging read by www.tomorrow.sg., a daily log of the best Singapore blogs. But it also led to some of her fellow JC mates and even teachers cautioning her over her writings in her blog, which touched on political and social issues. She wrote about the warnings in a subsequent entry. What was interesting in this instance was the response from the Second PS. He responded via email that there was 'no need to tone down her criticisms. 'He apologised for using "strong language" to get the attention of the audience during his speech, but hoped it did not distract anyone from his essential message that the world is becoming far more competitive and Singaporeans will have to stay ahead of the game or go down' (The Straits Times, May 17, 2006).

The case demonstrates the shift needed — from concern for control toward openness and engagement — if Singapore is going to sustain performance while technology advances at an increasing rate. It is important that the younger generation are engaged in ways that enable them to understand the historical, economic and cultural dynamics of Singapore and her place in the global marketplace.

THE DYNAMICS OF CHANGE

From a 1st Generation to 3rd Generation Army, from a one-size fits all educational system to 'Thinking Schools-Learning Nation' approach — Singapore is a place of constant change, a place where work is always in progress. Fear of being left behind seems to be a powerful motivation in the Singaporean culture. Is this healthy? Would Singapore cease to exist if it did not change?

Pfeffer and Sutton (2006) have commented that:

> *...no one in the business world ever says that you, your people, or your company are good enough and you can rest on your laurels. The not-so-subtle message is that if you aren't constantly getting better by generating new products, services, and business models, or aren't borrowing and installing best practices, then you deserve to be mocked and fired, and your company deserves its inevitable, swift, and certain death...These slogans and beliefs aren't exactly wrong, but they are half-truths. Change and innovation are nasty double-edged swords (pg. 159).*

They suggest steps that one can take to reduce the risk and pain associated with change.

Peter Senge (1990: 154) says that there is a mistaken belief that 'fundamental change requires a threat to survival.' The crisis theory of change is a dangerous oversimplification and yet it is remarkably widespread. The tension is that 'we fear and seek change'. When change happens there is resistance. Maurer (1996: 23–24) draws our attention to the fact that we need to understand the nature of resistance and learn how to deal with it. A 'natural and expected part of change, any system whether the human body or an organisation, resists any change that it believes will be harmful. As much as you might wish for it, progress without resistance is impossible. People will always have doubts and questions.' People need time to adapt. Trying to shortcut change leads to an increase in stress levels, and other social consequences that make performance unsustainable.

Staying ahead of change requires us to be critical in our observations and analysis of events. Learning needs to be seen in the context of the cultural and historical evolution of societies and organisations. Encouraging reflection, deep learning, and the shared views of current realities that does not led to negative reprisals are some of the powerful-approaches to change that are not based on fear. Consider three promising approaches: learning journeys, collaboration, and planning for scenarios.

Learning Journeys: In the case of Singapore, Ministers and senior officials from time to time embark on 'learning journeys'. Learning journeys are nothing new: travel has always broadened the mind. Journeys now tend to be more formal, resulting in action plans.

Journeys are a powerful learning method because they expose us to new data and enable us to surface assumptions and beliefs we would otherwise take for granted. Arie de Geus (1997: 31) offers an analogy.

> *A tribal chief who was brought to Singapore by a group of British explorers at the beginning of this century. The explorers had found him deep in the high mountains of the Malaysian Peninsula, in an isolated valley. His tribe was literally still in the Stone Age. Its people had not even invented the wheel. Nonetheless, the chief was highly intelligent, and a delightful man to talk to...So, as an experiment, they decided to convey him to Singapore. It was at the time already a sophisticated seaport, with multistorey buildings and a harbor with big ships. Economically, it had a market economy with traders and professional specialisations. Socially, it had many more layers than the society from which the tribal chief came. They marched the chief through this world for 24 hours, submitting him to thousands of signals of potential change for his own society. Then they brought him back to his mountain valley and started to debrief him. Of all the wonders he had seen, only one seemed important to him: He had seen a man carrying more bananas than he had ever thought one man could carry. What the mind has not experienced before, it cannot see. The tribal chief could not relate to multistorey buildings or giant ships; but when he saw a market vendor pushing a cart laden with bananas, he could make sense of it. All other signs of potential change were so far outside his previous life experiences that his mind could not grasp what his eyes were telling him.*

The Singapore government has long recognised the need to examine what others do. Ministers and civil servants go on "learning journeys" aimed at enhancing their learnings and building their capability in responding to external environmental changes. For example, it has also established a Research, Innovation and Enterprise Council: a group consisting of 18 best thinkers: leading experts in fields such as in academia, business and industry. The council meet to discuss research and development proposals in three areas: biomedical sciences, environmental and water technologies, and interactive and digital media. Led by the Prime Minister, the Council aims to chart Singapore's research efforts over the next five years, using this as the basis for on-going learning and improvement. Council member Peter Schwartz, Chairman of Global Business Network 'suggested that more acceptance of those who don't conform to the mould of, say, model worker or successful professional was needed, so that they had the space to let their creative juices flow'. Professor Claus Weyrich, head of corporate techonology at Siemens AG, commented that Singapore was in a good position to capitalise on the changes due to its excellent networks and the ability of its people to learn new technologies (The Straits Times, 7 July 2006).

What are the implications for learning in Singapore? What impact will mental models have on the efforts of the Research, Innovation and Enterprise Council?

Ngiam (2006: 199) who had served in the Singapore Administrative Service shared his experience on the different mindsets of a civil servant and a businessman. He says that 'civil servants and businessmen may look at the same set of facts or data, yet the civil servant looks at the half that is empty, and concludes that there is a gap. A businessman, on the other hand, will see the half filled with water and conclude that there is an opportunity. The difference in perception is because of the difference in their mindsets. The calculus of the civil servant is cost and benefits analysis, taught in schools of public administration. The abacus of businessman is profit and loss, taught in business schools. My guess is that the civil servant and the businessman march to different drumbeats. The public sector strives to produce goods and services at the lowest possible cost so that the most number of people can afford them.'

One of the challenges for the council will therefore be to value the diversity of mental models they encounter. This diversity will be present not only amongst the exemplary researchers and innovators they uncover, but also within the Council itself. There is a danger in assuming there should be a best mental model of innovation. Rather, the lessons learned need to be understood within the context of the mental models from which they spring. If Ngiam is right, research and innovation within a civil service context is likely to be very different from research and innovation in a business context. The Council will need to be open to exploring the "assumptions, generalisations and images" that shaped the work of the various researchers they find.

Arie de Geus contends that 'learning begins with perception. Neither an individual nor a company will even begin to learn without having seen something of interest in the environment. That is why surviving and thriving in a volatile world requires, first of all, management that is sensitive to the company's environment' (pg. 22).

Collaboration: Another issue that I would like to touch on relates to the often under utilised capacity of individuals, organisations, and countries to network, collaborate and cooperate. The SARS episode is one example where cooperation worked. Singapore was one of the countries affected very much by the spread of the disease. Surowiecki (2004) comments that what made the SARS research effort successful was the scope and speed of various research labs around the world working together to find a solution. There was sharing of data and information that allowed them to check on and learn from one another's work. They took part in daily teleconferences, discussed strategies for future investigation and debated the results. They were able to work at the same time and on the same samples, multiplying their speed and effectiveness. In this instance, he asserts that 'collaboration works because, when it works well, it guarantees a diversity of perspectives. In the case of the search for the SARS virus, the fact that different labs had different initial ideas about the possible origin of the virus meant that a wide range of possibilities would be considered. And the fact that different laboratories were doing parallel work on the same samples, while it ran the risk of producing too much duplicated effort, also produced rich results in the form of unique data' (pg. 200).

Organisations and countries would therefore need to seriously revisit the notion that we compete to win is what matters at the end of the day. Technology for one has given us a more interconnected, interdependent, globalised world. A shift in mental models and in acquiring collaborative skills would be critical for long-term qualitative and quantitative growth and survival. Some of the challenges for collaboration within organisations will be discussed in the architecture of performance and learning section.

Planning for Scenarios: Singapore has a Scenario Planning Office in the Prime Minister's Office. Scenario planning is used as a tool for planning 'what if' situations in the public sector. It is one way of anticipating changes and shifting mindsets. However, there will always be challenges for scenarios to be translated into strategies and action plans.

Bobbitt (2003) mentions that, 'only one country has made extensive use of scenario planning.' He does acknowledge that fact that getting governments — and I suspect even organisations — to adopt scenario planning is not easy: it requires well-organised dialogue between decision makers at many levels, and a political culture that is tolerant of uncertainty. Poor stakeholder ownership, lack of commitment and the unskilled use of scenario planning tools can also undermine efforts.

No system or tool is foolproof especially when we are dealing with the dynamics of change that take place in the environment beyond our control. Anticipating change and preparing for the worst case scenario helps to reduce uncertainty, risk and at times safe lives, money and improve performance. When countries and organisations repeat the same mistakes does that mean they have not learnt from experience? There is sufficient amount of literature that explores the issues relating to what prevents organisations from learning (e.g. Argyris, 1990, 1991, 1994; Senge, 1990). Pfeffer and Sutton draw attention to research done by Amy Edmondson that 'if you want better performance instead of the illusion of it, you and your people must tell everyone about problems you've fixed, point out others' errors so all can learn, admit your own errors, and never stop questioning what is done and how to do it better' (pg. 107).

The continuous learning approach to improving performance suggest inquiring into: What worked and did not work well?; And what should we do differently the next time? From my experience organisations and teams tend to review their learning at the end of a project rather than at every iteration of processes within the project. They also tend to avoid documenting what they learn. They do not see the value of a disciplined approach, and the results it would yield over time. Rather, they tend to be more influenced by factors such as fear of being evaluated, confusion and unsafe environments for sharing knowledge. Over time the reluctance to engage in disciplined review leads to a loss of institutional memory, a repeat of the failures and a decrease in performance.

Harvard Dean, Dr David Ellwood argues that New Orleans was destroyed by the dykes that gave way and not Hurricane Katrina. The failure in this instance was the slow and ineffective government action costing lives and money (The Straits Times, 31 March 2006). Prevention would have been far better than cure! We could learn from the Japanese who are located in one of the most active earthquake zones in the world and yet their casualties are minimal. Earthquake preparedness is evident throughout their culture, people, systems and processes.

With change, complexity and perpetual advances in techonology whoever learns faster than their 'competitors' has an added competitive advantage. Even organisations such as the al Qaeda have learnt to apply learning disciplines: continuously reducing the learning curve from planning, implementation and action to generating the desired results.

ARCHITECTURE OF PERFORMANCE AND LEARNING

How do we know that learning has taken place? How we measure the impact of learning on performance? Sometimes it is evident in the direct results produced.

Singapore's per capita gross national income grew from S$1,618 in 1965 to S$44,455 in 2005(www.singstat.gov.sg), a remarkable 2,747 per cent growth. This success is powerful evidence that during this period Singapore was investing heavily in the systems architecture needed to support learning.

Disasters and crises can be seen as evidence that learning has *not* been happening: that the architecture for learning is missing or flawed. The Columbia Accident Investigation Board mentioned that the Space Shuttle Columbia accident occurred because 'the organisational structure and hierarchy blocked effective communication of technical problems. Signals were overlooked, people were silenced, and useful information and dissenting views on technical issues did not surface at higher levels' (pg. 201).

Pfeffer and Sutton (2006: 99) highlight the need to have effective systems in place rather than just focusing on individuals.

Given all the evidence on the importance of systems, something that W.Edwards
Deming and the quality movement emphasised for years, why do so many

227

companies still place so much emphasis on getting and keeping great people and so little on building and sustaining great systems? A big part of the answer is that Western countries, like the United States, glorify rugged individualism so much that we make a cognitive error. We forget that history, organisational goals, rewards, and structure are potent causes of what people and organisations do. We give too much credit to individual heroes when organisations do things right and place too much blame on individual scapegoats when things go wrong. This perceptual blindness pervades the talent mind-set, and you see it in story after story in the business press, in corporate histories, and in advice given by gurus and management consultants. This tendency to over attribute success and failure to individuals can be overcome, but to do so requires focusing on locating and dealing with systemic causes of performance issues.

Singapore has always placed a high premium on upgrading education and skills. These would always be one of the key drivers of sustainable performance and growth for countries. It is especially critical for Singapore given its only 'natural' resource is an educated, creative and nimble workforce. On education, Kelly (2006: 212–214) observes that 'with characteristic determination, the Singapore government has introduced a number of changes to stimulate a reorientation of the system. It has reduced curriculum content by 30 percent to free up free up time for thinking, reflection, and cross-disciplinary and self-directed learning and to signal to teachers that something different is expected of them... After a recent inspection visit, the International Academic Advisory Panel praised Singapore for the transition it has made, for the absence of the strong and stifling bureaucracy they had expected to find, and for the confident, outward-looking, and world-ready students who so impressed the visitors. Robert Brown, provost of MIT, said: "The changes in the Singapore higher education system in the last five or six years have been aimed at increasing the breadth of the students. Those are really good changes and necessary, in a world where you need to create very highly educated but very flexible human beings.'

We need to take a systems view of learning, understanding the level at which it is happening (Kumar, 2003) (see Figure 1). Learning can be understood from the perspective of an individual, group, organisation, nations and including supranational systems (e.g. the United Nations). Given the pace of change, gaps in learning

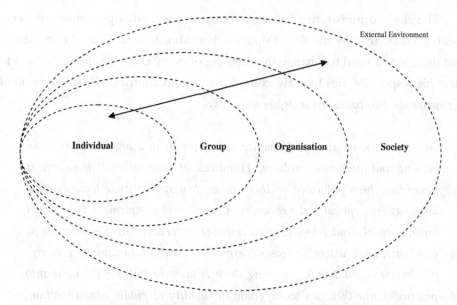

Figure 1. Learnings Within & Across Systems.

and understanding between different actors in a system will widen where there is a tendency for quick solutions and fixes. Hence, the need to balance learning and performance cuts across all levels and dimensions of human work. Fundamentally, learning generates change at a personal level. The brain therefore restructures and reorganises the thought processes. Successful learners would develop strategies for self-awareness and reflection. Over time people can become independent and life-long learners (Bransford *et al.*, 1999). At the societal level, Singapore needs to become a life-long learning nation. And it needs to be a nation made up of life-long learning individuals and organisations.

Having effective and efficient systems and structures is one part of the equation. Having 'wisdom' is an even more important talent for sustaining organisational performance. "Organisations need people who think quickly and well when they work alone on problems with known correct answers — that is what IQ tests measure. But having people who know the limits of their knowledge, who ask for help when they need it, and are tenacious about teaching and helping colleagues' is even more important as a basis for constant improvements in an organisation, technical system, or body of knowledge. Wise actions help people become smarter and smarter" (Pfeffer and Sutton (2006: 103)).

The elite Administrative Service in Singapore is made up of mostly government scholars. In 1999 the then Deputy Prime Minister Lee Hsien Loong stated that there was a need to 'change the thinking of every civil servant, to get him to view his responsibilities broadly, come forward and contribute'. On the issue of performance, he shares his insights as follows:

How to get maximum performance out of people and organisations is an ancient and universal problem. Hundreds of inspirational management tomes have been published on this subject. My own attitude towards these formulas is sceptical but pragmatic. Consultants complement but cannot replace capable leadership. Empowerment is important, but it is not a magic word that, when uttered, releases energies undreamt of. Buzzwords are helpful, but more vital than repeating them is actively putting the ideas into practice. Only then can we upgrade the quality of public administration, bring Singaporeans closer together, and guide Singapore safely through what will be a bracing and demanding phase of nation building' (The Business Times, April 6, 1999).

Reaching out to the people and employees in organisations involves not only the mind but also winning the hearts. Issues of alignment will always be a challenge to organisations and societies due to the speed of change and diversity of views.

Subsequent speeches by other Ministers over the years have emphasised the need to take risks, understand the nature of business and to work as a team across Ministries (The Straits Times, March 31, 2004). The challenge in organisations of all sorts is getting departments to see beyond their immediate boundaries. The Deputy Prime Minister again stressed the need for the administrative service to take the lead in developing an integrated approach in government and to avoid thinking in silos (The Straits Times, 31 March, 2006). This is a recurring theme amongst those concerned with balancing performance and learning.

Schwartz too highlights the importance of putting in place structures that focus on learning. His thesis is that we should "place a very, very, high premium on learning. Most failures to adapt are, in effect, failures to learn enough in time about the changing circumstances. And there will be more to learn in the future. If advances in science and technology are any indication, work will be increasingly knowledge intensive, and the value of scientific knowledge in particular will be all the greater (Schwartz, 2003: 223–224).'

Singapore has frequently been criticised for not facilitating 'an unhindered civil society'....since 'a clear lesson from Singapore that has relevance to other states is that to become global players, states should not only give more space and influence to markets, firms, and universities, but they should also involve the larger public to expand the "innovative capacity" of nations. States must also realise that civil society will flourish only under full democratisation of all facets of society. Informal networks and alliances are key ingredients of innovation and the creative economy (Parayil, 2005:67)'.

Deputy Prime Minister Lee Hsien Loong addressed some of the key issues during his speech at the Harvard Club's 35th Anniversary in 2004. He acknowledged that over time Singapore society would have to open up further:

...Government needs to be open to different views, so too must the participants. Individuals and civic groups are entitled to expect every serious proposal to be considered, but they must also accept that not all views can be accepted by the Government or other Singaporeans.

...to promote civic participation is to debate policies and national issues rigorously and robustly. Some people are afraid to speak up for fear of saying the wrong thing, or being taken to task...it has to be rigorous and not held back out of concern for egos or sensitivities. It has to be issue-focused, based on facts and logic, and not just on assertions and emotions. The overriding objective is to reach correct conclusions on the best way forward for the country.

The final way to build a civic society is for the Government to continue playing an active and leading role in taking Singapore forward. We will expand the opportunities for the public to give inputs, develop a more vibrant media, and pull back the Government from more areas, but the Government cannot abdicate its responsibility to lead from the front.

In Singapore, after independence, our national goal was to survive, prove to the world that we could make it, and make ourselves a First World Country.

> *That powerful drive united and motivated a whole generation of Singaporeans*
> *to achieve the vision within one generation.*

To move ahead of change requires preparing for the future. Schwartz (2003: 229) offers the following on what is required to stay ahead.

1. Build and maintain your sensory and intelligence systems.
2. Cultivate a sense of timing.
3. Identifying in advance the kinds of 'early-warning indicators' that would signal that a change is rapidly upon you.
4. Put in place mechanisms to engender creative destruction.
5. Try to avoid denial.
6. Think like a commodity company.
7. Be aware of the competence of your judgement, and the level of judgement that new situations require; and move deliberately and humbly into new situations that stretch your judgement.
8. Place a very high premium on environmental and ecological sustainability on financial infrastructure and support.
9. Cultivate connections.

Hence, the architecture for performance and learning requires a constant work in progress and quality of review mindset for developing and strengthening the systems and structures coupled with rigorous measurement tools. These cannot be achieved without the quality of leadership at each level of organisational systems and values required to drive it.

CONCLUSION

For organisations and countries, continuous learning and performance involves strengthening their internal systems and human resource capabilities. There is no magic bullet or short cut to achieving the desired performance and results. Time and again we find the same issues surfacing and without the necessary discipline and focus, coupled with a continuous learning culture, inefficiencies and wastage will continue.

Singapore has experienced remarkable success over the past 4 decades. This success can be a trap that prevents further learning, unless disciplined attention is given to mental models, the dynamics of change and the architecture of performance and learning.

The key issues discussed in this chapter and throughout the book are by no means exhaustive. Balancing performance and learning is a dynamic process with new demands and approaches emerging over time. It is hoped that these will spur more detailed and rigorous dialogue on learning and performance and its impact on individuals, organisations and countries.

The views expressed in this paper are the personal views of the writer and do not in any way represent the views of the organisation.

REFERENCES

Argyris, C. (1990). *Overcoming Organisational Defences: Facilitating Organisational Learning*, NJ: Prentice-Hall.

Argyris, C. (1991). Teaching Smart People How to Learn, in *Harvard Business Review*, May–June 1991.

Argyris, C. (1994). Good Communication that Blocks Learning, in *Harvard Business Review*, July–Aug 1994.

Bobbitt, P. (2003). Op-Ed: Seeing the Future, in *The New York Times*, December 8, 2003.

Bohm, D. (1994). *Thought as a System*, London: Routledge.

Bransford, J.D., *et al.* (1999). *How People Learn: Brain, Mind, Experience, and School*, Washington, D.C.: National Academy Press.

Ellinor, L.and Gerrard, G. (1998). *Dialogue: rediscover the transforming power of conversation*, New York: John Wiley & Sons.

Geus, A. de. (1997). *The Living Company*, Boston, MA: Harvard Business School Press.

Harold W.G. *et al.*, (2003). *Columbia Accident Investigation Board: Report Volume I*, Washington, DC: Government Printing Office, August 2003, http://www.caib.us/.

Isaacs, W. (1999). *Dialogue and the Art of Thinking Together: A Pioneering Approach to Communication in Business and Life*, New York: Doubleday.

Kelly, E. (2006). *Powerful Times: Rising to the Challenge of Our Uncertain World*, New Jersey: Pearson Education.

Kumar, P. (2003). Organisational Learning with a Purpose, in *Organisational Learning for All Seasons*, Kumar, P (ed) Singapore: National Community Leadersip Institute, 32–42.

Maurer, R. (1996). *Beyond the Wall of Resistance: Unconventional Strategies that Build Support for Change*, Texas: Bard Press.

Ngiam, T.D. (2006). Minds and Mindsets: The Civil Servant and the Businessman, in *A Mandarin and the Making of Public Policy*, Singapore: NUS Press, pp. 199–209.

Parayil, G. (2005). From "Silicon Island" to Biopolis of Asia: Innovation Policy and Shifting Competitive Strategy in Singapore, in *California Management Review*, 47, 2, Winter 2005, 50–73.

Pfeffer, J. and Sutton, R. I. (2006). *Hard Facts, Dangerous Half-Truths, and Total Nonsense: Profiting from Evidence-Based Management*, Boston, MA: Harvard Business School Press.

Schwartz, P. (2003). *Inevitable Surprises: Thinking Ahead in a Time of Turbulence*, New York: Gotham Books.

Senge, P. (1990). *The Fifth Discipline: The Art and Practice of the Learning Organisation*, New York: Currency Doubleday.

Simons, D. J. and Chabris, C.F. (1999). Gorillas in our midst: sustained inattentional blindness for dynamic events, in *Perception*, *28*, 1059–1074.

Surowiecki, J. (2004). *The Wisdom of Crowds: Why the Many are Smarter than the Few*, London: Abacus.

Swanson, R. A. and Holton III, E.F. (2001). *Foundations of Human Resource Development*, San Francisco, CA: Berrett-Koehler Publishers.

The Business Times, People, Public, Private Sectors as Partners, April, 6, 1999, pg. 1.

The Straits Times, Exchange between ACJC and Ministry Bigwig Creates Buzz, May 17, 2006, pg. H10, Singapore.

The Straits Times, Can 'Mavericks' fit into orderly S'pore?, July, 7, 2006, pg. 3, Singapore.

The Straits Times, Think Beyond Own Turf: Jaya, March, 31, 2006.

The Straits Times, Public Servants Must Think More Like Insurgents, March, 31, 2006, pg 20.

The Straits Times, Global Challenges Worsened by Government Inaction, March 31, 2006, pg. 24.

Wind, Y. and Crook, C. (2005). *The Power of Impossible Thinking: Transform the Business of Your Life and the Life of Your Business*, NJ: Pearson Education, Wharton School Publishing.

Contributors

CONTRIBUTORS

PETER BLYDE, Ph.D., is Founder of CATALYST4 — a consulting organisation that stimulates development in the areas of vision and strategy, leadership and people change. His main areas of focus include leadership development, visioning and strategy, executive team development, executive coaching, and emotional intelligence. Dr Blyde has over 14 years consulting experience and has consulted to a wide range of private and public organisations in Australia and New Zealand. His Ph.D examined Executive Perceptions of Leadership in New Zealand and Australia. In addition to his consulting role with CATALYST4, Dr Blyde is the lead designer and facilitator of the Hillary Leadership Programme (an 18 month, cross-sectoral leadership programme for senior executives) with *Excelerator: The New Zealand Leadership Institute* (part of the University of Auckland Business School). He can be contacted peter.blyde@catalyst4.co.nz.

JOHN SEELY BROWN is an Advisor to the Provost and Visiting Scholar at USC, prior to that he was the Chief Scientist of Xerox Corporation and the director of its Palo Alto Research Center (PARC) — a position he held for nearly two decades. While head of PARC, Brown expanded the role of corporate research to include such topics as organizational learning, knowledge management, complex adaptive systems, and nano/mems technologies. He was a cofounder of the Institute for Research on Learning (IRL). His personal research interests include the management of radical innovation, digital culture, individual and organizational learning, ubiquitous computing and the management of radical innovation.

He serves on numerous public boards and private boards of directors. He has published over 100 papers in scientific journals and was awarded the Harvard Business Review's 1991 McKinsey Award for his article, "Research that Reinvents the Corporation" and again in 2002 for his article "Your Next IT Strategy". In 2004 he was inducted in the Industry Hall of Fame. He is an avid reader, traveler and motorcyclist. Part scientist, part artist and part strategist, JSB's views are unique and distinguished by a broad view of the human contexts in which technologies operate and a healthy skepticism about whether or not change always represents genuine progress. His website is: www.johnseelybrown.com.

MARILYN DARLING is a partner in Signet Research & Consulting, LLC, which she founded in 1989. Signet's research and consulting focus is the intersection between leading, learning and execution. Ms. Darling's particular focus is leaders and teams who must perform complex work in dynamic environments, where no amount of training can possibly prepare them for their perpetually fluid and unpredictable world. Ms. Darling's clients have included a wide range of organizations in different sectors, from the Federal Aviation Administration, the Transportation Security Administration and the World Bank, to the Aspen Institute, The Nature Conservancy and Harvard Medical School, to Shell Oil, DTE Energy, BankBoston and Green Mountain Coffee Roasters.

Ms. Darling and her partners created the field of Emergent Learning and tools like EL Maps™ to support this work. She uses EL Maps to design and facilitate large and small knowledge growing conferences and meetings and to help organizations tackle complex problems by bringing everyone's best thinking to the table. She uses a robust set of leadership practices, including After Action Reviews (AARs), to help organizations create line-of-sight and accountability for both immediate results and for building the capacity to produce better results in the future. Previous publications by Ms. Darling and her colleagues include a study in 2000, *"From Post-Mortem to Living Practice: An in-depth study of the evolution of the After Action Review,"* and "Learning in the Thick of It," *Harvard Business Review* (July/August 2005). She can be reached at: mdarling@singnetconsulting.com.

PROFESSOR AMY C. EDMONDSON is the Novartis Professor of Leadership and Management at the Harvard Business School. Edmondson's research investigates leadership behavior and psychological safety as influences on learning in teams and organizations. She has published articles in academic journals including *Administrative Science Quarterly, Organization Science,* and *California Management Review,* and was co-editor with Bertrand Moingeon of *Organizational Learning and Competitive Advantage* (Sage, 1996). Edmondson received the Cummings Award from the Academy of Management Organizational Behavior division for outstanding achievement in early mid-career. Before her academic career, Edmondson worked as Chief Engineer for architect/inventor Buckminster Fuller in the early 1980s, and her book, *A Fuller Explanation,* clarifies Fuller's mathematical contributions for a nonscientific audience. She received her PhD in organizational behavior, AM in psychology, and AB in engineering and design, all from Harvard University. Her email address is: aedmondson@hbs.edu.

DAVE FLANIGAN has 33 years of global business experience in the automotive and financial service sectors. Mr. Flanigan has extensive background in strategic planning; acquisitions, mergers and divestitures; managing transnational joint ventures and integrations; and establishing start-up operations around the world. He has acquired 14 companies, created 9 joint ventures and launched 12 new businesses in 11 countries. He specializes in leading business transformations. He created numerous enterprise turnarounds and built exceptionally high performing teams at Ford Motor Company and Ford Credit as well as in non-profit organizations with which he serves.

Mr. Flanigan is a Consultant Member and Trustee of the Society for Organizational Learning — a global community of educators, researchers and business leaders dedicated to the study and practice of systems thinking, organizational learning and learning-based leadership. As a consultant to SOL, he has facilitated ongoing action learning and research collaboration of member institutions such as Intel, Shell, AT&T, DTE Energy, Ford Motor, the World Bank, Unilever, and NSA. Additionally, he has been active in developing communities of practice within SoL that focus on executive coaching and large system change. Mr. Flanigan earned a BA in Economics and Psychology and an MBA from the University of Michigan. He has been a guest speaker and panelist at the University's global business seminars and has lectured at graduate business courses. His email is: DavidCFlanigan@tampabay.rr.com

ESTEE SOLOMON GRAY is an inveterate boundary straddler and broker. Estee has spent a long and varied career at the intersection of technology, markets, practice, learning and sociality. She has been a biomechanics researcher, a software systems engineer, a corporate strategy and marketing consultant, a social architect, and most recently, retail/service entrepreneur. She has worked with technical and engineering teams, customer communities, senior Fortune100 executive teams, startup management teams, corporate and non-profit boards of directors, distributed leadership networks and both authorized and emergent communities of practice. Estee holds a B.S.C. in neurophysiology and biomechanics from Yale University, an M.S.E.E. in computer architecture and an MBA from Stanford University. She is a veteran of the pioneering technology marketing practice created in the 80's by Silicon Valley legend Regis McKenna and was a member of the highly influential Xerox PARC — Institute for Research on Learning (IRL) community during the '90s. She currently serves on the Board of Peer Networks, Inc.

She is a Wexner Heritage Fellow and been recognized many times for her local and national leadership, including receiving both the "Young" and "NextGen" Leadership Awards from the JCC Association of North America, 10 years apart. Her current focus in the Jewish community is on realizing new, "network" models of engagement and identity through organizations like Hillel at Stanford.

PROFESSOR PETER JARVIS is Professor of Continuing Education at the University of Surrey. He has written and edited about 30 books, one of which gained the CO Houle Award for Adult Education Literature from the American Adult and Continuing Education Association. He has also written about 200 papers, chapters of books and so on. His work has been widely translated. He is also founding editor of The International Journal of Lifelong Education. Peter Jarvis has been invited to lecture and teach in many countries throughout the world on the lifelong learning, the education of adults and on learning and teaching. Peter Jarvis can be contacted at: P.Jarvis@surrey.ac.uk.

PROFESSOR ANEEL KARNANI is faculty member of the Strategy group at the Stephen M. Ross School of Business, University of Michigan. He received the Teaching Excellence Award in 1991, 2001, 2006 and 2007. He has held visiting appointments to teach in the MBA and executive development programs at many universities including the Northwestern University, London Business School, INSEAD (France), HEC France), CEIBS (China), Indian Business School, Chulalongkorn University (Thailand), and INCAE (Costa Rica), among others.

His interest is focused on the basic question in strategic management: Why do firms succeed? He studies how firms can leverage existing competitive advantages and create new ones to achieve rapid growth. He is also interested in global competition, particularly in the context of emerging economies. He studies both how local companies can compete against large multinational firms, and how multinational firms can succeed in these unfamiliar markets. He has published in and is a member of the editorial boards of several professional journals, such as Management Science and Strategic Management Journal. His email address is: AKARNANI@UMICH.EDU.

PROFESSOR D. CHRISTOPHER KAYES is a Professor of Management at The George Washington University, School of Business and Visiting Professor at The University of Hull, UK. He is the author of *Destructive Goal Pursuit: The Mount Everest Disaster* (Palgrave-Macmillan) as well as over 35 articles on learning and leadership including "Destructive Pursuit of Idealized Goals", which was recognized as the first ever most significant contribution to the practice of management by the Organizational Behavior division of the Academy of Management. His article, "The 1996 Mt. Everest Climbing Disaster: The Breakdown of Learning in Teams" was named best paper in 2004 in the journal *Human Relations* and is one of its most frequently downloaded articles. His second book *Leadership, Loyalty and Deception: Lessons from the search for Weapons of Mass Destruction* (Palgrave-Macmillan) will appear in 2008.

Dr. Kayes consults and conducts executive education world wide. He is working with a team of researchers to develop practical tools to enhance learning including *The Kolb Team Learning Experience* published by the Hay Group. He previously taught in the Executive Leadership and Singapore Institute of Management Programs at GWU. He held a Visiting International Scholar position with the Helsinki School of Economics and Visiting Lecturer position at Butler University. He is co-owner, with his wife of The Oakton Group, an executive education and consulting firm. Their web-site is www.theoaktongroup.com.

ART KLEINER is the editor in chief of strategy+business, the management magazine published by Booz Allen Hamilton. His column, "Culture and Change," appears regularly in strategy+business, the quarterly management magazine published by Booz Allen Hamilton, and he has also profiled leading management thinkers for the magazine.He is a writer, lecturer and editorial consultant with a background in management, interactive media, corporate environmentalism, scenario planning and organisational learning.

He is a co-author (with Peter Senge *et al.*) of the best-selling Fifth Discipline Fieldbook (1994), The Dance of Change (1999) and Schools That Learn (2000), and author of The Age of Heretics (Doubleday, 1996; Wiley, new edition forthcoming) and Who Really Matters (Doubleday, 2003). He has also taught at New York University's Interactive Telecommunications Program. His email address is: kleiner_art@bah.com and website: www.artkleiner.com.

PREM KUMAR, Ph.D., is Principal Trainer with the National Community Leadership Institute, Singapore. He has been involved in human resource, organisational development and consulting in a broad spectrum of environments. His experience has spanned across a wide range of industry sectors in both the private and public sectors, designing organizational systems at the individual, group and organisational level. He has a doctoral degree from the University of Surrey, Master's Degrees in Tertiary, Adult & Continuing Education from the University of Hull and in International Relations from The Fletcher School, Tufts University. His email is: drprem@signet.com.sg.

ROBYN MASON is a doctoral student in Human Resource Management at Massey University, Palmerston North, New Zealand. Mrs Mason has taught in the areas of human resource development, equity, diversity and discrimination, and strategic human resource management. Her research interests are in human resource development and diversity. Her Honours research developed a model of Balanced Adjustment used in assessing the effectiveness of a cross-cultural orientation programme for international students — the 'Massey Kiwi Friend Programme'. Mrs Mason's current doctoral research is examining the relationship between organisational learning environments and young vocationally-skilled workers' orientation to learn. Mrs Mason is a recipient of several scholarships including Massey University Doctoral Scholarship (2006–2009), New Zealand Department of Labour Postgraduate Sponsorship (2007), Human Resource Institute of New Zealand Postgraduate Scholarship (2007), and Massey Scholar (Massey University, 2003). She can be reached at R.L.Mason@massey.ac.nz.

ANDREA NEEDHAM worked as human resource management strategist for more than thirty years. She worked with the Hay Group in London and the US, before starting her own consultancy in Southern California. Her consulting focused on organisations undergoing major strategic and organisational change and has worked successfully with client firms in many different industries. Ms Needham has held the position of Head of Human Resources in four organisations in New Zealand and the United States where she has developed strategic leadership and HR programmes. Since returning to New Zealand in 1996, Ms Needham has worked in change leadership, human resources and general management, and consulting and facilitation roles with a variety of organisations. Ms Needham is the author of *Workplace Bullying — the Costly Business Secret* (Penguin 2003). She believes that organisations need to focus on developing talented leadership and management individuals who are able to progress the people perspective and ensure long term sustainability. Where there is strong successful long term leadership, Workplace Bullying cannot exist.

DEB RAMSEY is a Director of Incite Learning, a New Zealand-based consulting company. She has taught in the area of communication for over 20 years; this has involved teaching children, at university level, and on executive development programmes. While working at Massey University in New Zealand, she developed an innovative programme for helping international students adapt to study abroad by breaking down barriers between them and domestic students. Mrs Ramsey has pioneered work on the use of improvisational drama as a method for uncovering unconscious conversational patterns and learning new ways of engaging in dialogue. Her recent research has involved work with gifted and talented young people, helping them to understand and challenge some of the dysfunctional attitudes associated with perfectionism.

PHIL RAMSEY, Ph.D., is a Senior Lecturer in Organisational Learning and HRD at Massey University in Palmerston North. Additionally, he is a Director of Incite

Learning, a New Zealand consulting organisation that helps leaders deal with the challenges of complexity and change. In his research and his consulting, Dr Ramsey aims to utilise concepts that are both powerful for addressing leadership challenges, and practically teachable. His research interests have included leadership in schools and school effectiveness, the impact of culture on organisational learning, and ways of increasing the effectiveness of on-the-job training. Much of his consultancy currently involves the application of systems thinking and organisational learning concepts to school leadership. He is the author of several books, including the 'Billibonk' series of books, designed to teach systems thinking concepts to gifted children (and their parents).

MYRON E. ROGERS is an author, speaker and consultant with a practice in large-scale organization change and leadership development. As *Myron Kellner-Rogers*, he co-authored the best selling *A Simpler Way* (Berrett-Koehler, 1996, 2002) with Margaret J. Wheatley, his long time former consulting partner. His work has also appeared in many edited books. He has authored or co-authored numerous articles in scholarly and trade publications, and he has been a regular columnist for *News for a Change* (AQP) and *The Journal of Strategic Performance Measurement.*

He has served as visiting faculty for the M.S.O.D. program at Pepperdine University and the executive development programs of Cornell University. Myron has been named a Global Thought Leader by both the Peter Drucker Foundation and the Fetzer Institute. He is a co-founder of The Berkana Institute, an educational and research foundation supporting public inquiry into the new organizational ideas, forms and leadership required for the future. He is also a founder and executive vice president of HealthString LLC, an innovative start-up provider of dynamic, web-based personal health records. Myron can be reached by email at mekrogers@msn.com, or at +773 929 8814

SARA J. SINGER, M.B.A., Ph.D., is Assistant Professor of Health Care Management and Policy, Harvard School of Public Health, and in the Institute for Health Policy, Massachusetts General Hospital. Her research uses organizational safety, organizational learning, and leadership theories to understand and address the causes and consequences of errors and adverse events in health care organizations. Dr. Singer has published 30 articles in academic journals and books on healthcare management, health policy, and health system reform. She has provided strategic and technical expertise, including Congressional testimony, to U.S. and international policymakers and health industry leaders to promote health care financing and delivery reform and innovation.

Previously, Dr. Singer was a Senior Research Scholar at Stanford University's Freeman Spogli Institute for International Studies, where she was also a Lecturer and founding Executive Director of the Center for Health Policy. She is currently co-principal investigator for a Stanford-based grant entitled, "Improving Safety Culture and Outcomes in Healthcare," funded by the U.S. Agency for Healthcare Research and Quality. This and related projects involve a national consortium of 135 hospitals, recruited to participate in this research, which examines safety climate, its relationship to safety performance and variation within organizations. The project also implements and evaluates an intervention that seeks to engage senior managers in learning-oriented leadership that strengthens safety climate by exposing them to frontline work. Singer holds an A.B. degree in English from Princeton University (1986), a M.B.A. degree with a Certificate in Public Management from Stanford University (1993), and a Ph.D. from Harvard University in Health Policy/Management with a concentration in organizational behavior. She can be reached at: ssinger@hsph.harvard.edu.

BETH TOOTELL is a lecturer in Human Resource Management at Massey University in Palmerston North, New Zealand. Before joining Massey in 2001 Mrs Tootell was employed by Otago University as an Assistant Lecturer, and was the co-convener of the 7th National Postgraduate Conference. She is the author and co-author of a number of conference papers, book chapters and academic journal articles on work-life balance and valuing Human Resources. Mrs Tootell has a particular interest in different needs of a diverse workforce, and is currently researching the role of diversity in the formation of sub-groups in governance teams.

MARGARET WHEATLEY, Ph.D., writes, teaches, and speaks about radically new practices and ideas for organizing in chaotic times. She has been an organizational consultant and researcher since 1973 and a dedicated global citizen since her youth. She is President emerita of The Berkana Institute, a global foundation serving life-affirming leaders around the world. Her newest book, *Finding Our Way: Leadership for an Uncertain Time,* is a collection of her practice-focused writings, where she describes both the organizational and personal behaviors that bring her theories to life. Her classic book *Leadership and the New Science* has just been published in a revised and updated third edition, and now appears in 20 languages. Her other books are *Turning to One Another: Simple Conversations to Restore Hope to the Future,* and *A Simpler Way* (with Myron Kellner-Rogers). Her articles appear frequently in a wide variety of magazines and professional publications.

She received a doctorate from Harvard University's program in Administration, Planning, and Social Policy, and an M.A. in systems thinking and Media Ecology from New York University. She has served as faculty at The Marriott School of Management, Brigham Young University, and Cambridge College, Massachusetts. In 2003, The American Society of Training and Development awarded her their highest honor, the "Distinguished Contribution to Workplace Learning and Performance." See www.margaretwheatley.com, for her most recent articles and listing of seminars.

INDEX